DIRECT
AND
DATABASE
MARKETING

D1078851

110892

'There are very few people who really know as much about direct marketing as Graeme. To get all that experience in 320 pages for less than the cost of a decent lunch is probably one of the greatest bargains you will ever come across. You're crazy if you don't rush out and buy it now.'

John Watson, Chairman, WWAV Rapp Collins

'Immensely valuable! The first book of its kind, as far as I know. And probably only Graeme McCorkell could have written it. The case histories alone make it worth the price.'

Drayton Bird, Managing Director, Drayton Bird Direct and author of Commonsense Direct Marketing

'When I first met Graeme McCorkell 20 years ago, I was impressed by his approach to direct marketing – innovation, imagination combined with common sense and commercialism. Having read his book I'm pleased to say he hasn't changed.'

David Jones, Chief Executive, The Next Directory

DIRECT
AND
DATABASE
MARKETING

GRAEME McCORKELL

THE INSTITUTE OF
DIRECT MARKETING

KOGAN
PAGE

YOURS TO HAVE AND TO HOLD
BUT NOT TO COPY

The publication you are reading is protected by copyright law. This means that the publisher could take you and your employer to court and claim heavy legal damages if you make unauthorised photocopies from these pages. Photocopying copyright material without permission is no different from stealing a magazine from a newsagent, only it doesn't seem like theft.

The Copyright Licensing Agency (CLA) is an organisation which issues licences to bring photocopying within the law. It has designed licensing services to cover all kinds of special needs in business, education and government.

If you take photocopies from books, magazines and periodicals at work your employer should be licensed with CLA. Make sure you are protected by a photocopying licence.

The Copyright Licensing Agency Limited, 90 Tottenham Court Road, London W1P 0LP. Tel: 0171 436 5931. Fax: 0171 436 3986.

First published in 1997
Reprinted 1997, 1998 (twice), 1999, 2000

Apart from any fair dealing for the purposes of research or private study, or criticism or review, as permitted under the Copyright, Designs and Patents Act, 1988, this publication may only be reproduced, stored or transmitted, in any form or by any means, with the prior permission in writing of the publishers, or in the case of reprographic reproduction in accordance with the terms and licences issued by the CLA. Enquiries concerning reproduction outside those terms should be sent to the publishers at the undermentioned address:

Kogan Page Limited
120 Pentonville Road
London N1 9JN

© Graeme McCorkell, 1997

The right of Graeme McCorkell to be identified as author of this work has been asserted by him in accordance with the Copyright, Designs and Patents Act 1988.

British Library Cataloguing in Publication Data
A CIP record for this book is available from the British Library.
ISBN 0 7494 1952 0 (Hardback) ISBN 0 7494 1960 1 (Paperback)

Typeset by Northern Phototypesetting Co. Ltd., Bolton
Printed and bound in Great Britain by Biddles Ltd, www.Biddles.co.uk

CONTENTS

PART 2   CREATING AND USING MARKETING INFORMATION SYSTEMS

FOREWORD

There are many books written by direct marketing practitioners which purport to explain how direct marketing works. Many, however, almost isolate direct marketing as a distinctive discipline.

Graeme's book is different. It does not dismiss the fundamental concept of marketing but skilfully demonstrates how this concept has evolved and changed as we approach the millennium. The driving force behind this change has been the information technology revolution, which has enabled marketers to focus on individuals rather than segments or masses. Customer marketing databases are a central theme in this text. They allow marketers to analyse, implement and control plans which are geared to gain 'share of customer' rather than share of market.

The targeting, interaction, continuity and control formulae developed in this book symbolise a new, dynamic approach to modern marketing. Most of the 'classic', predominantly American, marketing textbooks tell you how to develop your marketing strategies and plans, but tend to assume that you are starting a business and do not have existing customers. Other, more recent, books on relationship marketing discuss ways to build customer satisfaction. Graeme's is the first authoritative book to bring together both aspects as a continuous process of marketing.

An important theme in the book is that of return on marketing investments which can, for example, be quantified by setting customer marketing objectives and measuring the life-time value of customers. This ability to value customers as an asset is portrayed as being as important as brand equity to a business, but is still to be recognised by some senior management.

If you are a marketing practitioner you should read this book. In it you will recognise the essentials of good marketing practice, and you will learn how direct marketing can enhance your current practice, from researching new products to delivering enhanced customer satisfaction.

If you are a direct marketer you should read this book. It will demonstrate how direct marketing has evolved with technology to become central to modern marketing practice. And you may learn some new points about marketing you didn't know before.

If you are a marketing student you should read this book. There are good marketing books, but they teach you only half the story and do not fully reflect what modern marketing practice is today, particularly regarding the implementation and application of customer marketing databases.

Graeme's book reflects the most balanced view of today's modern direct marketing practice. It is written by a man who has been a mentor to hundreds of young people in direct marketing through his career. He has been Chairman of the Institute of Direct Marketing and I have been fortunate enough to have him as my mentor in this period. If you asked the ten most senior practitioners in direct marketing who they would most like to work with, it would be Graeme.

He has dedicated two years of his life, between consultancy work, to this book. No one has more authority or knowledge than Graeme. If you don't read it, cover to cover, you will be missing what is destined to become *the* classic text on direct marketing.

D A Holder
Managing Director, Institute of Direct Marketing

PREFACE

A century ago, in 1897, an Italian economist postulated a theory of income distribution. His name was Vilfredo Pareto and his theory – or a loose adaptation of it – is used by every direct marketer to explain why mass marketing doesn't work very well and why direct marketing works a lot better.

The diagram below illustrates Pareto's principle applied to marketing. I have never found an exception to this principle, although sometimes it operates more extremely than the diagram indicates.

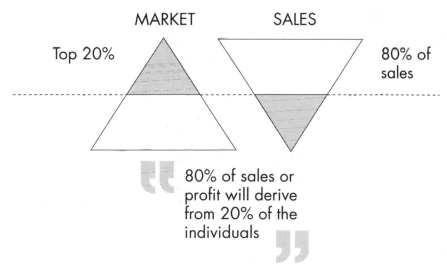

MARKET   SALES

Top 20%   80% of
                                            sales

> 80% of sales or
> profit will derive
> from 20% of the
> individuals

Pareto's principle – applications in direct marketing

Of course, marketers have always known, or at least suspected, that some customers are worth a great deal more to them than others. However, there was very little they could do about this until the computer came to their rescue.

Now customers are valued. Literally. Their lifetime value is projected and, in best practice direct marketing, they are treated accordingly. This book tells you how it all works. If you already know, I think you will find some new things in the book anyway.

Warning to purists: media *are* but data *is* throughout the text.

Graeme McCorkell

ACKNOWLEDGEMENTS

Writing is a solitary occupation. Only when it's all over does one realise how many people have helped.

For a start, the book was conceived by Derek Holder and was mostly written to a specification drawn up by Derek Holder and Neil Woodcock.

Most of the charts and tables are borrowed from the Institute of Direct Marketing and a number of the IDM crew have been involved one way or another, always helpfully. Particular reference must be made to Janice Pickard's help, without which there would have been no case histories, always the most valuable part of any marketing book.

I am truly grateful to those who have provided case history information and given permission for it to be used.

Finally, I must mention the special contributions of Simon Hall, Angus Jenkinson and Paul McCarthy. They reviewed the first three sections of the book very thoroughly, giving me many suggestions for improvements. This enabled me to make what I believe are useful revisions and to avoid repeating the mistakes in the last section.

My thanks also to the many others who have provided help and encouragement.

Graeme McCorkell
The Gables
Wistanstow
Craven Arms
Shropshire
SY7 8DG

PART ONE

MARKETING IN THE DATABASE AGE

1
WHAT IS DIRECT MARKETING?

IN THIS CHAPTER

Once upon a time there were people who knew exactly how to do marketing. They worked at Procter & Gamble. Then along came the silicon chip and the old certainties vanished.

In 1995, the Marketing Council surveyed 373 senior UK marketers. They were asked which firms they rated highest for their historical importance in marketing. The top four were:

- Procter & Gamble;

- Unilever;

- Coca Cola;

- Mars.

You will see from this list that all four are known as creators of fast-moving consumer goods, that three are American, and that three are chiefly known *for* their brands, not *as* brands – although it is true that Mars is known as a brand, too. The very homogeneity of this list is what is so striking about it. It suggests the packaged goods boys and girls know how to do this marketing stuff, especially those with an American accent, and the rest of us better copy them.

Things have changed. The same respondents were asked who they rated for their present-day importance. The four companies mentioned most often were:

- Virgin;

- British Airways;

- Tesco;

- Direct Line.

Of course, all four are brand names, not just corporate names. Otherwise the companies on this list have little in common beyond the fact that, unlike any on the previous list, they …

… all deal direct with the public, at least in their main businesses.

The 'new' list includes companies that are not yet mature and we can be pretty sure that this list will not be as stable as the first. Respondents clearly recognised these companies as innovators, not as the masters of a formulaic system of marketing. All four had found ways to reward customers for their business, in ways more or less reflecting each individual customer's contribution.

Every ten years 100 times as much information can be compressed onto a disk and the amount of information that can be transmitted rises equally dramatically. The implications of this are immense. It becomes feasible to know as much about the behaviour of every single customer as we used to know about an entire market segment, perhaps comprising a million customers. But how should we use all this information? The pace of change is so fast there is no perfect model to copy, no infallible formula for doing marketing right.

The big question in marketing today is not 'Who will buy this new product?' nor even 'Where is there a gap in the widgets market?' It is:

What will our customers want to buy from us next?

This change – from a product marketing strategy to a customer marketing strategy – is occasioned by the realisation that it is cheaper to identify and sell to established customers than to keep finding new customers. Direct marketers, or rather their ancestors, the mail order entrepreneurs, knew this 100 years ago. That is because they had to know who their customers were so that they could arrange deliveries.

Goodbye to stereotypes

When the makers of washing powders ruled the marketing world, there were two kinds of customer, wholesalers and retailers. There were three main kinds of consumer. They were called men, women and housewives. The mass marketers subdivided the three sexes into two age groups, under 35s and over 35s, and four socioeconomic groups, ABs, C1s, C2s and DEs. This enabled them to recognise as many as 24 kinds of people. Your behaviour pattern was explained by which pigeon-hole you occupied. For marketers selling business products there was also a special category called AB Businessmen. They were all called this, irrespective of their sex, age or social class.

This simplistic view of the world of consumers prevailed when the admired marketers were those who sold soap in quantity. Yet, even then, the direct marketers occupied a world in which consumers were customers and were described by their behaviour, not by their social class, age or sex.

What they want, not what they ought to want

Marketing is getting more interactive. Now that customers are getting promiscuous, marketers want to go steady. They talk about customer dialogue and relationship marketing. But they must learn to listen.

The customer conversation is very different conceptually from mass marketing. It reflects the needs of a sophisticated and confident market in which the customer expects his or her voice to be heard. There is no perfect model for this, but the most advanced working models we have are derived from direct marketing.

Direct marketing's contribution owes less to our skill at creating direct mail campaigns and more to the fact that the technological revolution hit us first. What had been simple customer mailing lists became customer databases recording the source, purchase history and profiles of individual customers. We had learned how to manipulate large volumes of customer data through modelling to group customers into broadly compatible behavioural segments, to predict their future behaviour and estimate their lifetime value to our business.

At one end of the scale, an independent shop can keep a customer database on a single PC and use it effectively with a minimum of training or technical knowledge. At the other end, a marketing manager can use a PC to fish data from a data warehouse containing many millions of records. This almost miraculous feat is performed with the aid of a processor and middleware to forge the link between alien mainframe technology and the cheery, familiar image presented by Windows.

In this chapter we will see that, however rapidly technology advances, the principles of direct marketing remain the same. There are four building blocks:

- *Targeting* – who will be interested in this now?

- *Interaction* – how did they respond to our last offer?

- *Control* – what was the return on our investment?

- *Continuity* – how can we build the customer relationship?

We will see how *interaction* provides the data that guides a customer marketing strategy, informing everything we do – not just direct mail, telemarketing or other direct response activity. Interaction provides the dynamic data for the marketing database. It tells us how we are doing and, together with direct marketing's other building blocks, is relevant throughout an integrated marketing campaign. It is direct marketing that has supplied us with the tools to plan and monitor integrated marketing campaigns.

So who will win the battle of the giants? The global brand proprietors, so admired for their historical importance in marketing? Or the retail technocrats whose access to customer data can give them unrivalled customer knowledge? This book will help you decide. But the winners in every market will not always be those with the most data. They will be those who listen best to what their customers are telling them.

Direct marketing is tailor-made marketing. Of course, you can't devise a unique marketing strategy for every customer or prospective customer. But neither does a tailor design a suit for each customer. The tailor merely ensures that a basic design is adapted to match the shape, size and taste of the customer. The tailor's efforts are perfectly focused on the individual customer.

The degree of tailoring is almost infinitely varied. A Motorola pager may be tailored to the exact specification of a customer. No other customer may choose the same specification. On the other hand the Glenlivet whisky drinker does not expect his or her whisky to be served up in a unique recipe. Tailoring will be reduced to marketing communications and, perhaps, the offer. These may be varied according to what is known about the consumer. For example, is the consumer a user of another Seagrams brand? Is the consumer a user of other single malt whiskies? Or premium quality blended Scotch? Little may be known about the consumer other than one piece of factual information. But even this will be enough to drive communications and offers that are likely to be more relevant than if our whisky drinker were treated merely as a member of a broad 'target group'.

According to Marshall McLuhan, 'One of the future aspects of advertising is the custom-made, the tailor-made. Instead of peddling mass-produced commodities, advertising is going to become a personal service to each individual.'

Both Motorola and Seagrams could, if they so decided, use direct marketing to the exclusion of other marketing methods. But they are more likely to take the view that volume sales and profit will be maximised by employing direct marketing within an integrated marketing plan.

MARKETING WITH INTELLIGENCE

The origins of direct marketing are in mail order. Long before the microchip enabled direct marketing to become tailor-made, mail order firms already made sharp distinctions between some potential buyers and others. They were categorised into unconverted enquirers, current customers and lapsed customers. Within these broad categories, more refined value indicators might be used. For example, the recency, frequency and value of past transactions were found to be predictive of the likelihood and value of future transactions.

Thus customers could be typecast, not by their membership of a group, such as an age group or social class, but by their previous *behaviour*. Since behaviour could be recorded on an individual basis, it was possible to select people to receive future offers on an individual basis, too. Thus the targeting of direct marketing became based not on how people *ought* to behave (as 18–24-year-olds or whatever) but on how they had behaved previously.

Now that membership of any kind of grouping is so much less predictive of people's behaviour than in the past, direct marketing methodology is at an overwhelming advantage. But, to employ it, we must gather the facts about customers' behaviour.

Let's see how direct marketers think. Here's a case based on the launch of a car servicing and repair shop.

Launching a business – the garage

Bang in the middle of the overgrown village where I once lived is a useful little business whose proprietors and sole employees service and repair cars. One of the two partners is trained on Renaults and the other on BMWs. How would you have advised them to market their business when they started out?

Would you tell them to advertise in local directories? A good idea, perhaps, but suppose they would have to wait for six months before their first ad appeared. Would you tell them to take local freesheet advertising or hire distributors to drop leaflets through letterboxes? If so, what about the 93 per cent of households in the area where there is no Renault or BMW parked outside the front door?

Let's assume we have looked at their business plan, discovered they have next to no money to spend in advance of generating cash from their business, that they have invested in a PC with a good bundle of software and that they have decided which partner is in charge of their information system. This is the advice we could give them.

Creating a marketing database

The vast majority of the first year's business will come from private owners of Renault and BMW cars. We estimate that about 85 per cent of the households within the natural catchment area for the business own at least one car and that at least 90 per cent of these are responsible for the maintenance of at least one car. Our business partners believe that the aggregate Renault and BMW market share is above the national average and could be as high as 10 per cent. This gives us a penetration of 7–8 per cent of all households. The return on their new business investment will therefore depend on targeting these households as accurately as possible.

Our partners must now build a street directory to be held on their PC. They could buy a copy of the Electoral Register but they don't have money to burn. A local street map will suffice as a reference. They must now tour the neighbourhood, preferably on their bikes, hitting the most promising streets on Sunday mornings and leaving the others to weekday evenings and other times. They will note down each address at which a Renault or a BMW is parked. Of course, the cars will not always belong to the residents and they will miss cars that are out and about. But, if they do the work thoroughly, they will succeed in data capturing the addresses of about three-quarters of all owners.

They will have created a 'suspect' file, that is a file of potential prospects for their business. This file will now be used both as an addressing medium and as a reference tool for management information as response and business is created. As addresses convert to customer status, they will be flagged on this file and the customer names will be added. However, the full customer data will be held on a separate file, cross-referenced by URNs (unique reference numbers) to the suspect file.

The new business offer

When we looked at our partners' business plan, we naturally established that they had undertaken a rudimentary competitive analysis. This was not difficult as each partner had been Head Service Engineer at the local main Renault and BMW dealerships. They had estimated they could undercut main dealer service charges by 20 per cent, offering free collection and delivery, or by 25 per cent if they cut service to the bone. As marketers, we recommend superior service at the higher price because superior service will lead to greater customer loyalty and more customer referrals (recommendations to friends).

However, to overcome human inertia and to encourage suspects to take a chance on the new service, we need an introductory offer. We decide on an introductory discount of £10 on an oil service or £20 on a full service. Combined with free collection and delivery, a free wax and polish, and a saving of around 20 per cent on the normal service cost, this should prove to be a powerful inducement. Unfortunately, the majority of our suspects' cars will not yet be due for servicing. So we need a mechanism to get them to identify themselves to us. We can do this by holding our offer open until their next service in exchange for confirmation of name, address and car ownership data, and details of when they think the next service will be due. As part of the offer, we promise to mail a service reminder before this date. As well as starting some mutually beneficial customer relationships, our new business programme will also convert a number of our suspects into prospects. These, too, will be flagged on the suspect file and the full data will be transferred to the customer file. This file will permit our partners to mail out service reminders. In fact, it will be a diarised file and the reminders will be created automatically.

Using the word processing software, our partners must now create a 'mailing' which they will deliver by hand. The mailing will not be personalised because we do not know the names of the suspects. Nor will the mailing be written as if we knew the recipients were Renault or BMW owners. The mailing must make the offer clear, must convey that the offer is open until the next service is due and advise the recipient how to respond. If a service is due within the next four weeks, the recipient will be advised to book this by phone. If not, the recipient will be asked to return a pre-paid postcard giving the details we want. We may even put a second class stamp on the postcard as this will save applying for a business reply or Freepost licence and it will increase the response rate. The copy must also establish the name and location of the business and the credentials of our partners. These, of course, are impeccable and will be known to some of the recipients.

Forecasting the result

This is difficult because we have no back data, but we need it for the final business plan. We estimate that there are 16,000 addresses in the catchment area and that our suspect file will be around 1000. Inaccuracies will reduce this to about 800. Of the 800, about 130 will own cars due for a service within the first month. We hope to secure 10–15 per cent of these services and add a few more from walk-in business and former customers who the partners know. We also hope to get 7–10 per cent response from those whose cars are not yet due for a service. This will give the partners between 13 and 20 attributable jobs in the first month and 45–65 convertible prospects for the next five months. The out-of-pocket expenses will be about £500, excluding the cost of the introductory discount.

Managing customer relationships

For each customer the car, service and payment details will be recorded as well as the due date for the next service. Incidentally, the accounting database will be separate from the customer marketing and service database but will be linked by the customer's URN. An important part of data capture, for both customers and prospects, will be the daytime and evening telephone numbers. These will be used to make reminder calls when the customer does not respond to a service reminder. Less obviously, they will be used to make courtesy calls within a week of each job to check that the customer is satisfied with the work.

All that remains is to surprise and, we hope, delight each new customer with an unexpected gesture of appreciation. A small present, such as a large-scale soft-back road atlas or a bottle of windscreen wash liquid, will be placed in each returned car together with a card giving the business address and contact details. This will be the first shot at becoming famous for service and attracting business through customer recommendations.

We may also recommend that the partners spend some money on signage and on local advertising but the database will be the heart of the marketing programme, making targeted and timely communication possible and providing a wealth of marketing data. In due course it will be possible to confirm the catchment area, the accuracy of the suspect data collection, the split of Renault to BMW to other business, the source of each new customer and the payback on each marketing activity. There is no reason why our partners should not become as sophisticated in their marketing planning and execution as a business many times bigger.

THE DATABASE IS THE NERVE CENTRE

In our homespun example of the motor engineers, we have used the term 'database' rather loosely. More accurately, a database is a collection of files. The suspect file and any prospect and customer files together make up the marketing database. In Chapter 6 we will see how these can be organised to allow relevant information to be plucked out of each file to supply the answer to any enquiry we may wish to make.

If you have learned your marketing theory from the classical texts, you will have found no reference to the central role of a one-to-one marketing database. That is not because we are now advocating 'alternative' marketing. On the contrary, data-driven marketing is becoming the mainstream. It is simply that the classical texts were written in advance of a technological revolution. Every 20 years, the computational power that can be bought for one pound has increased by a factor of 1000. Marketing information is almost the only marketing cost that has moved downwards. It is not moving steadily down. It is hurtling down. Little wonder, then, that the practice of marketing has lagged behind the rate of technological advance. The cost of information processing is now one thousandth of what it was when most of today's marketing directors were trainees.

Back in 1975, it would have been possible for our motor engineers to follow our proposed marketing strategy. But it would have been immensely laborious and their information system would almost certainly have collapsed under the strain. Now it is possible for a business with, say, 5 million customers to know their preferences as well as a convenience store proprietor knows his customers' preferences.

Addressing the first Institute of Direct Marketing Symposium on 28 June 1995, Keith Martin-Smith of Dell Computing revealed that the company received 50,000 telephone calls a day from its customers. Every call received since 1987 had been logged and the essential details had been data captured. The resulting data was used to make changes to pricing and inventory, no item in the 9600 product inventory having been on the market for more than four months. The data volumes involved are mind boggling and a common solution is to keep raw data in a data warehouse rather than risk discarding original bits of information by summarising them. Once a working system is in place, it is no harder to make marketing decisions based on immense volumes of individual customer data than on small volumes of market research data.

We will discuss the impact of this technological advance in the following two chapters. For now, it is enough to say that the database provides a central information system that can be used to drive and assess the contribution of each marketing activity, whether this activity is labelled 'direct marketing' or not. It is the very centrality of a one-to-one marketing database that has impeded the adoption of the technology in the past. For marketing people who have mastered longer-established methods, it has been hard to accept that what used to work so well may no longer be good enough and harder still to begin learning a new game with apparently more complex rules. Yet it is the database that makes integrated marketing possible, that is to say, marketing in which diverse sales channels and communications channels work in harmony to create a sum bigger than the constituent parts. Furthermore, the basic design of a one-to-one marketing database is very simple to understand.

THE FIVE-MINUTE GUIDE TO DATABASES

'Advertising', says Regis McKenna (1991), 'serves no useful purpose ... The new marketing requires a feedback loop; it is this element that is missing from the monologue of advertising but that is built into the dialogue of marketing.' The database provides the feedback loop.

At its simplest, as in Figure 1.1, the database answers three questions: *Who? What?* and *Where?* The 'Who' question enquires about the identity of the customer. The 'What' question asks what the customer bought (or enquired about). The 'Where' question refers to the sales channel used by the customer. This might be a dealer, a branch, a salesperson, an advertisement, a mailing or a telephone call. If the database gave us no more than the answers to these three questions it would very useful. But we marketers are demanding and we want our database to achieve stardom.

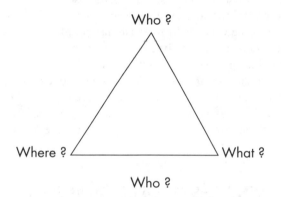

Figure 1.1

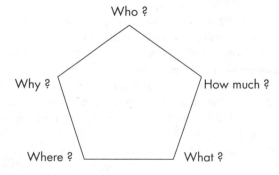

Figure 1.2

So, in Figure 1.2 we turn our triangle into a star, or pentagon. Now we can get our database to provide two more useful answers. The first of our extra questions is *How much?* That is, what was the value of the transaction? The second is *Why?* That is, what did we do, if anything, to provoke the customer's purchase? There's no need to worry about *When?* Our system will record, in retrievable form, the timing of each event.

We must now be sure that our computer stores this information until we decide it is no longer relevant and are prepared to archive it. In this way we can build up a historical picture of the customer's dealings with us, thus establishing the customer's value, enabling us to recognise this in our future dealings and warning us when there is any discontinuity in our customer's transactions.

Never satisfied, we will want to string a host of reference files to the core of our database. The core is good enough to tell us how our customer relationships are developing, how our sales channels are performing, which products our customers are buying and what is working in our marketing mix. The reference data we will add merely increases the functionality of the database. For example, we need to string contact data to our customer identity so that we can mail or telephone the customer. We may also use the postcode or add a SIC (Standard Industrial Classification – see Chapter 8) for customer profiling. A discussion of the value of postcodes in targeting will begin in Chapter 5.

We know what the customer has bought but we may wish to add more detail, such as colour preference or dress size. We may wish to add margin to the 'how much?' data. And we are almost certain to want to add the cost of the promotional stimuli to the 'why?' information. But, important as they are, these extra bits of information do not interfere with the basics of our database design. This remains simple.

PRINCIPLES OF DIRECT MARKETING

Direct marketing and its information systems focus on what the customer or prospect does. To put it another way, information about past behaviour is used to predict future behaviour. This information is processed on an individual basis and can be analysed and acted upon on an individual basis, even if the number of customers reaches millions. This does not render marketing research obsolete, as we will see in Chapter 11. However, if we can rely only upon marketing research information, we are forced to make assumptions about customer behaviour which may be generally right but may be wrong in an individual case.

We may suppose that because our customer is female, belongs to socioeconomic group B, is aged 30 and lives in the South East she 'ought' to behave in a particular way. But people do not all conform to type. Why should they? We should try to recognise and respect our customers' idiosyncrasies. To fail to do so is the antithesis of good marketing.

More than 20 years ago I worked on the advertising and direct marketing for a small chain of quality shoe shops. It was run by twin brothers, one of whom, Adrian Elliott, was responsible for marketing. The central plank of their marketing communications strategy was a direct mail programme to their customers. Even in those days, their selection system permitted 16 variations of the content of the mailings they sent out. Mailings were so crucial to profitability that they tried, unsuccessfully, to take action against the Post Office for failing to settle a labour dispute that continued for six weeks. Among the items of customer information they data captured was age group. I asked, 'How do you know their ages?' The answer was that they didn't. The age captured was the age group for whom the shoes bought were deemed appropriate. 'The customer's real age is no business of mine,' Adrian told me. His logic was impeccable and logic drives the best direct marketing practice. If a 50-year-old woman wants shoes that lie about her age, why should the marketer spoil her harmless deception? Her choice of shoes reflects who she wants to be and that choice should be respected. If Elliott had nosily enquired about her true age they would have made the wrong assumption and sent her the wrong mailing. What customers buy is the most important clue to what they will want in the future.

A few years later the brothers sold the business to a company which considered the customer database to be a useless extravagance. The new owners bankrupted the business within two years.

Targeting, interaction, control and continuity

Successful direct marketing is based on four features. These are *targeting*, *interaction*, *control* and *continuity*, or *TICC* for short.

You will see from Figure 1.3 that we are back to triangles. The diagram can be looked at either as four triangles or alternatively as one triangle inside another. *Interaction* has been placed in the centre. It includes the stimuli we marketers produce in the hope of eliciting a response from the people in our target market. Their response is also included in the interaction triangle. In all cases we will attempt to attribute a response to the correct stimulus. Thus the results of our activities form the core of our information system and enable us to become progressively more efficient at *targeting*, *control* and *continuity*. That is because we are learning by experience.

Targeting refers to our selection of the recipients of our message, whatever media we may use, be it broadcast media, print advertising, direct mail, telemarketing or sales calls. We may be targeting our established customers, identified prospects or a much larger audience of 'suspects'. In all of these cases our targeting decisions will generally outweigh in importance decisions about what to offer and how to frame our message. By examining the results of our previous attempts to target correctly, we can keep on refining our future targeting.

Control is the management of our marketing. It includes setting objectives,

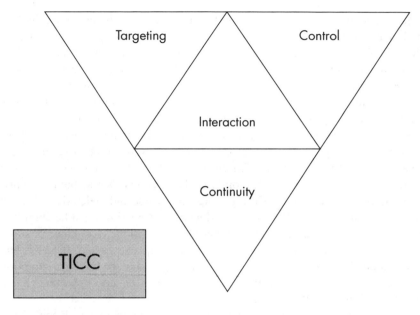

Figure 1.3

planning at the strategic and operational levels, budgeting and assessment of results. The process is cyclical, future planning being informed by past results. The completeness of our data within the *interaction* triangle will be crucial to the exercise of control.

In the vast majority of business enterprises, the bulk of profit arises from dealings with established customers. *Continuity* is about retaining customers, cross-selling other products to them and uptrading them. Our painstaking care in recording *interaction* enables us to communicate with customers, recognising their interest and showing appreciation of their past custom. When I started out in direct marketing, the importance of continuity was very largely unappreciated by general marketers. Yet I found in all the industries for which I was able to derive comparative selling cost statistics that the cost of making a sale to an established customer was a small fraction of the cost of acquiring a new one. A figure which kept recurring was one-fifth and this figure certainly applied within the new car market. Yet, even in the 1980s, car marketers appeared obsessed with 'conquest' sales far more than with brand loyalty.

In their book *The Machine that Changed the World*, Womak, Jones and Roos report that:

> Toyota was determined never to lose a former buyer ... it could minimize the chance
> of this happening by using data on its customer database to predict what Toyota
> buyers would want next ... Unlike mass-producers who conduct evaluation 'clinics'
> on randomly selected buyers, Toyota went directly to its established customers ...
> Established customers were treated as members of the Toyota family.

In one generation Toyota went from small producer to World's Number One in the automotive market. In survey after survey, Toyota have recorded higher satisfaction scores from owners than rival manufacturers.

Taking the example of a car maker with a 5 per cent market share and a 60 per cent customer loyalty rate, it is clear that the chances of making a sale to an established customer are likely to be many times greater than to a competitor's customer. Is it not logical to construct research samples from the people most likely to buy the car?

Our customer database makes this easier but it also gives us an unfair advantage. We can use it to communicate with our customers both discreetly and discretely. We can pave the way to future sales by keeping our customers informed and listening to what they have to say to us. If we do these things better than our competitors, our loyalty rate will be superior to theirs and so our eventual return on new business investment will also be better. Our aim, like Toyota's, will be to maximise *lifetime customer value*, that is the total net revenue each customer will contribute to our business.

Lifetime customer value or share of customer?

The lifetime value of a customer clearly has two dimensions, one being the customer's loyalty measured by time. Yet, in many markets, customer loyalty can be measured on a very short-term basis. For example, in packaged goods, retail and business-to-business markets, buyers may select from a portfolio of brands, shops or suppliers. It is no less important in these markets to employ the techniques of direct marketing to converse confidentially with customers, and not rely solely on out-shouting the competition in a crowded marketplace. The concept of lifetime customer value remains important in these markets but may be re-expressed as 'share of customer'.

Since it is cheaper to make sales to existing customers than acquire new ones, it is more profitable to increase market share by gaining more business from *each* customer than by increasing the *number* of customers. It costs less to keep in touch with one customer who spends a million pounds than a million customers who each spend one pound.

In the next chapter we will examine the rise and fall of mass marketing. We will also see how the four Ps, *product*, *price*, *place* and *promotion*, are no longer fixed-point decisions. That is to say, all of these elements can be varied to suit customers, and reflect their value to us, on a one-to-one basis.

Automating the four Ps

There is nothing fanciful about this. It is already happening. A complex manufactured product such as a car can be delivered in an almost countless choice of specifications. The cost of insuring it will depend on an automated decision system driven by your answers to 20 or more questions. The system has the capacity to sort through millions of permutations to make a precise calculation of the risk you and your car represent. The bank may have already offered you a pre-agreed loan to buy the car. This offer will have been driven by another automated decision system that has decided there is a better than, say, 98 per cent chance you will repay the loan. The system will have done this without troubling you to answer a single question. It is more accurate than a traditional bank manager's assessment.

Today you can bank at home or through any branch in a network. The depth of your relationship with your bank will be decided by you. Their charges will reflect, increasingly, your profitability (or lack of it) to them. You decide how much you will tell them about yourself. You decide how often you want statements and whether or not you want to receive marketing communications. As time progresses, you will be choosing and paying for bank services on an à la carte basis, not on some pre-set formula they have created for 'people like you'.

Already, decisions on the four Ps are increasingly being made on a one-to-one basis. Whenever they are, the direct marketing principles of targeting, interaction, control and continuity will drive these decisions. Marketing is becoming a tailor-made process, but one automated by computer.

When cherry-picking doesn't work

In borrowing from direct marketing experience, many who are interested in integrated marketing or integrated marketing communications, in particular, have been selective in their use of the TICC principles. Some have become preoccupied with targeting, others with interaction or with continuity through customer loyalty programmes. But it is the whole TICC formula that makes direct marketing work and it is the whole formula that must be imported into integrated marketing strategy.

In case you are in doubt, reread our example of the two motor engineers. You will see that this simple case exploits all four principles that are the basis of successful direct marketing. Direct marketing empowers the small business to market in a sophisticated fashion and empowers the large business to recognise its customers as individuals. That is the future of marketing.

TO SUM UP

The future of marketing depends on recognising the individuality of customers. The model for this is derived from direct marketing. Direct marketing analysis began by organising customers into behavioural categories because it was found that past behaviour was a reasonable basis for predicting future behaviour.

As information technology has advanced it has become practicable to gather more information about customers on an individual basis. The information may be held in its raw state in a data warehouse or it may be organised and, when necessary, summarised in a marketing information system comprising different elements or files. A single PC may hold both transactional data and the marketing database in a small business.

The customer marketing database answers the questions *Who? What? Where?* and, probably, *How much?* and *Why?* Information about what customers do provides much of the dynamic (constantly changing) data for our database. The results of interaction between customers and the marketing organisation enable the direct marketer to exercise *control*, make informed decisions about *targeting* and securing *continuity* of custom (*TICC*). Product, place, price and promotion decisions are no longer necessarily fixed-point decisions. Each of these elements may be varied within an acceptable range.

In a world of rapid change, the fastest change of all has been in the development of information technology. This has upset a well ordered marketing apple cart. Marketers are having to learn to live in a world where the customer answers back. Or chooses not to, of course.

2

THE RISE AND FALL OF MASS MARKETING

IN THIS CHAPTER

Procter & Gamble, Unilever, Coca Cola, Mars ... these were the ultimate mass marketers according to the Marketing Council's survey respondents. But what was it that worked so well about mass marketing ... and why can't it work again?

Not many years ago, 20 million people in the UK read the same Sunday newspaper, read the same weekly magazine and watched the same TV series. There wasn't much choice. Advertising cheerfully patronised its mass audience. It featured such characters as Katie, the Oxo lady, and Persil mums. Conformity was rife.

In this chapter we trace the rise and fall of mass marketing and its companions, mass production and mass media.

Mass production is essentially a nineteenth-century idea, its great pioneer being Samuel Colt who died in 1861. Although Colt benefited from the Mexican War of 1846, he took no part in starting it and therefore cannot be considered a mass marketing pioneer. On the other hand, Henry Ford, who applied Colt's ideas to making cars instead of guns, had the vision to see that demand for cars would increase exponentially if they could be produced faster with less labour and, therefore, more cheaply.

Theodore Levitt, in 'Marketing Myopia', an article in the *Harvard Business Review*, argues that we should celebrate Ford for his marketing vision, not his adaptation of Colt's production principles. When the first Model Ts rolled off the production line, Colt had been dead for 48 years. The interval between the development of mass production technique and the marketing realisation was long.

For some time it has been technologically possible to drive high-speed automated processes with individualised data, in other words to mass produce goods that are not identical. In fact each unit may differ from the last one off the line. The producers have been waiting for marketing to catch up with the immense opportunity this creates but, understandably, the marketers have found it difficult to arrive at a rapid solution.

Individually made packaged goods may be some distance away but here, too, the trend is towards micro-market segmentation. William Hesketh Lever, who built Lever's fortune on soap made from vegetable oils instead of tallow, mass producing it under the brand name Sunlight, might well have been astonished to discover that Persil Automatic is produced in at least 40 varieties. How, he might have asked, are you going to explain who or what each one is for? It is a question some feel the marketers have yet to answer convincingly.

Electronic control of automated production and the configuration of services enables the consumer to be offered almost infinite choice. It is no longer necessary to accept that products and services must be the same as the next door neighbour's if they are to be affordable. Functional efficiency, reliability and hygienic standards of products are no longer an issue. Mass production and its partner, mass marketing, are outmoded.

In October 1993, the renowned pioneer of direct marketing, Lester Wunderman, delivered a paper to the Direct Marketing Association Conference in Toronto. He proposed: 'The new definition of a brand will be that it represents a cluster of a consumer's needs. It is each customer who is becoming the brand.' He quoted the example of the National Bicycle Industrial Company in Japan. This company made 11,231,862 variations of bikes, customised to buyers' individual measurements and preferences at a cost 10 per cent higher than that of a mass produced bike. 'And, therefore, what would be the brand name on the bicycle if I bought one? Not National but Wunderman. I am the brand.'

THE FUTURE FOR BRANDS

Brands will not disappear and the need to promote their values will not diminish. The proliferation of choice made possible by technology will tend to increase the value set upon the brand that stands for a whole company, or range, as opposed to the single-product brand. When a producer can serve up the product the way we want it, we must still exercise a choice of producers. Our concern will increasingly be directed towards the values which a producer represents. The more we take product quality and obsolescence for granted, the more demanding we will become of other virtues, such as service standards, ethics and environmental responsibility. Shell experienced this painfully when its plan for deep-sea disposal of a North Sea oil platform was disrupted by consumer response to Greenpeace pressure.

Research undertaken by the Henley Centre showed that the consumer's faith in nationally advertised and well known brands actually increased between 1981 and 1993. Yet the same study showed an increase in the perception that retailers' own-label products represented the best value for money. This apparent conflict was explained by the increasing strength of retail corporate brands. Own-label products had always been perceived as cheaper. They had less often been perceived as representing better value.

In *The Popcorn Report* (1991), Faith Popcorn wrote: 'The general direction corporations have taken over the last decade has been to retreat behind their products, leaving them, in effect, to speak for themselves. Promoting products over their makers. What corporations need to do next is form relationships with their consumers. Relationships based on trust.'

REMEMBER WHEN BATHTUBS WERE WHITE ...?

The socioeconomic and demographic changes that prompted the mass marketing revolution have been well documented and the end of mass marketing has long been predicted. As long ago as 1970, Alvin Toffler introduced 'demassification' to the vocabulary in his book *Future Shock*. When mass markets cease to exist, mass marketing becomes redundant. The desire to conform, at least in some respects, exists in all of us. But the degree of conformity we practise has become a matter of individual choice to more people than at any time in the past.

The greatest example of mass conformity was 'the melting pot' of nineteenth- and early twentieth-century America. In exchange for protection and opportunity, the new American was expected to learn English, uphold the Constitution and lead the American way of life. At the time it was a reasonable contract and one which has had a lasting effect on Western culture, making English the predominant world language. Today, it would be unacceptable to melt down immigrant cultures and attempt the creation of a monoculture. Today, advertising which is in the English language is incomprehensible to millions of American consumers.

In far more subtle ways conformity was enforced in all industrialised societies. Blue-collar workers predominated, wore identical working garments and, except in wartime, were mostly male. They went on holiday in the same weeks to the same places. For the most part, women were chained to the sink. The vast majority of the population were subject to the same cultural influences and knew how they were expected to conduct themselves.

Their aspirations were similar and their buying behaviour was predictable. It was a mass marketer's paradise. Everyone wanted a TV set, a refrigerator, a washing machine, a telephone, a car and a packaged holiday abroad in a predictable sequence.

By 1995, less than 27 per cent of the workforce were engaged in blue-collar jobs, about 48 per cent of those in gainful employment were women, the nuclear family had become a minority group and the growing population segments were mainly in the age groups of 35 years and over. A major survey conducted by J. Walter Thompson, Millward Brown and the Henley Centre (1993) described the 1990s consumer as 'The Thoughtful Butterfly', literate, sceptical and thoughtful about the choice of a brand and even disdainful of mass media advertising techniques.

From the end of the Second World War, conformity had been enforced by lack of choice. Now, for 20 years or more, consumer choice has increased faster than disposable incomes, reducing market shares and customer loyalty. 'Remember when bathtubs were white, telephones were black and cheques were green?' asks John Naisbitt in *Megatrends* (1982). When the possession of any of these desirable commodities was a status symbol, the consumer did not complain about the colour.

WHEN MASS MEDIA RULED

The pervasive influence of mass media has been given less attention than it merits. In the UK, immediately before the advent of commercial television, it was possible to reach more than half the adult population by placing one advertisement in *The News of the World* and another in *The Radio Times*. The former peaked at a circulation of just under 8 million and the latter at just over 8 million. By the time ITV offered national coverage, it was possible to reach half the adult population with one commercial. The commercial breaks were dominated by ads for fast-moving consumer goods, by brands for which continuous exposure on TV became unaffordable in the 1970s.

People read the same things and watched the same TV programmes. Television offered the advertiser extraordinary value for money. It was possible to make a new brand famous in a matter of weeks. When Procter & Gamble launched Camay on the toilet soap market in the late 1950s using heavyweight national TV, it became brand leader almost overnight. In the process, it drove down the long established Cussons' Imperial Leather market share from 6 to 2 per cent. When Cussons retaliated by doubling spend and switching to TV, they restored their 6 per cent share in only two months and eventually took over brand leadership.

Terrestrial television has long ceased to exercise this extraordinary power. In February 1988, Eric Nicholl, Managing Director of UB Brands, was quoted as saying: 'Since 1980 our advertising expenditure has grown more than 100% ... our media weight has declined by 25%.' The mass media coverage and frequency required by mass marketing is being priced out of the reach of most brands. Meanwhile the brands themselves have had to spawn more varieties to preserve their market shares, rendering the marketing communications task more difficult. When Procter & Gamble launched Camay, both this product and Imperial Leather came in one formula, one colour and two sizes.

The power of television to generate awareness of products has had a profound effect on marketing communications. Advertising messages have been refined, polished and simplified because that is what the medium dictates. The information content of most commercials is minimal, unsatisfying to the more thoughtful and sceptical consumer of today. In their book, *The One-to-One Future*, Peppers and Rogers (1993) remark: 'The only reason "awareness" advertising plays much of a part at all in marketing today is that the mass media available for promoting a product electronically and inexpensively are not very good at doing anything else.'

To be sure, there will always be a role for simple advertising messages but simple advertising messages are no longer sufficient. They must now form part of an integrated marketing communications strategy that offers the consumer the means to exercise an informed choice. The proliferation of magazines to aid car buyers and PC hardware and software buyers is an example of the increasing demand for more substantial information. Better nutritional and ingredient information on product packs is another example. These same packs increasingly carry the offer of a helpline to call for yet more information and advice.

COLLABORATIVE MARKETING

In his influential paper, 'Marketing is Everything', Regis McKenna (1991) postulated that marketing must become a collaborative process. Only through dialogue and collaboration is it possible for the consumer to exercise a choice between many alternatives. According to McKenna:

> Marketing today is not a function; it is a way of doing business. Marketing is not a new ad campaign or this month's promotion. Marketing has to be all-pervasive, part of everyone's job description, from the receptionists to the board of directors. Its job is not to fool the customer nor to falsify the company's image. It is to integrate the customer into the design of the product and to design a systematic process for interaction that will create substance in the relationship.

Such a view would seem idealistic in a media environment that offers only the opportunity for monologue and no opportunity for dialogue. But the humble telephone and the newer interactive media are changing the media map. Of course, dialogue needs to be simplified. But by touching a screen it is possible to choose between, say, four alternatives. As the next menu appears, another choice can be exercised by touching the screen again. Within a matter of minutes, a choice can be made between thousands of alternatives. The technology permitting this is familiar, at least in its application, to most schoolchildren and the majority of office workers.

Participation, not passivity

In the early to mid-1990s, sales of printed encyclopaedias were savaged by the new availability of Encarta, Grolier and other encyclopaedias available on CD-ROM. Although the content of these works was not extensive, they employed multimedia presentation and encouraged active participation. The Nintendo generation prefers active media and participation was the seductive element attracting users to the Internet.

In the same period, Advanced Promotional Technologies (APT) were installing multimedia touch-screen terminals in US supermarkets. The shopper could touch the screen for a recipe idea or cookery demonstration, receive money-off coupons by inserting a membership card, pay by inserting a credit card and even receive a personalised 'mailing'. The contents of the mailing and the brands to which the offers applied would be determined by the items she chose in last week's shop. No two shoppers would necessarily receive exactly the same offers. The technology was used to introduce differential pricing so that loyal shoppers who elected to join a membership scheme could buy at lower prices than occasional shoppers. The terminal allowed the occasional shopper to touch the screen, receive information on the benefits of membership and to join by entering a few personal details. By collaborating with each other, the store and the customer each benefited.

The database as a defence system

An independent supermarket, we'll call it Wilsons, used APT's Vision Value Network to fight off competition from a new multiple opening within its catchment area. The first step was to review the purchases of members of the scheme against those of non-members. It was discovered that members represented one-third of all customers but three-quarters of all sales. The top 5 per cent of all customers accounted for 25 per cent of sales and the top 10 per cent for 40 per cent of all sales. A programme of benefits was devised for members only immediately before, during and after the competitive launch. In the week before the competitive store opened purchases by members increased 15 per cent over the six-week average, they dropped 2 per cent below the average in the competitive launch week and recovered to 4 per cent above the average value a week later. In the same weeks, sales to non-members remained level for week one, dropped by 18 per cent in week two and by 20 per cent in week 3.

Wilsons lost some members during this period, but the extra benefits offered allowed them to recruit two new members for each one lost. The new members spent an average of $90 per shop compared with $75 for the lost shoppers. Since the identities of the lost members were known, the highest spenders among them were mailed. They were offered a 10 per cent discount on a $200 shop. Of these 80 per cent responded, on average spending more after they returned to Wilsons than they had before they defected.

The scandalous wastage of untargeted sales promotion

Studies from a number of countries indicate that between 70 and 90 per cent of mass-distributed money-off coupons are redeemed by regular users of an established store or brand. A study conducted by Ehrenberg, Hammond and Goodhardt (1991) for the London Business School used the raw data from consumer panel research to track the relationship between pre-promotion, promotion period and post-promotion buyers of established brands. It was found that promotions were largely ineffective in reaching new buyers and, although they might cause temporary shifts of preference within a consumer's chosen brand portfolio, they had no discernible residual value.

The wastage involved in untargeted promotion is becoming unacceptable. The net effect may be little more than to drive down margins as consumers switch between two or three favoured brands when one of them is offering a discount.

Wilsons' experience is one example of the additional marketing power customer collaboration offers. The store that knows who its customers are (and, therefore, who they are not) within its catchment area can target its promotion for both customer retention and customer acquisition to the best advantage. If, like Wilsons, the store knows who its *best* customers are and what their buying preferences are, then its marketing will become yet more effective and more beneficial to the customer. Furthermore, stores with customers' previous purchase data can offer suppliers the opportunity to target genuine competitive brand users with their offers, thus resolving the problem highlighted in the London Business School study.

THE END OF THE FOUR Ps?

The beginning of the end for mass marketing was signalled in the 1970s with a wave of market segmentation. But few marketers recognised that market segmentation would increase to the point when the ultimate market segment becomes one individual company, household or individual. It may be convenient for the purposes of forecasting and 'suspect' targeting to group people together into clusters sharing recognisable characteristics. But in terms of delivering customer choice and satisfaction, there will be no substitute for recognising the individuality of each customer.

The Head of Automotive Design at Toyota, Hiroyuki Yoshida, said: 'We now live in an age of diversity. There is apparently no limit to the amount of differentiation or the diversity of preferences. If we cannot keep pace with the growth of this diversity we are bound to decline.'

Within the same 1993 paper in which he quoted National Bicycle's 11 million varieties of bike, Lester Wunderman referred to Motorola's choice of 29 million varieties of Bravo Pager. Does this spell the end of the first of marketing's four Ps, P for product? Surely not, because varieties have to be devised around a basic design, formula or recipe. However, the ability to programme choice into the design and to control production so that no two items at the end of the line need be the same becomes as important as the original concept. The amount of choice becomes a potential competitive advantage. Furthermore, less assumption about consumer preferences is required when we are not committed to producing a large number of identical products.

Price decisions, too, must still be made. But as we saw in the example of Wilsons, the price may depend not simply on the precise variety of the product the customer has specified, but on what the individual customer is worth, or predicted to become worth, to the marketer's organisation.

Increasingly, place is becoming a matter of choice and the extent of this choice will increase with the growth of interactive media. Consumers are increasingly opting to deal with travel, banking, insurance and, even, mortgages by telephone. There has been rapid growth in the ordering of goods by phone, fax and, more latterly, by e-mail. Marketers are beginning to question the logic of moving the customers to the goods instead of moving the goods to the customers. Many customers take a similar view. Since no one avenue will be right for every customer, competitive strategy may well dictate that choice of distribution channel is a necessity.

Promotion decisions will remain critical and are getting harder to make. However, at the individual level, many of these are already automated. The offers received by customers, the information sent to them and the timing of marketing communications are already driven by computer in many companies. Again there is no technological barrier to delivering a programme that is unique to each customer although it will include elements which may be delivered to every customer.

FAREWELL TO MASS MARKETING

In less than one century mass marketing enabled the widespread distribution of goods and services to a more egalitarian society. It was so effective that many have found it hard to accept that its days are all but over throughout the developed world.

Information technology, on which direct marketing depends, is the only resource delivering an exponential growth in capability while reducing raw material and energy costs. An ordinary electronic wristwatch has more processing power than a mid-range computer of the 1960s. By 1995, a PC had more power than a mainframe computer of ten years earlier. In the same year, 65 per cent of the world's telephone calls and over 90 per cent of the UK's telephone, fax and data transmissions were by optical fibre, a medium with vastly under-used capacity. The Internet encouraged thousands to get lost in cyberspace and putting integrated and interactive entertainment and information systems in the home depends more on demand than technology.

Meanwhile, the average American consumes eight times the energy resource that is sustainable. Much of the wastage is in journeys that technology can render needless. In the UK alone, the 1995 cost of transporting people to work was £15 billion.

At the same time, multiple retail groups were spending up to £40 million to open one new superstore. Like any retail outlet, this serves the three functions of providing information about goods, storing them and permitting transactions to take place. Within a short time it will be possible to provide the information on-screen, warehouse less expensively in fewer sites, permit touch-screen transactions round the clock and deliver to the customer's home. The environmental cost-saving is potentially enormous as is the convenience benefit. That's why marketers are beginning to question the wisdom of bringing the people to the goods instead of bringing the goods to the people.

Of course, not everyone will want to shop remotely for everything they buy. But, to protect their market franchises, retailers will have to offer a choice of channels and make shopping more pleasurable. They have no choice but to use the new technology to help them get to know their customers better.

Today the marketer must adapt to meet the needs of consumers as individuals instead of *en masse*. The extent of change may be much greater in some markets than others. The least change in the near future may be expected in the marketing of fast-moving consumer goods, although even that will be considerable. So far, the greatest change has been in markets where it is most practicable to identify every customer and keep a running record of each customer's worth. Many of the 'new' marketing disciplines involved have been derived from mail order, subscription marketing and other businesses which have always known their customers by name. In the next chapter we will look briefly at how these businesses grew up and the technological advance that enables other businesses to know their customers too.

TO SUM UP

The link between mass production and mass marketing is well understood. Less prominence has been given to the role of mass media, without which mass marketing would have been impossible. Like almost every other market, the media market has splintered and now offers diversity where once there was conformity.

The day of the one-product brand has gone. Today's brand must represent an ethic, a mindset, a lifestyle or some other banner under which a diversity of products can be sold. Above all, the brand, whether corporate or not, must be accessible, willing to engage in dialogue and to collaborate with the customers. Interactive media will gain from this.

Important as these changes are, the most significant development of all is that of the microchip. Every ten years the amount of data that can be stored on a disk increases not by 100 per cent but by 100 times. If this seems remote, a desiccated fact lacking in social significance, think of the computer's power to turn production lines into producers of tailor-made products. Just as mass marketing was needed to create demand for mass-produced products, so one-to-one marketing is needed to introduce consumers to products that are tailor-made to their requirements.

3

THE RISE AND RISE OF DATA-DRIVEN MARKETING

IN THIS CHAPTER

From its humble beginnings in the mail order business, computer power helped direct marketing to become a sophisticated method of distribution ... combining economies of scale with an ability to track the purchase and payment behaviour of customers on a one-to-one basis. As recently as the 1980s direct marketing was defined as a method of distribution:

> Direct marketing is a method of distribution ... in which transactions are completed between buyer and seller ... without the intervention of a salesperson or retail outlet.
>
> (Rapp & Collins presentation)

Direct response advertising and customer file management for companies using sales forces or dealer networks would be excluded from this definition. Yet the services of direct marketing agencies, address management bureaux and other direct marketing practitioners were in heavy demand from companies having no intention of making their sales forces redundant, closing their branches or firing their dealers. What these companies wanted was the targeting, interaction, control and continuity provided by best direct marketing practice.

In this chapter we trace the development of direct marketing and suggest how the new direct marketing might be defined.

The mass marketing pioneer, William Hesketh Lever, once remarked that he knew half the money he spent on advertising was wasted but that he didn't know which half. Even as he spoke, there were already marketers who had a better notion of which individual advertisements were paying their way and which were not. These were the mail order pioneers, the originators of the principles that still govern much of the direct marketing of today.

Better informed these mail order pioneers might have been, but it would be a gross over-simplification to suggest that their marketing was data-driven and that all indirect marketing was conducted in an information vacuum. By the 1930s marketing research was well established and, before long, panel research started to give fast-moving consumer goods manufacturers a model of their marketplaces. By the 1950s, marketers of grocery and pharmacy brands had access to both retail and consumer panel data, to press media readership data and to television audience data, as well as to both qualitative and quantitative *ad hoc* research. What they did not have was information about each of their customers or end users to help them to isolate the effect of individual advertisements. It was even difficult to separate the effect of a complete advertising campaign from external factors which might have influenced sales or market share.

Although the mail order operators knew how much it had cost to acquire a customer from each advertisement they placed (the advertisements carried code numbers within reply coupons) it was another matter to track any subsequent buying behaviour of the new customers. If profitability depended on winning customers, not just on making the initial sale, the mail order operator might be little better informed than the indirect marketer. Unlike the packaged goods manufacturer, the mail order operator might have little or no information on competitors, beyond seeing which media and advertisements they continued to use. However, since competition would only repeat advertisements that worked and pay for space in media that were relatively efficient, such simple competitive information was, and still is, extremely useful.

Great Universal Stores is the largest mail order group in the UK. In 1963, one of their advertising agencies lent GUS a statistician to track the buying and payment behaviour of customers recruited through direct response advertising. The only way to do this was manually and in real time. At the time, *The News of the World* was the most used advertising medium for the GUS catalogue brand under investigation. After nine months' work, the statistician reported that advertising in this medium appeared to be unprofitable whereas advertising in other, less heavily used media, was profitable. The work was not continued because it was so labour intensive. Today, the profit arising from any advertisement can be predicted with a fair degree of accuracy before the response has ceased to come in. What used to be almost impossible is now routine. The value of each component of a campaign can be individually assessed although, even now, the interaction between different components of an integrated marketing campaign is not always easy to quantify precisely.

FIVE HUNDRED YEARS OF MAIL ORDER IN FIVE MINUTES

Figure 3.1 shows the key dates in the early history of mail order. Six years after Columbus sighted San Salvador, the Venetian founder of the Aldine Press, Aldus Manutius, published the first book catalogue showing prices. In 1667, William Lucas published the first gardening catalogue in England. Sixty years later came Benjamin Franklin's Junto mail order library in Philadelphia and, in 1833, Antonio Fattorini started a mail order watch 'club' in Bradford. This was the beginning of Empire Stores, a mail order catalogue company still in business under the

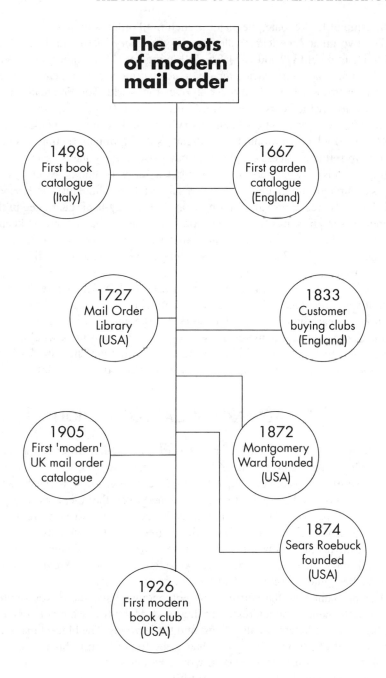

Figure 3.1 The roots of modern mail order

ownership of La Redoute, the major French mail order company.

The two great American catalogues, Montgomery Ward and Sears Roebuck, started to trade in 1872 and 1874. The following year Montgomery Ward's Spring and Summer catalogue carried the first recorded money-back guarantee, an idea which was to popularise mail order all over the world. The Freemans catalogue (now owned by the Sears Group) was launched in 1905.

In 1926, Sherman and Sackheim launched the first modern book club in the USA, The Book of the Month Club. Already subscription marketing was in place, mainly to sell magazines, and this idea gave rise to a number of *continuity* marketing models in which consumers bought a series of books, records, cookery cards or limited edition reproductions on subscription. These models depended on the device of free approval, differing from the money-back guarantee in that no money was required in advance. Free approval enabled the marketer to keep mailing out products to the customer until the order was cancelled or the customer stopped paying. For the first time, marketers began to measure the lifetime value of a customer.

Only one piece of the jigsaw was now missing, that piece being the introduction of mail order credit. This grew out of Fattorini's 'club' idea. Christmas Clubs proliferated early in the twentieth century. If 20 members each saved a shilling a week, a pound's worth of merchandise could be ordered. A draw would determine which member would be lucky enough to receive their merchandise first. Eventually, the offer became 20 weeks' free credit, an offer still used today.

THE ADVANCE OF DATA COLLECTION

The Reader's Digest Association and the Littlewoods Mail Order Group were pioneers who recognised the value of area marketing data even when such information was difficult to collect and hard to analyse. Subscription marketers and mail order operators had long used rented lists and even the telephone directory to direct mail people who were not already customers. Lists were rented or exchanged by non-competing companies. Direct mail to such lists was effective because the people on the lists had exhibited a previous inclination to respond to offers through the mail or in direct response advertisements. Previous behaviour was the best guide to future behaviour.

The problem was that there were not enough lists, there was duplication between the names and addresses on the lists and the lists were not large enough for big scale marketers like the Digest and Littlewoods. The biggest list of all was the Register of Electors, but a way had to be found to turn this into a selective medium. Mailing people at random would be unprofitable. The solution was to collect census data by ward and use multivariate regression analysis to assemble the census data items in order of their discriminatory power. By adding in customer penetration data and household composition data, it was possible to build on the census data. The wards could now be arranged in order of their potential and, using the Electoral Register, streets or individual addresses of low potential from within each Ward could be eliminated. Both the Digest and Littlewoods were selecting names for direct mail on this basis by 1970.

At around the same time, the requirements of credit control were dictating that the mail order business had to become more selective in accepting credit risks if it was to continue its expansion profitably. The American company, Fair Isaacs, was a pioneer in this field and Littlewoods' competitor, GUS, imported the skills of this company before going on to develop credit risk assessment tools which were more sophisticated still. The Register of Electors was the primary reference source because it enabled the group's own bad debtors and those whose names appeared in County Court Judgments to be plotted. Using similar methods to those employed by Littlewoods to assess the likelihood of unknown mailing recipients becoming good customers, GUS could assess the likelihood of their falling into bad debt.

Geodemographics and ACORN

Before long, GUS recognised that overlaying information about good customers and using census data for marketing purposes could, when combined with credit data, turn the Electoral Register into a powerful direct mail medium. The process was completed when a deal was struck with the American-owned research company, CACI, to ally their geodemographic cluster analysis system, ACORN, to the Electoral Register.

Hitherto, ACORN, an acronym standing for 'A Classification Of Neighbour-hood Types', had been used mainly for stratifying market research samples, the main example being the British Market Research Bureau's Target Group Index. ACORN used census data, like The Reader's Digest and Littlewoods, but the system differed in two important respects. Firstly, it used cluster analysis, not regression analysis. As its name suggests, regression analysis is only suited to arranging items in a preferred order. Here, the purpose was to pinpoint similar neighbourhoods that recurred all over the country. To do this, a statistical technique to find families of neighbourhood types that were most similar to each other was needed. This technique was cluster analysis. The second difference was that ACORN used the smallest areas for which census data was available, these being enumeration districts, comprising an average of around 150 households. A major difficulty was the attribution of, often, odd-shaped enumeration districts to postcodes, there being no direct relationship between census and postal geography. The first census used for ACORN was that for 1971.

Of no less importance has been the introduction of postcodes. Because there are so many, about 1.3 million, these have become extraordinarily useful in refining area marketing data. Postal geography has for some time been overtaking less sensitive methods of categorising consumers and, to a lesser extent, business markets. The use of postcodes in marketing has brought British practice more closely into line with American practice. The Americans had long used location in much the same way as the British had used social class to categorise consumers into broad groups expected to share similar circumstances or aspirations. Today's consumer is challenging the usefulness of all such crude classifications, but they remain relevant to marketing planning.

The creation of scorecards

Following a Monopolies Commission ruling against a proposed takeover of Empire Stores (on the unusual grounds that GUS credit data and technology would place the enlarged group at an unfair advantage) GUS opened the doors of its internal credit bureau to other companies. Before long the expertise built up in mail order was being used by every major bank, by credit card companies, by finance houses and by store groups offering card-based credit to their customers. Soon, these companies recognised the power of personal and micro-market data to drive marketing communications and site outlets, not simply to guide credit decisions.

The term 'scorecard' is becoming increasingly familiar in marketing. Using regression analysis, a scorecard may be built to assess any individual's propensity to become a bad debtor, to respond, to become a profitable customer, or whatever else is relevant – provided, always, that there is sufficient data to make it reliable. In its most developed form, the credit scorecard, it enabled mail order operators to pre-score names on the Electoral Register so that almost 100 per cent of the credit applications produced through direct mail could be accepted. The banks have taken the technique on a stage and, exploiting their superior customer information, have started to offer customers personal loans of up to £7500 by direct mail, guaranteeing acceptance. The bad debt cost is said to be lower than that arising from branch manager approved loans.

ENTER THE TELEPHONE

The introduction and widespread acceptance of plastic credit did much more than forge a link between mail order and financial services. Credit cards revolutionised the ordering of goods, services, travel and, even, theatre tickets. Store cards (credit cards restricted in use to purchases from the sponsoring retailer) made remote ordering simpler and allowed stores to challenge mail order's competitive advantage of credit.

The most significant effect in direct marketing has been the obvious linkage between the credit card and telephone ordering (see Figure 3.2). Today, the term 'mail order' is a misnomer. Nearly 80 per cent of the goods are ordered by telephone and delivered by company-owned or independent carriers. The telephone

Diners Club	– 1950
First Visa card	– 1958
American Express	– 1958
Barclaycard	– 1966
Access/Mastercard	– 1972
Store cards (eg M&S, Burton)	

Figure 3.2 The plastic money revolution

is becoming the preferred method of response by consumers for making enquiries as well as ordering goods. The telephone is transforming service quality in personal banking, general insurance and other areas in which information exchange is critical. Telephone service, at its best, is immensely popular with customers.

Interactive voice response systems, which do not depend on human operators, become more widely accepted with familiarity. The instant service that can be accessed by telephone has begun also to popularise response by fax and e-mail. With the spread of fibre-optic cable networks, there is no apparent technological limit to the possibilities for increasing the level of interaction in remote dealings.

In business-to-business marketing, telemarketing has replaced the sales representative in high-frequency, low-value transactions. PCs, computer peripherals, software, stationery, office equipment and office furniture are ordered by phone, fax and e-mail. Using the telephone, it is possible to give the PC hardware and software buyer superior after-sales support. In this field, the distinction between the business buyer and the consumer has become blurred. A customer is a customer, although some spend more than others.

Telephone response has widened the media opportunities available to direct response. Television, radio and even outdoor advertising have become direct response media and the distinction between 'brand' advertising and direct response has become blurred.

THE ADVANCE OF PERSONALISED COMMUNICATION

In the first chapter I referred to the extraordinary reduction in the cost of data processing, enabling companies to track the ongoing purchase behaviour of millions of customers, measure their reaction to marketing stimuli and store relevant personal data.

The marketer has two distinct uses for this information. The first is to aid decision-making by providing better, or more complete, data on what is happening in the business. The second is to drive person-to-person communication, the subject and frequency of messages being varied according to the customer's present status and presumed interests.

Until the late 1970s the production of personalised messages in quantity was limited by crude technology. Mainframe computers drove massive impact printers which clattered like demented typewriters, churning out 600 blurred words a minute or 400 words in less than letter quality. If the printers were permitted to reproduce the message all in capital letters, they could run faster. To cut costs, personalised paragraphs were often inserted in pre-printed letters. When the receipt of a personalised message was a novelty, the ugly result was acceptable, even rather exciting, to most recipients. It was, however, resented by a sizeable minority as an invasion of privacy. Nevertheless, there were huge gains in response over direct mail using pre-printed text in most markets.

By the time laser printing was introduced in the late 1970s, personalised direct mail had long ceased to be a novelty. The initial effect of laser printing was to increase the speed with which letters could be mass produced using continuous stationery. Shortly afterwards, the Xerox 800 printer enabled sheet-fed letters to be produced for shorter runs, but in far superior quality. Surprisingly, the faster continuous stationery machines had been designed to capture the billing market, not the much larger direct mail market, and adaptation was required. Before long, the problems of fugitive, poisonous ink and format limitations were overcome and it became possible to produce high-quality personalised print in innovative formats.

Primitive deduplication

The limitations of impact printing was not the only problem facing the user of personalised direct mail. The reference tools and statistical techniques for recognising that two similar, but not identical, names and addresses belonged to the same person were far less well developed than they are today. This problem had to be overcome in order to prevent irritation by mailing the same person twice, to cut the wastage involved, to prevent customer data and dealings being confused by duplication and, even, to prevent credit fraud.

Although there is no 100 per cent solution as yet, it is now reasonable to expect a 98 per cent level of accuracy using a list of names and addresses of people the direct mailer has never dealt with before.

The use of personalised communications is not confined to direct mail. As we saw in Chapter 2 personalised communications can be produced instantly from a terminal in a shop. More commonly, they may be delivered by telephone. Outbound telemarketing to customers has also been impacted by the advance of technology. An auto-dial system may dial numbers in order of priority, thus saving operator time and selecting customers in order of their estimated propensity to respond favourably to the call.

Exactly the same data may be used to drive telemarketing as is used to drive direct mail. However, telemarketing is at an advantage in delivering time-sensitive messages, engaging in dialogue and in permitting changes of call content according to hour-by-hour results. Because the telephone is potentially a highly intrusive medium, its use must be tempered with discretion and many marketers believe that its use is most appropriate to dealings with established customers or enquirers. It has been remarked that no one gets out of the bath to answer a direct mail shot.

The growth and pre-eminence of mass media had a profound influence on the success of mass marketing. Personal marketing was already working when the tools available to the direct marketer were crude in the extreme. Now that the growth and increasing sophistication of personal and interactive media permit precise targeting and dialogue, the customer will increasingly expect to be respected as an individual.

THE NEW DIRECT MARKETING

As recently as 1980, it was accepted that direct marketing was a method of distribution, just like shops or vending machines. A commonly accepted definition was: 'Direct marketing is a method of distribution ... in which transactions are completed between buyer and seller ... without the intervention of a sales person or retail outlet.' Although this definition is now too narrow to embrace all the uses of direct marketing, it remains true of a great part of direct marketing and a growing form of distribution. Direct marketing, as a form of distribution, will grow all the faster with the widespread adoption of interactive media.

Yet the influence of direct marketing is far more widespread than this definition suggests. It is to direct marketing that we owe the introduction of the customer marketing database, now the principal marketing information resource of banks, building societies, airlines, stores, insurance companies, automotive distributors, computer manufactures and dealers, magazine publishers and a host of other businesses. In business-to-business marketing and in mail order, some companies have data-captured their entire market universe, not simply those who are enquirers, customers or former customers.

The heart of the marketing information system

Figure 3.3 provides a checklist of the benefits of information flowing from the database. The uses of this information range far beyond permitting and provoking remote transactions. Marketing databases are used to track the progress of customer relationships, the market penetration of products, the success of marketing investments and to forecast the likely success of future marketing investments. They are used for these purposes whether customer transactions are remote or face to face.

Marketing communications using the personal media of direct marketing are now employed to build business for dealers, to secure appointments for sales people, to deliver information to enquirers and to keep customers informed. Direct marketing has wormed its way into the integrated marketing mix. Arguably, it would have done so far more quickly if its role had been less significant. The central position of the marketing database, informing the whole range of marketing decisions, made it difficult to accept by people who had mastered other marketing disciplines. The philosophy of 'If it ain't broke, don't fix it' prevailed until the conventional marketing mix was seen not to deliver any more.

The techniques borrowed from traditional direct marketing are highly appropriate to dealing with the desired and real individuality of today's consumer. They are appropriate to collaborative or relationship marketing. They exploit our new-found ability to capture, manage and use large volumes of marketing data. They are in tune with our new capacity to engineer products and design services around an individual customer's needs.

Direct, data-driven marketing is the star in the integrated marketing firmament. As other stars have complained before, it has waited a hundred years to become an overnight success. In the next chapter we will see how it works in practice.

TO SUM UP

In this chapter we have traced the progress of direct marketing, giving a definition of the activity that was acceptable until a few years ago. But how would we re-define direct marketing today? Actually, definitions abound. Unfortunately they are mostly incomplete or incomprehensible without several paragraphs of explanation. So here is another attempt to bring a collection of activities together under one umbrella:

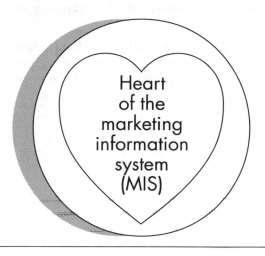

Improves targeting

Measures results

Facilitates continuity and dialogue

Identifies key customers/segments

Analyses financial performance

Provides predictive information

Triggers marketing communications

Aids market research

Figure 3.3 The database in a nutshell

Direct marketing is the process in which individual customers' responses and transactions are recorded ... and the data used to inform the targeting, execution and control of actions ... that are designed to start, develop and prolong profitable customer
relationships.

This new definition describes what we might consider to be real direct marketing
as opposed to direct mail advertising or customer communications not obeying
the full set of targeting, interaction, control and continuity disciplines.

4

DIRECT MARKETING IN ACTION I

IN THIS CHAPTER

Now we take a closer look at direct marketing in action. The opportunities to collect personal data and forge relationships are not always the same. To assist in understanding why this is so, we need to understand more of the practicalities of collecting and using customer information. So, here we consider the situations of a retailer, a business-to-business marketer and a fast-moving consumer goods manufacturer. Each of these three businesses has very different opportunities to capture and exploit information about customers.

In Chapter 21 we provide eight real-life cases of direct marketing in action. These cover a wide variety of situations in both consumer and business marketing.

THE RETAILER

Modern stores employ EPOS or EFTPOS (electronic point-of-sale) terminals, giving the customer an itemised printout of the transaction. The terminals form part of an information loop that provides accounting and stock-control data. All that is usually missing is the identity of the shopper. The missing link to the customer can be joined by means of a membership scheme, such as Tesco's Clubcard. Alternatively, the retailer may have an account card such as the Marks & Spencer card. In either case it may be difficult to secure universal acceptance of the card and there will be a gap in the customer information (see Table 4.1).

Not all outlets experience this problem. For example, the identity of the retail banking customer is always known. The same may apply to a store that operates a compulsory membership scheme, such as Costco or many other cash-and-carry warehouses, in which the distinction between a genuine trade buyer and a consumer bulk buyer may be blurred.

As the benefits of data-driven one-to-one marketing become obvious, we may expect to see more retailers aspiring to know the identities of all their customers, or as many of them as possible without data collection costs getting out of hand. An obvious advantage is the ability to poll customers on added-value services, changes of opening hours and levels of satisfaction with various aspects of the shopping package. Involving customers in the planning and enhancement of service and range leads to greater customer commitment and this is closely related to loyalty.

Table 4.1 The retailer database

Must sell membership/account to capture customer ID	*Can't cover all customers*
EPOS links transactional data to customer ID	*Can provide lifetime value data*
Purchase patterns can be tracked	*Corrective actions can be taken*
Customer preferences can be recorded	*Relevant offers can be made*
Customers can be consulted and involved	*Customer commitment can be increased*
Catchment area and non-user data can be obtained	*Competitive strategy can be precisely targeted*
Customer base can be 'bribed' on a tactical basis	*Impact of competitive launches can be minimised*

Who are the non-customers?

A less obvious motivation for collecting individual customer data is that the store which knows who its customers *are* also knows who its customers are *not*. This is because the locations of customers can be plotted, so arriving at a clear definition of the catchment area. According to the customer penetration within sectors of the catchment area, the entire area can be segmented into primary, secondary and tertiary divisions. It does not take a marketing genius to work out that it is more efficient to employ sales promotion and other techniques to entice identified non-customers from the primary catchment area than to make offers to the world at large. Making offers to the world at large means that most of them will be redeemed by regular customers.

However, acquisition targeting can be more sophisticated than this. High spending customers can be profiled. For example, families may spend more than single occupants. People within prosperous postcodes may spend more. This information can be derived from the transactional histories of regular shoppers. Now it becomes possible to target similar people within each catchment area segment.

Of course, few people are completely loyal to any one store. There aren't just shoppers and non-shoppers. There are shades in between. Here again transactional history reveals any breaks in continuity. If a shopper has been making one trip a week but doesn't appear for three weeks, the store can be alerted to this. If the weeks of non-appearance were in August, it is more likely that the absence is due to holidays than if the non-appearance is in April. Either way, the wealth of accumulated historical data will permit a calculation of the odds. These odds will be calculated routinely by computer and an appropriate 'welcome back' offer can be generated, again by computer, without human intervention. The customer may even be telephoned to find out if he or she is dissatisfied.

The customer's phone number may be selected and dialled automatically, a screen showing the telemarketer who he or she is about to talk to and why the computer thinks the customer has defected. The computer may even advise the telemarketer what offer to make, according to the customer's previous value.

The technology to permit relationship marketing of this level of sophistication has been in place for years. You, the reader, may find it extraordinary that a store whose customers may spend £2500 a year each with it doesn't collect and use such information assiduously. Having spent some time attempting to instruct retailers in the error of their ways, I remain as surprised as you are.

The same customers may spend one-tenth of this amount with a mail order company. Yet this company will use automated decision systems to drive mailed or telephone messages to defecting customers. The difference in attitude is surely explained by history and habit. People find it hard to stop doing what used to be so successful for so many years. Now the wastage inherent in mass marketing methods is no longer acceptable.

Actually, the retail store able to data capture the universe of its customers is better placed than the mail order company. The mail order company cannot so easily identify its potential customers. Its catchment area is at least national and the large majority of the market universe shop elsewhere. It can only know those who have enquired, but never bought, and those who used to buy but no longer do so.

THE BUSINESS-TO-BUSINESS MARKETER

This marketer may be in the happy situation of supplying direct to end customers or may rely upon distributors. The company may use a mixture of channels, supplying direct to large users and via distributors or wholesalers to small customers (see Table 4.2).

It is sometimes overlooked that the purchasing power of businesses varies enormously. One company may have several thousand times the purchasing power of another. This provides an even more significant distinction between business and consumer marketing than does the difference in the number of customers. If ever there has been such a being as an 'average' consumer, there has never been an average business customer.

In most markets it is practicable to capture the identities of the companies that account for 80 per cent or more of the market in value terms. If the business marketer supplies these large companies direct, it is possible to maintain a full transactional history for each customer, estimate the share of the customer's purchases that is leaking to competitors and identify uptrading or cross-selling opportunities. It is also possible to target those large companies that are providing no business, even estimating their potential value in advance.

Table 4.2 The business-to-business database

Company size and classification data available for non-customers	Market penetration and targeting data
Full transactional data for all customers	Database is primary source of marketing data
Complex business relationships, eg use of multi-sales channels	Data coordination problems
Use of sales channels for data collection/updating	Data integrity problems
Multi-sited customers, differing degrees of devolvement	Complex data management
Group decision-making (decision-maker units)	Customer companies must be 'populated' accurately

Multi-channel customer relationships

It all appears delightfully simple. Unfortunately it is not. The first complication may be internal. We may be negotiating sales through more than one channel. We may have more than one technical sales team with different teams specialising in different product lines. They may be dealing with different departments of the same client company. We may also maintain an inbound telemarketing department that takes orders for lower value items and, perhaps, an outbound team that sells such items over the telephone. Some customers may mail, fax or deliver orders electronically.

All of these sales channels are in a position to collect customer data and, if they have free access to the marketing database, to corrupt data by replacing correct information with erroneous information. Maintaining the integrity of customer information and clear rules of customer contact requires good management.

Externally, the complications are even greater. Large companies have their own ways of doing business and these ways may be as numerous as the names on the customer file. In-depth customer knowledge is essential. Furthermore, many purchasing decisions are not made by a single individual. Often, they are made by a person or team that does not have a buying department job title. Many business-to-business marketers attempt to define the decision-making unit in their client companies and then identify the members of this unit in each case. But the names we are most likely to capture in the ordinary course of business are those of buyers and people in the accounts department.

We may depend on our sales or telemarketing teams to collect the names and job titles of the real decision-makers. This means we must give them rights of access, though not necessarily direct access, to the database. We need a quality control procedure to ensure they don't enter incorrect information.

We may also want to communicate with decision influencers and end users in the client company. Business marketing is becoming increasingly collaborative and we may wish to consult end users on how we can improve the product or the service support. It is a major task to identify these people but, if the company's business is worth hundreds of thousands of pounds, it is a task worth undertaking. We need what Regis McKenna, in *Relationship Marketing* (1991), describes as a feedback loop so that we can see how the business relationship is developing.

As if these complications were not enough, people change their jobs more often than their home address. Individuals get promoted, moved sideways and fired. Others leave to get a better job elsewhere. Our goodwill may be with the individual as much as it is with the company. If we are on the ball we can welcome a defecting executive's successor to their new post and contact the defector at their new employer's.

In some cases, companies will devolve purchasing power to branches or sites. We may need to treat each site as a separate customer but also aggregate the purchasing data of the whole company, perhaps identifying sites that give us no business.

Many business marketers build files of indirect customers. The object is to establish a dialogue so that the marketer is not at the mercy of the distributor or wholesaler. Often the product information offered by intermediaries is poor. A common example is the creation of files of indirect retail accounts who buy from cash and carries. These files are built with the aid of telephone research.

Although it is impossible to collect full transactional data for indirect accounts, it is possible to make offers that can be redeemed through a wholesaler and to track redemptions on the database. Even a small business customer, whether direct or indirect, is usually worth many times more, in sterling value, than a consumer. It would be quite illogical for a packaged goods manufacturer to collect data about individual consumers and neglect to do so about small convenience outlets or off-licences, for example.

THE PACKAGED GOODS MANUFACTURER

We have referred to the fast-moving consumer goods (fmcg) manufacturer as an indirect supplier to small retail outlets. We have pointed out the logic of maintaining a file of these shops. But why is it logical to build a file of end consumers? What use is such information? And how can we collect it? (See Table 4.3.)

Table 4.3 The fmcg database	
Depends on buying data – directly or via offers	Data collection costs high in relation to value
Can capture competitive brand user data	Permits targeted market share stealing
Cannot capture all own-brand users	On-pack and media customer communications still needed
Only promotional response data available	Limited value as management data. Decay problems
Can ally to panel data	Benefits of database marketing can be measured
Can use for stablemate brands	Strong share-of-customer potential

The reasons why fmcg manufacturers began experimenting with one-to-one marketing communications were largely negative. That is not to suggest they were bad reasons. An early 1980s pioneer, Kraft General Foods, was concerned about the increasing cost and reducing value of coupon distribution. Initially, direct marketing was seen purely as an alternative to conventional sales promotion. Since coupon redemption rates were falling and the post-promotion sales value quickly fell back to the pre-promotion level, the company felt compelled to seek a new solution. If heavy users could be identified, if repeat purchasing could be stimulated and if cross-selling opportunities could be exploited, the high cost of one-to-one file building and contact could be clawed back.

The tobacco and drinks industries were influenced by the fear of an advertising ban. They saw the longer-term future of direct marketing as an alternative to conventional media advertising. If, they reasoned, they could demonstrate that their one-to-one messages were directed only to habitual smokers or drinkers, the new communications channel should escape legal restraint. Although one-to-one communications were seen as an alternative to other advertising, their initial use was largely predatory. *Competitive* brand users were targeted with highly aggressive promotional tactics in the tobacco field, but generally softer offers in the drinks market.

Others, for example Pedigree Petfoods, became interested because they saw their media costs rising, while coverage and frequency fell. There appeared to be no end to this trend. Meanwhile the only marketing cost they could see to be falling was that which depended on information technology. Again, direct communications were seen as a potential alternative to advertising, but were used in the rather more conventional advertising role of supporting brand values and reinforcing customer relationships among established users.

Finally, some smaller or newer manufacturers saw direct marketing as an alternative channel of distribution. They were shut out by the large corporations which had sewn up the available shelf space. One successful pioneer was Giorgio of Beverly Hills, using scent-strip inserts in magazines to sample their fragrance. Readers of the inserts could order direct. Other products to have been successfully marketed direct include disposable nappies, or diapers, and complete product ranges, such as cosmetics. Much depends on the potential lifetime value of the customer and the value:weight ratio of the shipment.

On many packages, you will see that you are offered the opportunity of speaking direct to a customer service department or advice centre. Increasingly, manufacturers are understanding the value of inviting dialogue. Even if we never take them up on their offer, it tells us something about their attention to delivering customer satisfaction.

As we have seen from these examples, consumer information and communications can be used to undertake selective sales promotion, to target competitive brand users, to reinforce brand values, to sell direct, to provide superior product information and advice, and to establish and strengthen relationships with users. They can also be used to cross-sell, introducing users of one brand to others from the same stable. Everything depends upon the gearing that can be obtained on the initial expense of data gathering and the subsequent expense of one-to-one communications.

Since consumers select from within a portfolio of brands, a brand with a 10 per cent market share may be purchased with varying degrees of regularity by 25 per cent of consumers. Forging direct relationships may increase market share by a substantial margin without winning a single new customer. If customer values are sufficiently high, the investment can readily be justified. If not, it may be justified by spreading the investment across a portfolio of brands.

Lack of transactional data

It is impossible for the fmcg manufacturer who does not sell direct to maintain a transactional database of all the end users. The data is inherently less valuable than the retailer's data. It will decay faster because there is no way of knowing which consumers have stayed loyal, which continue to buy more occasionally and which have defected. Unlike a bank's customers, fmcg customers will not bother to tell the company when they change address.

The best the fmcg company can do is maintain a transactional record of a *sample* of data-captured customers. One method is to have these identified as a subset on a consumer panel sample. This allows the fmcg manufacturer to follow the direct marketing discipline of *control*. By tracking the behaviour of a sample of customers, the behaviour of other like-minded and similarly treated customers may be inferred. In this way the return on direct marketing investments can be calculated.

Naturally, the fmcg manufacturer can also communicate with regular users on- or in-pack. These communications are severely restricted by space, by packaging limitations, by poor control of timing and the inability to communicate person to person. However, pack-based communications can reach every user. It is impossible for the fmcg manufacturer to build a database of all end users. On the other hand, it is possible to build a database of competitive brand users. Thus direct marketing communications find their place within a whole battery of communications opportunities which must be integrated and coordinated to maximise their cumulative effect.

Name and address sources

How is consumer information collected? A variety of means are employed. Firstly, it can be purchased from one of the lifestyle survey companies who distribute many millions of lengthy questionnaires in packs, door to door, as inserts in publications and by direct mail. The advantages are that the address data is already verified, competitive brand user data is obtainable, profiling and preferred outlet data is included, heavy and light users can be identified – and respondents are not necessarily compulsive coupon redeemers. A direct alternative is for the manufacturer to distribute similar questionnaires.

A second source is from coupon distribution or on-pack offers. By requesting address information, the manufacturer can collect consumer identities as a by-product of routine promotions. Product sampling is a more aggressive and effective technique, although much more expensive. The two usual methods are knock-and-drop and shopping mall distribution. The former uses teams of distributors to make door-to-door deliveries and collect customer data at the same time. This method is appropriate to household products. The latter uses teams to offer samples (or participation in a promotion) at or near point-of-purchase. This method is appropriate to tobacco, because only those observed to make a purchase are approached.

Consumer names may also be collected through advertising, from telephone advice lines, from recommend-a-friend offers and other media. Multi-media sourcing is most often employed because it is extremely difficult to collect data about enough consumers through any one mechanism. The cost of collection and replacement of old data is high and it may take one to two years to achieve a payback.

TO SUM UP

Enough of the abstract. What about the flesh and blood of direct marketing in action? In Chapter 21, thanks to the generosity of those responsible, we are able to look at some real-life cases. They are quite brief and have been chosen to give you the flavour of direct marketing, usually within an integrated marketing environment.

PART TWO

CREATING AND USING MARKETING INFORMATION SYSTEMS

THE HENLEY COLLEGE LIBRARY

5

CUSTOMER MARKETING OBJECTIVES AND STRATEGY

IN THIS CHAPTER

With some honourable exceptions, businesses have not been very good at providing for large numbers of small customers. The rise of the marketing department did little to improve customer focus at a person-to-person level, customer focus being seen as the vision to anticipate and cater for the needs of substantial market segments.

It was sufficient for the company to relate to consumers on a brand-by-brand basis or a division-by-division basis. Operations that affected customer relationships were divided by function, while products were turned into profit centres, each with its own marketing management. The transference of this type of organisation from manufacturing to service business had a negative impact on customer relationships.

The rise of information technology was seen as the opportunity to drive down the cost of transactions, this being seen as essential to maintaining competitiveness. Inevitably this led to greater centralisation and customer frustration in finding a point of contact to solve problems or resolve complaints.

In this chapter we look at how companies are now considering information technology as an aid to focusing on the needs of individual customers.

WHY THE SHIFT TO DIRECT MARKETING?

In marketing consultancy, I find that a good way to gain an understanding of the many complex issues confronted by a large company is to simplify, to boil everything we can down to its bare essentials. After years of experience I still find complex flow diagrams daunting. Furthermore, they arouse an uneasy suspicion. What, to a mathematician, are no more than aesthetically pleasing and graceful lines seem like plumbing. The real world, I suspect, has a way of ensuring that sooner or later there will be a blockage in all that pipework. The real world is inhabited by real people displaying a distressing tendency to do things their way, no matter what logic dictates.

A good way to simplify is to begin by imagining a large business as a small business. The simplest kind of small business is one that has only a few large customers. You can be sure its customer focus is pin-sharp. For the sake of familiarity, we can take the example of an advertising agency – not one of those multinational empires, just a comparatively immature outfit with one office.

The agency is our corporate brand. We also have products. These are, let's say, TV, Radio, Print Advertising, Outdoor Advertising and Collaterals (things like point-of-sale materials, direct mail, brochures, and so on). Inside our agency, we have functional interests. These are creative, media, planning, account handling, production and finance.

Our creative people have a good show reel of TV ads. They want us to pull in more TV work. The media people agree. We are under-represented in this profitable market segment because the 'establishment' agencies have an unfair share of this business. So what do we do?

Focus on the brand

If we follow the conventional marketing thinking I was brought up on, what we would do is focus on our TV brand. We would begin by trying to get on every pitch list we could for TV business. Our best resources would be devoted to speculative work on new business. We might even decide that our organisation impeded our progress. We might decide that we should reconfigure it around brands, putting our best people on the TV brand. Clients who wanted to use our services across a range of media would have to deal with different people for each of our brands.

This would be a very high-risk strategy. It might just succeed but the odds are not good. The one certainty is that our service to established clients would suffer. Too much of our most talented people's time would be spent on new business. Our finances would be stretched by the cost of speculative work. Even more seriously, it would now be harder to deal with us because we have reorganised our business to meet *our* objective, not our clients' objectives. Even if we retained our clients' business, we would miss opportunities to develop it. Our employees would have sectional interests and would see each other as competitors. They would not introduce a Print Advertising client to our Collaterals brand management. Why make them look good?

I hope this picture looks familiar to you. It is the way many large companies have configured their objectives, marketing organisations and strategies. It worked when the customer had little choice and it was easy to make money. But it never worked as well as it should have done.

So, what should our agency do? It should take stock of its strengths, weaknesses, opportunities and threats, just like any other business. To do this, it must compare its loyalty rate with the industry average. Is it performing better or worse than the industry at large? The average life of a client is about seven years. If the client loss rate is under one-in-seven each year, it is outperforming the industry. Then it must find out exactly what it is that allows it to outperform the industry. What do clients value most about the quality of service and work they are getting? Perhaps it is a dull but cardinal virtue, like commitment to the client's cause.

Where does the profit come from?

There are two crucial points here. The first is that it is better to be famous for something than nothing. It is better to play to the strengths of a business, not risk sacrificing them in the name of an apparently more desirable objective. The second point is, if anything, even more important. It is that *all* the profit arises from established clients. Even if a new business pitch is successful, the resulting client relationship will not generally become profitable until the second year.

The direct marketing way is to look first at where the profit comes from. The higher the loyalty rate, and the better the growth rate of existing clients' business, the more profitable the agency will be. Its success is bound up with its clients' success. There is a commonality of interest, the basis of a mutually profitable partnership. The main profit-driver is the lifetime value of a client. The greater this value, the more money the agency has to spend on new business and the higher the gearing on the resulting new business investment.

Because the agency has recognised that it must put its clients' interests at the top of the agenda, it revolves its organisation around each client's needs. Its understanding of these needs places it in an advantageous position to cross-sell other services which it can provide, but which the client is either not using or sourcing elsewhere. The agency's desire to push its 'brands' is subordinate to the offering made to each client. Brand interests and function interests are not allowed to get in the way of delivering the precise product and service mix the client needs and wants. The service is tailored to fit.

Not only have the funds available for new business investment increased – because the agency has increased the lifetime value of its clientele – but less of the new business is needed to replace lost business. More of the new business gains will be incremental. Furthermore, the task of making forward profit projections will have been eased because less of the future profit will depend on the lottery of new business pitches.

As I hope you will agree, the direct marketing way of looking at the issues makes sense. It will not guarantee greater profits than the high-risk alternative. However, the odds are very much better and the chances of survival, the primary aim of every business, are almost infinitely greater. A business that is focused on delivering what its established customers want is unlikely to fail unless technological or other change create a paradigm shift in demand. The balance between customer acquisition and retention in such a business is much healthier and this drives down costs.

If this makes sense for a small business with big customers, why does it not make sense for a large business with small customers? The answer is that it does. However, for many years the cost of tailoring the marketing and service effort would have been prohibitive. Large companies did the best they could. To do better than that has become a necessity, yet the technology to make this possible is still comparatively new. Inevitably, there is a lag between what has become practicable and its actual practice. Large companies have powerful functional and brand interests that may need to be dismantled to permit bespoke marketing. Brands have only recently become assets in the balance sheet. Customers, an even more important asset in reality, are not yet assets in an accounting sense. Nevertheless, customer databases are already traded. A bankrupt company's customer file may be purchased by another company which does not wish to take over the whole portfolio of assets and liabilities. The price paid will be related to the anticipated future value of the customers' business.

WHAT DOES LIFETIME VALUE REALLY MEAN?

Customer lifetime value means the anticipated future worth of a new customer. This value is calculated by forecasting the period over which the customer will remain loyal and the customer's spend within that period. Very often this spend will increase for a while, then reduce before the customer severs the relationship.

Lifetime value calculations are usually made in present-day prices. They may be made on a gross basis or a net basis. The gross basis values the customer on the basis of spend alone. Average product margin, marketing and service costs can then be applied to arrive at an approximate net value. Sometimes, however, these costs are applied within the calculation. This is particularly appropriate when customers may be projected to use very different product and service mixes, producing different net margins. Figure 5.1 shows the formula expressing lifetime return on customer acquisition.

Although it is the common practice to use present-day prices in these calculations, there is no reason why discounted cashflow (DCF) procedures cannot be used. The objective of this is to value money now more highly than money later. This is completely logical. Instead of using expenditure to recruit customers, the company could use it to invest in an interest-bearing account. Money left lying in an account increases. Therefore, money produced later is worth less than money available now. Figure 5.2 shows an example of discounting future customer values where sales occur (on average) 6, 18, 30 and 42 months after the acquisition cost had been incurred.

Most companies recognise that measuring a customer's value at present-day prices over a whole lifetime, while important, is somewhat theoretical. After all, the company is measured by its financial performance on a year-to-year basis. Therefore, if they do not use DCF procedure, they will usually apply an artificial cut-off after, say, two or three years. They will set a payback period to break even

$$\text{ROI} = \frac{\text{Future contribution less discount}}{\text{Net acquisition cost}}$$

ROI = Return on customer acquisition investment

Future contribution = Eventual profit

Discount = Allowance for deferred profit (discounted cashflow)

Net acquisition cost = Cost after allowing for value of initial transaction

Figure 5.1 The 'lifetime' return on customer acquisition

	Year 1	Year 2	Year 3	Year 4	Cum.
Margin on sales	£50	£60	£60	£65	
Retention rate	0.8	0.6	0.5	0.4	0.4
Net margin	£40	£36	£30	£26	
Discounted 1% per month	£37.60	£29.52	£21.00	£16.08	£104.20

Figure 5.2 Discounting future customer value

on new customer acquisition which falls within this artificially shortened customer lifespan. This also has the merit that it is easier to predict short-term values than long-term values.

The value of acquiring a customer

The lifetime value calculation helps the company to value its customer assets and to value each customer individually. This both permits better turnover, profit and resource forecasting and enables each customer to be treated on their merits – or, rather, their projected merits. Less obviously, perhaps, it enables the company to set a price on what it is prepared to pay to recruit a new customer. This price is determined by the estimated future value of a customer. It is the only realistic way to set customer acquisition expenditure at the optimum level. It is part and parcel of direct marketing philosophy to reduce marketing and other expenditures to a unit cost level. Instead of saying it will cost £5 million to mount a 'reasonable' campaign giving the company a 20 per cent 'share of voice', the direct marketer is more precise. Having calculated that lifetime value merits a spend of £50 to recruit a new customer, the direct marketer goes on to calculate how many customers can be recruited before this figure is exceeded. This calculation will be informed by past performance. A model will be built showing the anticipated return from deploying varying amounts of money in various different ways.

When the optimum plan is produced by such a model, much of the guesswork has been removed and the optimum expenditure is more likely to be deployed in the optimum way. Such a model does not have to exclude expenditures on marketing communications that fall outside direct response advertising. The cost of background advertising can be included, as can the cost of sales force or dealer activity and support. Direct marketing has supplied the theory and the practical experience for this, but it can and should be applied to any integrated marketing programme.

SETTING CUSTOMER MARKETING OBJECTIVES

Like the imaginary agency with which we started this chapter, most companies are obsessed with product marketing objectives. This is understandable in a manufacturing business when the investment in starting up a new product line may be huge. If a new car fails to capture its predicted market share, the financial consequences are severe. If a new fmcg brand fails to merit its footage in the superstores, it will be delisted and nosedive. However, the rewards and penalties represented by product launches are tending to diminish. Technological change has shortened the effective life of many products. Most launches today are just line extensions, aimed at highly specific market segments. More and more products are now services, often with short lead times to market, few economies of scale and little investment in research and development.

In these circumstances it makes less sense to follow a much admired Procter & Gamble philosophy, developed for a different market in another era. Yet that is just what so many large businesses have done, irrespective of its lack of relevance to their situation. In the 1980s, for example, we saw a plethora of branded service products emerge from the banks. Their customer research and their front-line staff told them it was service, not branded services, that their customers wanted but they had swallowed the wrong textbook. Product managers vied with each other for the customer's attention, causing confusion and, eventually, something close to rebellion.

In any business, profitability depends on maintaining and increasing the value of customer relationships. It follows that the *customer marketing objective* is more important than any product marketing objective. Yet few companies have set any customer marketing objectives, while all have product marketing objectives. The customer marketing objective focuses attention on securing as much profitable business from each customer as possible. This entails increasing *share of customer*. Few customers are 100 per cent loyal to any supplier. Of those companies who bother to measure customer loyalty at all, most do so in terms of longevity. But in many markets, *share of present-day business* may be more significant.

It is generally cheaper to become the preferred supplier to more established customers than it is to win entirely new customers. Becoming the preferred supplier will also increase the longevity of the average customer relationship. It will make cross-selling easier, so that the customer extends the breadth, not just the depth, of the relationship. It is well known in general insurance and other industries that a multi-product user tends to be more loyal than a single-product user, although separating cause and effect is not so easy.

Returning to our example of the car launch as a case in which the product marketing objective is critical, it is an industry in which the importance of customer retention has long been recognised. The success of the new launch will largely depend on how many established users of the make buy the new car. That is why Toyota conduct most of their research within their own customer database. It is why every manufacturer has a target retention level for its existing model owners. Car makers knew, even in the early 1980s, that the total cost of making a 'conquest' sale (a sale to someone new to the make) was five times as high as the total cost of making a repeat sale.

From this example we can see that product marketing objectives depend on customer marketing objectives. When Heinz launch a new soup recipe, its success will depend on how many Heinz users try it and continue to buy it. Its *raison d'être* is not really to win new customers for Heinz so much as to increase the company's share of the customers it already has.

Customer values are everything

The life of the company will depend on the lifetime value of its customers. A customer marketing objective is essential, otherwise there can be no customer marketing strategy.

The customer marketing objective does not have to be the same for every customer. It is more realistic to set achievable objectives for particular customer segments or, even, for individual customers. An airline may not wish to spend as much effort in marketing and service to develop an occasional flyer relationship as a frequent flyer relationship. A computer software company may want to spend more time in dialogue with corporate customers than with self-employed people using the same applications at home.

The customer marketing database enables these distinctions to be drawn and provides the raw data from which lifetime value calculations can be made.

THE CULTURE SHOCK OF CUSTOMER MARKETING STRATEGY

It is one thing to set an objective and another to reach it. I have mentioned that different groups of customers may be accorded different objectives. There may also be more than one objective for an individual customer. We may want that customer to entrust us with more business as well as simply remain loyal. In some cases securing prompt payments from the customer may be more important than securing extra business.

Whatever the objectives, we need to devise a strategy to achieve these objectives. The database will provide us with most of the information we need, although we may also have to use marketing research to gain a better understanding of how to motivate customers to give us more business. Our progress, once we are up and running with our operational plan, will be monitored on the database. Successful tests, conducted among small groups of customers, can be rolled out and unsuccessful tests can be aborted.

In most cases, obtaining the information to devise a sound strategy and develop a working operational plan will not be the main problem. The main problem will be in refocusing the organisation on customers and away from product or operational concerns. Conflict is inevitable because most product and operational objectives are based on a logical framework which is familiar. Hierarchies within the company will have been built on delivering to these objectives. Influential people will feel threatened by the new, flattened organisation chart depicting the customer at the centre and the front-line troops, such as telemarketers, very close to the centre.

It's not efficient if the customers don't like it

In one large home shopping company, I learned that the performance of the telemarketers handling inbound enquiries and orders was measured by the length of each call. This was because the function was seen as clerical and it came under the direction of an operational manager.

The manager's own performance was measured by his ability to drive down staff costs and maximise the utility of the equipment. Thus a telemarketer who cut a customer off abruptly instead of dealing with his or her enquiry sympathetically was helping the manager to appear efficient. Until a new marketing director came on board, few senior people ever bothered to listen to tapes of their own sales staff talking to the customers. Transaction costs can be driven down faster by satisfying customers than by saving a few pence on phone calls. The problem is that it is easier to measure the length of the call than to measure customer satisfaction and its causes.

In a large building society, it was recognised that future success would depend largely on broadening and deepening customer relationships. It was also recognised that the telephone was an excellent device for delivering good customer service and obtaining information from customers that would enable accurately targeted offers to be made to them. Unfortunately, the full consequences of refocusing on customer relationship development were much harder to take on board.

All the operational hierarchies remained in place, the staff interfacing with customers continued to be held in low esteem and the plan quickly degenerated into a crude, tactical effort to improve cross-selling. Even the marketing staff assumed that the society would be able to 'manage' the customer relationship. Scarcely anyone recognised that it was the customer who was in charge. A lifetime spent in a business where customers are looked upon as chattels does not prepare people for a new culture in which the customer comes first. The irony is that a building society is owned by its customers.

When First Direct was launched, the customer-interfacing staff were not recruited from any other bank or building society because a new culture had to be established. The telephones were answered after no more than two rings, even at midnight. Customers were accorded their due importance.

The working practices, the organisation, even the vocabulary of such large businesses has to change. They simply can't afford to be arrogant any more. The customer has too much choice and all the power he or she needs to exercise it. By focusing attention on customer behaviour the marketing database can play a valuable role in securing recognition of the importance of winning customer commitment.

In the next chapter we will begin our discussion of the database marketing system. We will do this from the user's point of view and not get lost in technicalities. The hardware and software of database management changes so rapidly that a monthly journal is more appropriate than a marketing textbook to describe the alternatives. The categories of data held and the management issues change too, but much less rapidly, and it is to these that we will direct our attention.

TO SUM UP

This chapter includes the formula for calculating customer *lifetime value*. See again Figures 5.1 and 5.2.

The notion of *customer marketing objectives* is also introduced. In this context we suggest that increasing *share of customer* may have more impact on profitability than increasing share of market. This is because it is cheaper to sell to customers than strangers. The more business a company can generate at low cost, the stronger its competitive position will be. Increasing share of customer pays off twice, because the greater the customer's dependence on the supplier, the less likely the customer is to defect. The multi-product customer will usually prove more loyal than the single-product customer.

We suggest that, while companies have displayed great interest in using IT to improve customer service, the transition to a true service culture may prove more difficult because of its implications for arrogant, status-conscious executives. In Chapters 19 and 20, you will find a much fuller discussion of customer relationship development and retention.

6

DATABASES: WHAT EVERY MARKETER SHOULD KNOW

IN THIS CHAPTER

It is crucial to grasp the contents of this simple chapter. Information about individual customers is our stock-in-trade … and, as you will discover, it is astonishing how much we can tell from just a name and an address.

We need to know where we can get data, roughly how it is organised and what it can tell us. We are not concerned with technicalities, however. Our concerns are, firstly, to ensure that bits of data are assembled into customer information; secondly, that we learn from the information, turning it into knowledge. The marketers who know their customers best will be the winners.

There are lots of clever management things we could do with the information. We will forgo the opportunity to discuss these and remain focused on direct marketing.

WHAT IS A MARKETING DATABASE?

There are many kinds of database. What concerns us is one kind only: the one-to-one marketing database. This is a way of recording what we know about individual customers or prospects that maximises the value of the information, enabling us to become more competitive.

As marketing people, there is no need for us to become too entranced by the technicalities of how this result is achieved. But we do need to understand the basic principles and we also need to understand what we have a right to expect from our database.

Sometimes we find information technologists (IT people) hard to understand. They seem to us rather pedantic and to converse in a coded language. Why can't they use simple English instead of impenetrable jargon? Perhaps we should be more sympathetic. IT people must be absolutely precise. Many of their words have a particular meaning. No other word will do to describe exactly how they want their IT system to function. Of course, we should never be afraid to ask them to translate for us, but we should respect their desire for precision because we are utterly reliant upon the accuracy of the information they organise and manage.

Ingredients of the excellent database

The excellent marketing database has three fundamentally important ingredients, as follows.

Firstly, all the data it contains is accurate. This means it was correct at the time of input into the system and that it was amended or deleted by the time it became out of date. The processes involved in achieving this depend on human intervention. Therefore 100 per cent accuracy is unlikely. Anything much less than 100 per cent is unacceptable. The quality of the data outweighs every other ingredient of the excellent database by at least ten to one. Gresham's Law applies. Just as bad money drives out good money, inaccurate data prevents us from exploiting the good data. We cease to trust it and stop using it. A file including incorrect inputs is said to be *corrupted*. Out-of-date entries on the database are said to have *decayed*. The corollary of this is not obvious and is worth stating: if our data is good, we can still send individually addressed marketing communications *even on a precisely targeted basis* without creating a database. We simply use modelling techniques (as we will see in a moment) to make inferences about the names on our customer file.

Secondly, the data is as complete as possible. There may be times when we will collect information about some customers (for example, information they volunteer) that we are unable to gather for all customers. Providing that we do this deliberately and for a good, specific purpose, we should not worry about it. But there will be other categories of information we simply must have in all cases. An example would be status (that is, customer or prospect). Another would be postcode.

Thirdly, the data should be so organised and managed that we can find what we need quickly and easily. In Chapter 1 we described the database as a collection of files. If we now imagine a file as a card index file, we can see that we must decide how to arrange it. Usually, we may arrange it in alphabetical order. If it is a telephone directory, that is highly appropriate. Since we remember the name of the person we want to call, we do not need any other way of accessing our file.

But supposing we needed to call everyone on our list who lived in Birmingham? Now we would need to rearrange our file so that it was in alphabetical order within towns. So far, so good. But, we decide, we only want to call those people who spent over £100 with us last year and have not given us any business this year. Using a card index filing system, we would need to buy another filing cabinet and repeat the information, organised by customer value and by elapsed time since their last purchase. It would be extremely cumbersome and hard to keep up to date.

The relational database

The principle of our information system is to record a piece of information once only but to allow us to access this piece of information through a number of different routes. The files in the database each contain different categories of information that can be linked together to answer any enquiry we wish to make.

Thus we can find out how many customers we have who spent over £100 last year, who have not bought anything this year and who live in Birmingham. We can find out who they are, where they live and their telephone numbers. We can also show these (lapsed) customers as a percentage of all customers in Birmingham who spent over £100 with us last year. We can then compare our customer retention rate in Birmingham with our performance elsewhere.

Files which are so arranged that we can make such enquiries without worrying about where each item of data is held are said to be *relational*. A relational database can be held on a mainframe computer or a PC disk (or a network of PCs). However, it will be much easier to manage and access if it is on a PC (see Figure 6.1). The only significant loss will be in processing speed, a problem that is being resolved so quickly that it may have disappeared by the time you read these words.

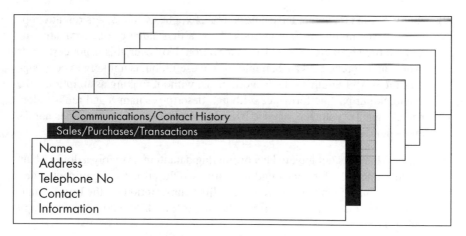

Figure 6.1 The card index comes of age

WHAT'S IN A NAME?

Direct marketing pioneers were adept at deriving a great deal of information from a few items of data. They had to be, because data was hard to collect and expensive to manage. Their skills in deriving a quart from a pint pot, to use old measures, remain relevant today. Let us try to wring the last drop of information out of what follows.

Mrs Emily Smith, Avalon Cottage, 33 Acacia Avenue, Shrewsbury SY2 3BB has bought plants by mail order from a horticulturalist within the last 12 months. She has permitted the horticulturist to release her name to firms who may make related offers to her. We wish to sell a gardening encyclopaedia by post but we cannot afford to mail everyone on the horticulturist's customer list. We have to decide, from what may seem to be one simple piece of information, whether Mrs Smith should receive our mailing. How should we decide?

In making our decision, we will be guided by a painstaking analysis of our previous experience in direct mailing our encyclopaedia offer. The one piece of information we have from the horticulturist actually comprises a surprising number of data items. These can be compared with the data items arising from our past activity.

1) *Mrs*. This is the title Emily Smith prefers to use. Without making any assumptions about her marital status, we can compare our previous success rate in selling to people using this title with our success rate in selling to people with the title Mr, Ms and Miss. We can accord a value to 'Mrs' on an index basis. If 'Mrs' is 20 per cent more likely to buy than the average of all other titles, we can attach a score of 120 to Mrs Smith.

2) *Emily*. Some first names have enjoyed brief vogues while others remain popular or uncommon for long periods. Thus a first name can be indicative of age. Matilda is likely to be older than Sharon. However, this is not certain. It is only an inference. As such, it may prove useful, but is unlikely to be as significant as Mrs Smith's title. Nevertheless, without making assumptions, we can track our past performance with age-descriptive names and rank 'older' names against 'younger' names. If Emily is an older name and older names are better, we can record this on our index.

3) *Smith*. This does not look to be a promising data item. Possibly a double-barrelled name or a foreign-sounding name would attract a significant index rating. If, on the other hand, we were selling subscriptions to the English-language *Time* magazine in Bulgaria, the name 'Smith' would produce a high index score.

4) *Avalon Cottage*. This indicates that Mrs Smith lives in a detached house which may well have a large garden. Again, we need not jump to a conclusion about this. All we need do is compare our previous success with mailing people in named houses against our average performance.

5) *33 Acacia Avenue*. Before the days of geodemographic and lifestyle targeting systems, we would certainly have seen this as good information. People living in long streets are likely to behave differently from people living in short streets or country lanes. There may be a significant difference between Street, Road, Avenue, Lane, Close and so on. By accessing Electoral Roll

data, we can see how long Mrs Smith has lived at this address. Long-term residents may be better buyers than people who have recently moved in.

6) *Shrewsbury*. The town name enables us to look at our regional data. Are we successful in Shropshire? Are county towns good for us? Is the size of town significant?

7) *SY2 3BB*. The full postcode enables us to access geodemographic or lifestyle data, of which more in the next chapter. It does not matter whether we have ever received an order from someone who lives in Mrs Smith's postcode before. Geodemographic and lifestyle data are used to typify neighbourhoods. Therefore we can find out if we are more or less than averagely successful in Mrs Smith's *type* of neighbourhood. This does not provide a fact about Mrs Smith as a person. She may be atypical of those who live in her neighbourhood type. But the odds are that her choice of neighbourhood reflects her lifestyle. This choice provides a useful inference. It allows us to make a statistical comparison between those who have made a similar choice and those who have made different choices. We can also use the front half of Mrs Smith's postcode (the outward postcode) to compare our success rate in SY2 with our success rate in all other outward postcodes.

Having done all this, we can aggregate Mrs Smith's index score. This aggregate score will place her in a league table of names on the horticulturist's file, enabling us to make an odds-based decision on her inclusion or exclusion. This process will be automated, the decisions (based on prearranged criteria) being made by computer while the prospects are being addressed.

To explain how much actionable information can be derived from a simple name and address, we have jumped ahead to the use of direct mail as a customer acquisition medium. However, our purpose is to highlight the value of data about individuals and to re-emphasise the importance of accurate data. Our clever analysis would be useless if our information were incorrect. This analysis also depends on our ability to access our past performance data.

To complete the analysis, we must record our previous contact history. We need to know about our failures as well as our successes. If we merely profiled Mrs Smith against our customer base, we would probably arrive at the wrong conclusion. Our customer profile will reflect all the biases in our previous marketing efforts. For example, we may have twice as many males as females on our customer file. But is that because we mailed three times as many men as women? If so, it indicates that women are more likely to order from us than men and we should change our targeting.

WHAT MARKETING DATABASE SYSTEMS DO

The word *system* is used to define the complete installation of computer hardware, peripherals and software that accepts, stores and manages data. The *marketing database system* may not be the only system that is related to marketing within a company. Nevertheless, it is the key repository of customer information.

Two other systems may be in use. There may be a *sales management system*. There may also be a *telemarketing and teleservice system*. The three systems may be linked as in Figure 6.2. Just to complicate matters, a company may have a consumer marketing database and a trade marketing database. For example, an fmcg company might need all three systems for trade customers and indirectly supplied outlets, but might use only a marketing database system for consumers.

The roles and features of the three systems (from the Institute of Direct Marketing's *Education Programme, Module 2*) are displayed below and on page 82.

Marketing database systems

What they are for:
Market research and testing
Segmentation and targeting
Loyalty and customer care programmes
Direct marketing (ie direct sales)

Cross selling
Customer account management

Essential features:
Flexible data structures
Data import from various sources
Name and address management
Research profiling and compiling facilities
Communications targeting
Campaign and promotion recording
Personalisation
Fast, volume performance

Some explanation of the features may be helpful. *Data structures* must be flexible enough to cope with new ideas about what information should be captured and retrieved. *Data import* may be from different departments within the company or include items that are bought in. *Name and address management* is crucial. A key requirement is the ability to recognise different variants of a name and address as belonging to the same customer. Otherwise there will be many duplicates, established customers will be treated as new customers, customers will receive duplicated messages and the resulting marketing data will be inaccurate.

Research profiling enables marketers to find clusters of behavioural types among customers and *communications targeting* enables marketing to take appropriate action. For reasons we have already identified with our example of Emily Smith, it is important to record who has been exposed to each *campaign and promotion* whether they responded or not. To recognise customers as people we know by name a *personalisation* facility is required. *Fast, volume performance* is

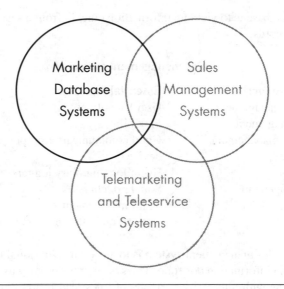

Market research and testing

Segmentation and targeting

Loyalty and customer care programmes

Direct marketing (ie direct sales)

Cross selling

Customer account management

Figure 6.2 Marketing database systems: the key to customer information

needed if a database is to yield up information quickly from a search of, perhaps, millions of records.

Sales management systems

What they are for:

Key account management
Territory management
Sales activity management

Forecasting
Contact management

Essential features:

User friendliness
Flexibility
Good communications – possibly hand-held devices
Event logging/diary joggers
Standard letters
Team involvement
Integration in the 'bigger' marketing picture

The role of a sales management system is to act as an operational front end to the total marketing information portfolio. The system must be easy to use, be flexible enough to cope with alternative methods of sales lead follow-up, be accessible away from base, provide reminders of time-sensitive tasks, save time by providing letters to customers, be understood and endorsed by all users and must be integrated into the bigger marketing picture.

Telemarketing and teleservice systems

What they are for:

Information fulfilment/provision
Appointment setting
Standard service requests
Customer research
Direct sales
After-sales follow-up

Essential features:

Access to inventory data
Prompts for questions
Sales/service diary management
Event logging/diary joggers
Order handling facility
Access to customer data
Integration in the 'bigger' marketing picture

Call centres and outbound telemarketing operations vary greatly in sophistication depending on their size and task list. Inbound operations (call centres) may be equipped and staffed so that the phone is always answered within a target time. As the call is taken, the operator may access the customer's credit status with the company and, on discovering that an order can be accepted, immediately access the inventory database to check that stock is available and confirm price or specification details. Calls from outbound units may be driven by automatic predictive diallers that select customer phone numbers on the basis of specified priorities. For example, they may be driven by a score-based selection system similar to the type we imagined using to select or deselect Emily Smith. The calls are passed to the operator only when there is an answer. Again, the telemarketing and service system is in the front line of operations but may often be put to more diverse uses, particularly in information-gathering, than a costly field sales operation. One of telemarketing's tasks may be to fill vacant fields when customer data is incomplete. Another may be to secure information volunteered by customers on their preferences. It is likely to be one of the most important information-providers to the marketing database.

It will be apparent that, if the three systems are all stand-alone systems unable to exchange information, the company's capacity to gather and use marketing information to the mutual advantage of its operations and its customers will be seriously impaired.

The purpose of all three systems is to permit the company to win business cost-effectively. Thus all three may be integrated with a fourth system, that which automates the handling of orders, enquiries or service requests … *a fulfilment system*.

Computer-aided fulfilment systems

Even companies that do not deal directly with their end customers must be able to handle enquiries and send out information or samples, as well as process orders from intermediaries. Orders, coupon redemptions and enquiries provide the transactional data that is the most significant information a company can acquire about its customers. Each interaction with a customer adds to and updates the information. Order or purchase data attaches a value to the customer and provides a basis for forecasting future value. A hiatus in the frequency of a customer's orders rings a warning bell that should trigger action. Not all of a customer's purchases will be prompted by any particular promotion, but all are important to record within the customer marketing data because, without a complete record, wrong assumptions will be made.

In Figure 6.3 we see the four systems linked together. This linkage permits an integrated marketing effort and makes each marketing function accountable. Salespeople can take orders on laptop computers and orders may be received by telephone, fax, e-mail and post. Integration of systems provides a complete picture of a customer's transactions and of the customer's preferred channels. It assists the company to avoid delivering conflicting messages to the customer through alternative communications channels. It improves the company's responsiveness in speed and accuracy.

The unfriendly-looking sentence at the bottom of Figure 6.3 refers to the fact these four systems, specified for different but related purposes, may be combined into a single *customer (or client) information system (CIS)* that pulls together all the relevant information and attaches it to a customer.

Alternatively, data from these separate and possibly incompatible systems may be held within a data warehouse. Middleware is then used to bridge between these disparate sources and the user's terminal or PC. The user may then be able to

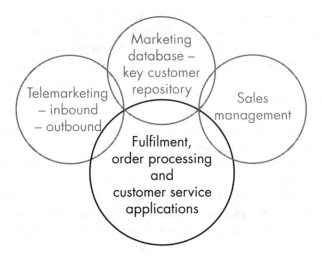

All systems need information about customers

Information needs to flow to where it is relevant

Data quality must be captured at source

Applications and tools can work as a partnership

Companies are writing multiple producer line servicing applications into central client-focused systems

Figure 6.3 Computer-aided systems for fulfilment

retrieve pieces of information, perhaps using Windows or Apple Mac, without even knowing which base the data comes from.

For the purposes of this book, we will now assume that any information on any of the systems can readily be imported into the marketing database or, alternatively, can be accessed for marketing enquiries. Although this will not always be so, for example when transactional data must be retrieved from the company's main accounting system, there is invariably a way round the problem. This will usually involve importing regular copies of the relevant data, like taking snapshots. In the inelegant language of computing, a file is dumped from the accounting database; that is, an unedited file is copied. This is then edited as required for the marketing database.

The accounting file from which the data was extracted may contain only current data. However, it can be matched through the customer's unique reference number, or name and address, to previous purchase data on the marketing database. The previous data will have been collected from earlier file dumps.

THE DATABASE FUNCTION

Figure 6.4 shows the four stages of database management and usage. Data is collected from all the sources of relevant information. It is then added together, edited (to remove inaccurate or surplus data) and deduplicated.

Deduplication nearly always refers to name and address deduplication. This is necessitated whenever there is more than one transaction attributable to a single customer, but may also occur even if the customers responsible for two transactions are not the same person. This is when the household, the address, the branch, the division or the company are considered to be the main customer unit. Aggregating data at household level may save postage and customer annoyance in direct mailing the same household on a non-confidential matter twice.

Stage three is the business of managing the data and making it accessible to users. The main users may be the marketing department but other managers may also need access. Some users may get all they need just by looking up information. However, outputs will generally be required when managers have made decisions. These outputs may include mailings, reports, tapes for high-speed laser printing, files for processing or telemarketing, or floppy disks. File processing may be for analytical purposes and, if the database is held on a mainframe computer system, this work will usually be done on a PC. If the database contains many millions of records, the file used may sometimes be a random sample of the whole file, selected on an nth name basis, eg every tenth customer.

In Figure 6.5 we see a more detailed picture, breaking down activities into 14 distinct functions.

1) *Data import*. This is the business of pulling in data from outside sources. The data may come from other systems within the company, like accounts, or may

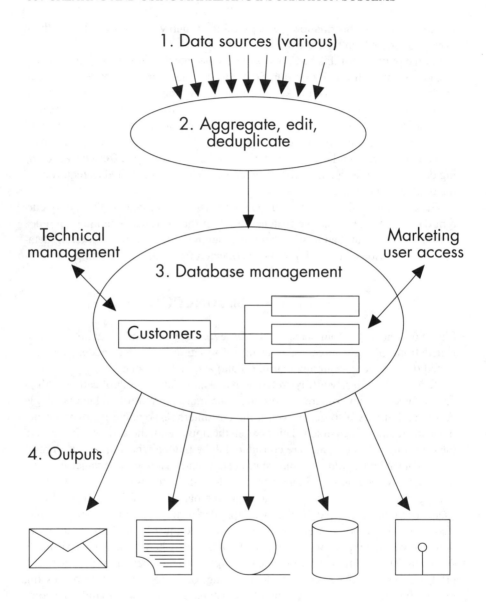

Figure 6.4 The four stages in database management and usage

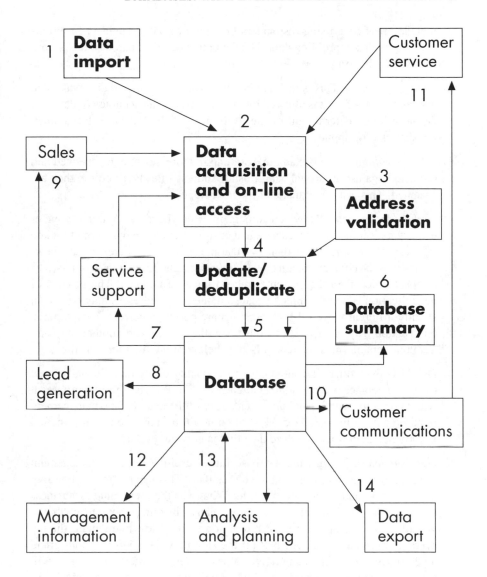

Figure 6.5 The database function

include press advertising responders or reference data bought in from out-side: for example, profiling data. The data must be reformatted so that it con-forms with the format used in the database.

2) *Data preparation.* This is the quality control stage in which data is validated and corrected before it is allowed into the database. The accuracy of data will be the primary determinant of the usefulness of the database. Remember, Gresham's Law applies.

3) *Address validation.* For example, residential addresses may be checked and corrected against the Royal Mail Postal Address File (PAF) before they are accepted. This is a prerequisite of the next stage.

4) *Update/deduplicate.* 'New' customers may not be new. A transaction or enquiry may come from an established customer even if it has been provoked by press advertising rather than by customer mailings. Therefore, all 'new' names must be compared with names already on file. If the transaction is, say, a repeat order, then the customer record must be updated. The process of deduplication is quite complex because names and addresses may be set out slightly differently even if both versions are perfectly correct. For example, one version may incorporate a house or village name and another may not. Yet both versions must be recognised as belonging to the same customer.

5) *Database.* Now there is confidence in the quality of the data, it can be used to update, replace and add to data already on file. Which of these purposes it will be used for will depend on the category of the data and the management requirements of the database. Most often it will be added to the information already held, but it may replace data that is now out of date.

6) *Data summary.* To turn the database into a useful source of management information, it is necessary to summarise data. This usually means totalling up, averaging and so on, for example: What was the total value of business generated by the last campaign? How many customers bought anything? What was the average customer transaction worth? How many items did the average transaction include? Not all the summary data will be about grand totals and averages. The cumulative value of each customer over a period will be an important piece of information, as will any summary data which indi-cates the customer's preferences. The resulting summary records are then incorporated within the database, making interrogation quick and simple.
Caution: when data is summarised the raw data may be discarded. This can cause a problem later if the raw data suddenly assumes significance when the database is being interrogated, perhaps while a new line of enquiry is being pursued. As it keeps on getting much cheaper to store information, we become less inclined to turf raw data out.

7) *Service support.* An important function is to supply information on-screen to

allow service and call centre staff to respond intelligently to a customer's requests. Any accurate information on the customer's last purchases and preferences may help to make the customer feel appreciated and understood. Complaints about the last purchase can be handled correctly without troubling the customer to spell out the precise details of the transaction. The information is already on-screen.

8) *Lead generation.* This function may include the provision of urgent contacts for sales people, such as timely follow-ups to enquirers. However, it also includes any time-sensitive communication prompts, however the communication is delivered. For example, it might be an anniversary mailing to a customer who bought their car two years ago, or it may be a telephone call to a customer whose last payment on a personal loan is due next month. The system has a wonderful memory and will never forget a birthday providing the data has been correctly captured. This is what more direct marketing communications could and should be about – messages that are relevant in time.

9) *Sales.* This is information about customer orders and purchases or non-orders and non-purchases. Our chart simplifies by assuming sales are always the result of lead follow-up. This is not necessarily so and the information may come from a sales team, telemarketing, a branch network or dealers. Some sales will be attributable to specific marketing activities and other sales will not. All must be correctly recorded.

10) *Customer communications.* These may be marketing or service communications and may result in direct orders or enquiries to a call centre (or by post). The call centre and post room are grouped together under customer service.

11) *Customer service.* Customer service may handle orders, simple enquiries or more complex enquiries that merit a sales call. Enquiries may also be passed on to branches or dealerships. Whichever route an enquiry takes, customer service will be generating data that must be used to update the database.

12) *Management information.* This will be derived from summary data and will show the performance of the sales team, customer service, marketing campaigns and so on. Some of the information will be produced in the form of regular standard reports on paper.

Increasingly, managers are using the data to make their own specific enquiries. This latter trend is most important. It should not be a function of the database to swamp busy managers with reams of standardised reports. If the data is truly accessible through a user-friendly system, the database should encourage managers to be imaginative and inquisitive, perhaps constructing scenarios from imagined tactical manoeuvres and using the data to assess their winning chances. The way the data is organised is critical to making the most of its information value, this organisation being the third essential ingredient we recorded at the beginning of this chapter. You will recall that middleware can be used to turn data held by unfriendly mainframe computers into information that a manager can use to answer enquiries while looking at his or her PC screen.

13) *Analysis and planning*. This includes interrogation of a type that requires skills the marketing manager would not usually be expected to possess. The main skill here is in statistical modelling. This may be used for establishing correlations between customer profiles and behaviour, for forecasting the results of future marketing activity and for segmenting the customer base in a useful way. We will deal with this subject in Chapter 7.

14) *Data export*. Data may need to be exported to specialist bureaux or laser printers. This is usually to create high-volume or technically complex direct mail. Sometimes it may be passed to a telemarketing bureau to make outbound calls. Or, sometimes, customers may have agreed to receive mailings from other companies making offers that might interest them; in that case name and address data would be exported to an approved bureau for processing. The names might be rented or they might be exchanged. Either way, the agreement would be for one-time use only.

CATEGORISING DATA

To a computer buff, data is data no matter what information we can extract from it. As marketing people, we are more interested in what it can tell us than we are in the technicalities of how it was collected, validated and assembled. The way we will categorise the kinds of data on our database may be non-technical but it will be purposeful and that is more important.

We have now described the differences between a marketing database system and other systems the company may use. We have noted that these are ideally integrated into a customer information system (CIS). We have described the functions of the marketing database and, before we continue, we can borrow the Institute of Direct Marketing's succinct definition of the database. It is:

> a comprehensive collection of relevant and interrelated data … serving multiple applications … allowing timely and accurate on-demand retrieval or manipulation of relevant data … and having a data management system independent of applications.

Our earlier description did not do justice to the last nine words of this definition so we should clarify these. The idea is that the specialised systems software used manages the data itself. The data can then be retrieved for applications, such as customer mailings, without the users having to worry about how it is managed. This is a complete change-round from the way customer databases were originated. Then, databases were a by-product of the need to undertake direct mail. The management of the data was driven by the requirements of direct mail without consideration of its other uses. Today, direct marketing is generally integrated and its technology is used to inform and make simpler other marketing decisions and tasks.

Now let us move on to categorise the data on the database, expanding a little on our capsule description from Chapter 1.

1) *Contact data*. This comprises everything we need to know to make contact with a customer, using individually addressable media. The records may include title, name, address, postcode, telephone numbers (day and evening) and fax number. For business addresses, job title will be a necessary inclusion. This is part of what we need to know to answer the 'who?' question referred to in Chapter 1. For business customers, our main customer unit may be the firm, not the individual. Therefore, the individual will be accessed via a reference directing us to the company. In some cases, the consumer unit may be the household.

2) *Classification data*. This is the supplementary 'who?' data and is independent of any transactional data. It may include information derived from a customer's postcode, such as a geodemographic code or lifestyle code. For a firm it may include a code indicating what the company does, such as the Standard Industrial Classification (SIC); it may include a size indicator, usually based on number of employees. This information may be used extensively in summary reporting, for example to permit market penetration analysis in various market sectors. It will often be used for profiling, usually to seek matches of unknown new customers or prospects against known customers, inferring from these matches how the unknown people may behave. This use is so important that direct marketers most often refer to classification data as profiling data.

3) *Transactional data*. This provides a history of the customer's dealings with us. It answers the 'what?' and 'how much?' questions. It tells us what the customer ordered and how much that transaction was worth. This would be simple if the company were never out of stock, goods were never returned as unsuitable and if all transactions were cash in advance. In most cases, however, it will be quite a lot more complicated than this and will involve drawing information from order processing, distribution and accounts.

A bank customer's transactional history will include hundreds of routine transactions occasionally punctuated by a major transaction, such as a mortgage agreement. In this case, it will pointless to import every routine transaction onto the marketing database. Instead, summary data will be used, perhaps opening and closing balances each month and the monthly turnover in the account. Access to the transactional history of each customer provides the company with a potential competitive advantage. What a customer does is more significant than the customer's profile.

4) *Channel data.* Does the customer buy from a salesperson, a call centre, by post, from a branch or order computer to computer? If the company markets through multi-sales channels, it must be able to answer the 'where?' question. The integration of this information with transactional data allows the contribution of each channel to be monitored and trends in channel use to be detected quickly.

5) *Promotional output and response data.* This is used to record the targeting, timing and cost of individually addressable marketing communications on a per-customer basis. Every message a customer receives is flagged against that customer's record. The customer's response, if any, is also recorded. Summary data for each campaign will usually include both the actual and forecast results.

In addition, any responses the customer makes to non-individually addressed promotions will be recorded. These responses may include responses to media advertising or money-off coupon distribution. Finally, the customer's use of services such as advisory hotlines will be recorded. The information that describes promotional output and response, when combined with classification and transactional data, helps to answer the 'why?' question: 'Why did this customer order that product?'

It also permits the monitoring of the effect and efficiency of marketing expenditures by target group, by product, by month and so on. It provides a sound information base for forecasting the results of planned activity.

In the next chapter we will see how these categories of data can be combined together and manipulated to help improve our marketing effectiveness and efficiency.

TO SUM UP

The chapter began by proposing that the three important attributes of direct marketing data were accuracy, completeness and retrievability. We then discovered the nuggets of gold the alert prospector can find inside a name and address.

The relevant information systems of a company were discussed and these were linked together through a customer information system or, alternatively, were held separately as stock in a data warehouse but accessed as if they were all one source.

The database functions were detailed and the IDM's preferred definition of the marketing database was given:

A comprehensive collection of relevant and interrelated data ... serving multiple applications ... allowing timely and accurate on-demand retrieval or manipulation of relevant data ... and having a data management system independent of applications.

Finally, we categorised the data as:

1) contact;

2) classification;

3) transactional;

4) channel;

5) promotional and response.

It is far more important to understand the categories of data and appreciate their uses than to memorise technicalities about how data is managed. The more technical stuff becomes dated very quickly in any case. However, the marketer must take some interest in checking the quality of data collection and management because everything in direct marketing depends on accuracy.

This is the chapter where you will find all the itemised lists of information system contents and functions when you need to refer to them again.

THE HENLEY COLLEGE LIBRARY

7

TESTING, MODELLING AND FORECASTING

IN THIS CHAPTER

This is the creative side of data. We have been through the hard grind of ensuring our data is accurate, as complete as we can make it and accessible. Now we have a sophisticated toy we can play with. Like child's play this has a serious purpose. It's all part of a learning process that will enable us to make or guide better marketing decisions. This chapter explains the formulae for conducting simple tests and describes the more sophisticated models used by marketing statisticians.

As far back as anyone can remember, direct marketers have tested their ideas in a controlled way. Testing is a subject to which we will return in Part Four of this book when we discuss marketing communications. Nevertheless, we must touch on this subject now because it is how we validate our theories, and testing has paved the way to the more refined modelling we must introduce in this chapter.

A database is not the prerequisite of testing but it may help us to drag the last drop of actionable information from the results. Direct marketing tests are head-to-head encounters between alternatives. It doesn't matter what the alternatives are as long as they are significantly different and we confine ourselves to including only one variable in each test. The alternatives might be products, prices, promotional offers, terms of business, headlines on advertisements, direct mail letters or outbound telemarketing messages.

The principle is to test two or more alternatives, each with only one significant difference, by addressing our message to matched samples of customers or potential customers. Usually, this is done by taking alternate names from a file and despatching alternative messages to them. But we can also test two alternative advertisements in one issue of a national newspaper. The newspaper prints our two different ads in alternate copies, providing for us two perfect random samples of their readership. The direct marketing terminology for such a test is an A/B split-run. In direct mail or in loose insert tests, the split-run may be divided between more alternatives and may become an A/B/C/D split.

Instead of testing two new ideas against each other, we will generally test a new idea against a proven idea. This test and control procedure is similar to that used in clinical trials. When the test is conducted outside the database, as in the case of newspaper ads, we need an identifying code (quoted by the responder) so that we know which of the two ads provoked each response.

STATISTICAL SIGNIFICANCE

There is no such thing as a statistical certainty. The degree of confidence we demand in predicting that A will be better than B will depend on what is at risk if we get it wrong. Traditionally direct marketers have liked to work on a 95 per cent confidence level. That is to say, there are 19 chances out of 20 that the result will be repeated within an acceptable margin of error. This margin of error may be sufficient to ensure that A is truly better than B, or it may have to be sufficient to predict future results to a tolerable level of accuracy. The notion of a tolerable level of accuracy arises because it may not be enough to determine that A will beat B 19 times out of 20. We may also need to be 95 per cent confident that A will be profitable on roll-out. (*Roll-out* means the application of the winning idea to a complete campaign.)

There is a formula for arriving at the correct sample size to ensure any given level of confidence. Very often in business-to-business or small-scale marketing it is unrealistic to work on a 95 per cent confidence level. This would require too large a sample. But the formula can handle any chosen degree of confidence, although it does not work for press advertising where response rates are too low. (The formula for press will be revealed in Chapter 18.) This is the standard formula:

$$\text{Sample size} = \frac{CL^2 \times \% \text{ response} \times \% \text{ non-response}}{(\text{Error tolerance})^2}$$

CL stands for confidence level. It is a number which always remains the same for any given level of confidence. For 80 per cent confidence, CL = 1.281, for 90 per cent CL = 1.645 and for 95 per cent CL = 1.960. (You may have seen the CL for 95 per cent expressed as 3.8416. That is because 3.8416 is the square of 1.960.)

You will see that the formula does not do all the work. It depends, firstly, on the accuracy of the response forecast. If the test is between a new idea and a control idea of known effectiveness, the forecast will be more accurate. However, we must still make a decision on how much better we expect our test idea to perform. If we knew the answer to this, we would not need to test. Therefore, we may well adopt a businesslike approach. If we are testing a price reduction that will cost 20 per cent in loss of margin we know the test must increase orders by at least 20 per cent. We also know that, plus or minus our error tolerance, we must be confident that the test price is at least as profitable as the control price. These considerations will drive the values we put into the formula.

Suppose we know our control has produced 5 per cent response. We think the low price will be more profitable, otherwise we wouldn't bother to test it. So we assume it will pull 7 per cent response; that is, 40 per cent more. If it pulls less than 6 per cent it will generate less profit so we want to be 95 per cent confident that a 7 per cent test result will not roll out at less than 6 per cent. We could say we need only test to a confidence level of 90 per cent. The reason is that our 7 per cent response forecast is just as likely to be an underestimate as an overestimate.

Therefore CL = 2.71 (that is, 1.645 x 1.645), response = 7 and non-response = 93. Below the line, ET = 1 (the difference between the expected 7 per cent and the acceptable 6 per cent). The formula is:

$$\text{Sample size} = \frac{2.71 \times 7\% \text{ response} \times 93\% \text{ non-response}}{1^2} = 1764$$

If our error tolerance were reduced to 0.5 per cent our sample size would need to be four times greater, that is 7056, because ET would equal 0.5 and the square of 0.5 is 0.25. Dividing 1764 by 0.25 we get 7056.

TARGETING AND EXTENDED TESTS

Although product, price, terms, offer and copy tests are important, testing is used more frequently to improve the accuracy of targeting or media selection, generally agreed to be the most important ingredient of successful direct marketing. Direct mail lists that are rented on a one-time use basis for customer acquisition have been tested for many years. List owners who rent their lists make samples available for testing. Testers must pay for a specified minimum quantity, usually 5000, whether they are all used or not.

The samples are selected on an nth name basis so that, if the whole list numbers 50,000 names, every tenth name would be selected to make up the 5000 sample. The user might specify a selection from within the list, such as the most recently acquired names only or women only. In that case, the sample would be representative of the restricted universe selected. Tests can then be conducted using the confidence formula already discussed.

Such tests have their limitations. What is being tested is the *average* pulling power of the list. Yet, if you remember the example of Mrs Emily Smith in Chapter 6, you will appreciate that some names within each list are more likely to respond than others. Large-scale direct mailers in the United States cottoned on to this many years ago. Their mailings had to be pre-sorted into zip code (American postcode) areas to qualify for the lowest postal rate. Why not analyse the results and check if some zip codes were consistently better than others? Using the statistical technique of regression analysis, it was possible to gauge the precise effect of zip code as a variable independent of list selection. Now, instead of using every name on the best lists and rejecting all the names on less useful lists, the direct mailer could take some names from every list. The analysis would show how far down the league table of zip codes the direct mailer could go on each list before the list became unprofitable to use.

This was an early step in moving away from using lists as an entity and towards micro-segmentation. However, as we saw in the case of Mrs Emily Smith, a name and address contains more data items than the zip or postcode. Gender information, title information and address type can all be included as independent variables and their effect measured using a standard statistical model. Now the direct mailer is getting close to targeting individuals instead of lists or market segments.

Simple A/B tests had become inadequate for targeting and were not always adequate for other purposes. In the example of the price test, the initial response is only part of the profit equation. The lower price may pull in 20 per cent more new customers and these extra new customers may generate further profits by making repeat purchases at full price. On the other hand the low price offer may attract customers who will buy only if a discount is offered. The extra customers may be unprofitable. Our test result will give us no pointers to their future behaviour. More sophisticated statistical techniques are needed.

STATISTICAL MODELS FOR MARKETING

A model is a simplified representation of a market that is used either for market segmentation or to help make predictions. Models can be considered as static or dynamic, the former providing a picture of a market that may be helpful in segmentation. Geodemographic targeting systems such as ACORN or MOSAIC are examples of static models. Dynamic models use interactions between variables such as price and demand, the notion being that one variable is dependent on the other or others; in this case, that demand depends on price.

There are also two kinds of model along a different dimension. There are micromodels and macromodels. Micromodels are frequently used in market research. Typically a sample of respondents may be asked if they would buy product A at price B. The results are then extrapolated into the predicted future behaviour of the much larger universe of customers. Such a procedure would be regarded as highly unsatisfactory by most direct marketers. That is because of the potential discrepancy between what people say they will do and what they will actually do. Direct marketers prefer the hard evidence of tests.

Macromodels depend on large volumes of back data, usually collected over a period sufficient to show trends and often describing an entire market or a company's entire sales volume. Many marketing people will be familiar with econometric modelling as an example of the macromodel. Econometric models, too, would meet with the disapproval of most direct marketers. That is because they generally depend on pulling together data from a good many sources of unproved compatibility and variable quality. Direct marketers are sticklers for accuracy.

There are, of course, occasions when there is no reasonable alternative but to use sample research micromodels or multi-source macromodels. Fortunately, the data on the database reduces the frequency of such occasions. The result is macro-modelling of an altogether higher quality.

Static models

Direct marketers use both static and dynamic models. Static models are used to segment markets into numerous small segments to which some sort of description can be attached. The models are borrowed from market research and were used in market research before anyone thought of applying them to targeted direct marketing. The most commonly used modelling technique is *cluster analysis*. For cluster analysis, data is searched to find natural groupings, the members of each group having more in common with each other than they do with the members of any other group. This method is used to create geodemographic systems that group together different neighbourhoods into recurring types, using census and other data. Static modelling is also used to generate lifestyle types among respondents to the lengthy "lifestyle" questionnaires such as The Lifestyle Selector, BehaviourBank, Facts of Living, Chorus and Lifestyle Focus. The key differences are that geodemographics cover the whole population but don't actually describe any individual, while lifestyle types cover respondents only but do describe them as people, not just as residents of a particular type of neighbourhood. A sort of hybrid of the two exists in the form of an extrapolation of lifestyle survey data; this works on the assumption that responders' neighbours are like the responders. Another example of a hybrid is Financial ACORN, using extrapolations from the annual Financial Research Survey in combination with geodemographic data.

The discriminatory power of geo-demographics can be tested by attaching the geodemographic code to the postcode of each customer. The number and value of customers within each code can then be checked. Figure 7.1 shows an example of how geodemographic clusters are arranged. Neighbourhood types are grouped within families and the families may in turn be subdivisions of broader categories. Thus, Category A in Financial ACORN, 'Financially sophisticated', is one of four families. Its two component groups, 'Wealthy equityholders' and 'Affluent mortgageholders', are two of 12 groups. The types within 'Wealthy equityholders' are 12 of 51 types. Category A represents 13 per cent of British households, Group 1 represents 7.7 per cent and Type 1.1 represents only 0.5 per cent. Users can choose the degree of refinement they need for their purpose. This application of cluster analysis represents a huge advance in marketing data for targeting.

The value of lifestyle survey clusters can also be checked, generally by sending a customer file sample to the lifestyle survey firm so that the two databases can be matched. The lifestyle survey firm is primarily interested in selling their products for customer acquisition. They do this by renting lists of people who match the best customers on the client's customer database. However, they also provide customer data enhancement services. Lifestyle survey data has been

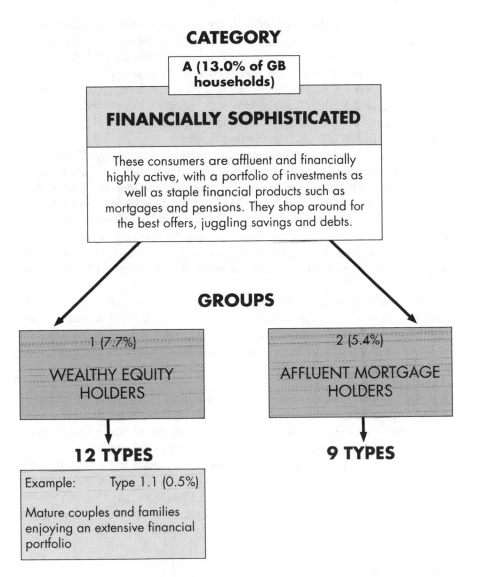

Figure 7.1 Geodemographic cluster example: financial ACORN
(Reproduced by kind permission of CACI Ltd. ACORN is a registered trademark of CACI Ltd.)

found to discriminate effectively enough for many customer acquisition direct mail programmes. It cannot (except in the extrapolated form) be applied so usefully to segment a database of established customers because not all the customers will be on the lifestyle database. A snag both with extrapolated lifestyle surveys and geodemographics is that they provide inferences rather than hard data. Thus, because a particular type of neighbourhood is populated disproportionately by loyal customers, we infer that anyone living there is more likely to be loyal than all those who live in disloyal neighbourhood types.

Experience shows that such inferences are rarely accurate enough for targeting individually addressable communications such as direct mailings. They are most useful when combined with other information, often as one component of a dynamic model (dynamic models will be described below). For example, geodemographics and extrapolated lifestyle data can be used as selectors within predefined catchment areas. Here, we are combining the inference with a hard fact. The hard fact might be that the potential customer lives within ten minutes of our shop. The data increases in value by being used in combination with other information.

The products of cluster analysis we have discussed have many applications to marketing beyond the targeting of individually addressable communications. They provide data that can be used in the siting of retail outlets, the fair division of sales territories and the description of market segments. Furthermore, they paint pen pictures of market segments that are useful aids to understanding, for example in creative briefings.

It is, of course, possible to employ this statistical technique to create tailor-made segmentations. Cluster analysis has been used by home shopping companies to form customer segments based on the customers' product preferences. The value of this depends on the stability of the clusters. It is most likely to work when there is an extensive inventory and customers' purchase frequency is very high. The data can be used to supplement trend data in the pattern of demand for specific product types, not merely to target merchandise offers. Another classic application might be the uses made of a credit card. In this and the home shopping case, the clusters are based on real data about customers' actual choices.

Dynamic models

The dynamic models in use imply a causal relationship between a dependant variable, such as response or purchase, and the interaction of a set of other variables, such as the number of previous purchases and the interval since the last purchase. Thus, we might say that customer A, who has bought three suits from us before, the last one a month ago, is more likely to buy another suit than customer B. Customer B has bought only one suit before and that was ten months ago.

The two types of model in most common use are very different. *Regression analysis* is used to build a scorecard in which the selected variables attract scores proportionate to their known influence on the dependant variable. In the example above, the frequency of suit purchasing may attract a bigger score than the recency of the last purchase. The scores may have a positive or negative value. The aggregate of the scores is used to define the relative probability of, say, person A responding to a mailing versus person B. It is conceivable, although not very likely, that no two individuals would attract the same score.

Regression analysis is particularly effective at handling *continuous* data values, like number of previous purchases (say, from one to ten) and drive time from a retail outlet (say, from under ten minutes to over 40 minutes). However, the score-card will also include yes/no variables, such as use of a credit card.

An example of a simple scorecard, using only yes/no variables, appears in Figure 7.2. This imaginary model is for a credit product, perhaps a personal loan, that is offered to members of an association by direct mail.

ELEMENTS	VALUE		MEMBER SCOREBANDS	
Constant	-34			
Member under 12 months	+77	**Band**	**Range**	**% File**
Member 12–33 months	+55			
Member 10+ years	-11	1	90+	12
Financial ACORN groups 2, 4	+24	2	60–89	15
Financial ACORN group 6	+12	3	40–59	14
Membership category A	+10	4	0–39	12
Membership category B	+11	5	Negative	47
Pay by direct debit	+12			
Postal regions AB, LS, NE, NG	+15			
Postal regions ED, M, YO	+22			

Figure 7.2 A response scorecard: theoretical example for credit product offered to members of association

A provisional approval scorecard could also be used. The provisional approval scorecard would be used to predict which members would be most likely to have their loan applications approved. The two scorecards could not be combined because there would now be two dependent variables. One variable (response) would describe who was most likely to want a loan and the other (approval) would describe who we thought was most likely to repay the loan. You can see how these two independent variables might conflict. We might therefore decide to select only those who achieved an acceptable score on our provisional approval score-card and build our response model solely for this population.

To build such a model requires back data to provide the basis for attaching a value to each variable. This underlines the importance of keeping a record of results. This is easy for a product that is promoted exclusively by direct mail and may only be purchased by mail. It is simply a matter of coding the reply forms. It is much more difficult when the product can be purchased through a number of sales channels. Now, the database can prove its value.

The *promotion history* data tells us who received the offer, *response* data tells us who enquired or ordered direct and *transactional* data tells us who bought. *Channel* data tells us which channel they used. By comparing the promoted population with the non-promoted population, we can tell how many extra purchases were provoked by our promotion. Naturally we are careful to maintain a control population of non-promoted customers who match the characteristics of those who received the promotion. This ensures our results are not distorted by comparing the behaviour of two unlike populations.

Regression analysis is a tried and trusted technique that has proven its worth over many years. It is not, however, always the most appropriate technique. You may remember that it is particularly strong with continuous data, such as customers' drive-time from a retail outlet expressed in minutes. But let us suppose that the influence of this variable may be strong in the case of one-car households but weak in the case of two-car households. Our scorecard model will not show this. Each variable will be accorded a score that reflects its average influence. It will therefore give us the wrong answer for both one- and two-car households.

The correct way of describing this weakness is that regression analysis is no good at handling interactions between the non-dependent variables. Unless we knew to build a separate scorecard for the two-car population we would come unstuck. (Later on we mention factor analysis and this can be used to help unscramble variables that could interact.) However, there is another popular technique that is better at handling interactions than regression analysis.

This is *tree segmentation*. Tree segmentation splits a customer population into segments that show a marked variation (for example, in responsiveness) from the average of the population. It goes on splitting the segments into smaller cells (see Figure 7.3). There are two variants of tree segmentation, AID and CHAID. AID stands for *automatic interaction detector*. This is used to handle quantitative target variables, while CHAID (*chi-square automatic interaction detector*) is used for categorical data, offering the particular advantages that it can handle more than amoeba-like binary splits and deal with dependent variables having more than two categories. Fortunately, we are not concerned with the technicalities here. All we need is an impression of what tree segmentation can do.

In Figure 7.3 we see a population of charitable donors broken down by tree

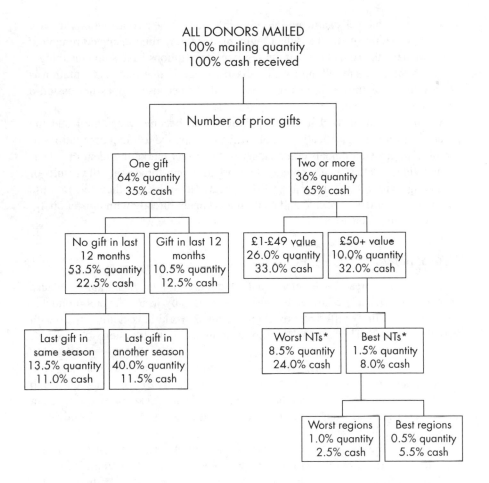

ALL DONORS MAILED
100% mailing quantity
100% cash received

Number of prior gifts

One gift
64% quantity
35% cash

Two or more
36% quantity
65% cash

No gift in last
12 months
53.5% quantity
22.5% cash

Gift in last 12
months
10.5% quantity
12.5% cash

£1-£49 value
26.0% quantity
33.0% cash

£50+ value
10.0% quantity
32.0% cash

Last gift in
same season
13.5% quantity
11.0% cash

Last gift in
another season
40.0% quantity
11.5% cash

Worst NTs*
8.5% quantity
24.0% cash

Best NTs*
1.5% quantity
8.0% cash

Worst regions
1.0% quantity
2.5% cash

Best regions
0.5% quantity
5.5% cash

*NT = geodemographic neighbourhood type.

Figure 7.3 An example of tree segmentation. This model demonstrates that 88.5 per cent of the cash could have been raised from 60 per cent of the donors by not mailing single-gift donors who had been inactive for over 12 months and who last gave at a different time of the year.

segmentation into cells showing the relative value of their contributions in cash terms. In using this method to select segments for future fundraising communications, we have the advantage that the segment descriptions have some meaning – we know who we are talking to. The disadvantage is that tree segmentation is potentially not as powerful as regression analysis because it does not assign a value to each variable.

A further problem is that cell populations can become very small and the process may not be statistically reliable when it is applied to small populations or samples. Regression models come closer to the direct marketing ideal of selecting individuals rather than segments. For targeting and forecasting the results of marketing expenditures, they are hard to beat. Nevertheless, they tell us little about the customers as people and so do not compete directly with cluster analysis or with customer research.

Neural networks

Neural networks present a direct alternative to regression models. That is because the end product, a scorecard, is the same. The means by which the end product is produced are entirely different, however. Neural networks have nothing to do with statistical method. They are the result of training a computer system to recognise patterns in data.

The model receives a training data set containing many variables that may contribute to an already known result (the dependent variable). This may be which individuals responded to a direct mail campaign. The model keeps on trying to get the answer right and stops being trained when it ceases to become significantly more skilful at the task.

Eventually, the common expectation is that neural networks will outperform statistical modelling but this is far from proven at the time of writing. They are a product of a fast developing branch of computer science, that of artificial intelligence, and it would not be a complete surprise if they were to supersede the more humdrum techniques in common use today.

Other models

Our list of modelling techniques is by no means exhaustive and two that are worthy of a passing reference are *factor analysis* and *discriminant analysis*. Factor analysis is useful for taking large numbers of variations and reducing them into a small number of factors or types. The computer looks for inter-correlations among the variables and, by taking linear combinations of variables, reduces their number. (This can be useful in assembling variables for regression analysis.) Factor analysis scores variables or attributes and classifies a market segment by its score. A segment called 'Empty nesters' might be the product of scores based on age, length of residence, type of housing and, as a negative correlation, family size. However, cluster analysis would be used to group together very large numbers of similar segments or neighbourhoods selected, for example from the 130,000 census enumeration districts.

Discriminant analysis is used in targeting. A description of good customers that can be replicated in describing non-customers can be used to find clones of these good customers. Unlike regression analysis, discriminant analysis does not set a value on the dependent variable. Discriminant analysis is concerned with the probability of an event occurring, such as the likelihood of your car being stolen or of your responding to a direct mailing. To do this it compares known characteristics of previous responders with known characteristics of the people to be mailed. Used in this way it can assist in refining mailing lists, most often by excluding those least likely to respond from the targeting.

CAUSE AND EFFECT

For the sake of keeping things simple, we have shown routine examples of the applications of the statistical techniques under review. They should not be dismissed as mere devices to assist in the planning of direct mail programmes as a result. The dependent variable can be almost any aspect of business performance. It can be profit, customer satisfaction, future demand for a product line or customer lifetime value.

A possible weakness from a purist viewpoint is the presumption of cause and effect. But this presumption has always been made in marketing, even when the available data was much less. Besides, what is the point of worrying about what it is not within our power to influence? Dynamic models are used in making plans that are designed to influence results. They work on back data that records actual customer behaviour. They establish connections between sets of known facts. They have been demonstrated to improve marketing effectiveness and efficiency. They allow the marketer to exercise the direct marketing disciplines of targeting, interaction, control and continuity at a higher level of productivity. What's more, they give hours of innocent amusement to marketing analysts and supply the rest of us with a few long words we can drop casually into conversation.

TO SUM UP

In this chapter we looked at some of the ways in which direct marketing uses back data (the past) to predict the immediate future. In particular, direct marketers are looking for ways to make informed choices between alternatives, whether these are alternative tactics or alternative customers. We discussed simple testing (used when there is only one variable, between a control stimulus and a test stimulus) and more sophisticated modelling (used when more variables have to be unscrambled and valued). You will find more on simple testing in Chapter 18.

The techniques we discussed were macromodelling techniques and were grouped under the classifications of static (cluster analysis) and dynamic (regression analysis and tree segmentation). Neural networks were not classified as statistical models but could be used to produce scores like regression analysis scores.

Modelling of this sort can be used to help the marketer exercise control over all kinds of marketing activity, not just direct response activity, with the proviso that the marketer maintains records of customer behaviour.

8

EXPLOITING DATA IN BUSINESS MARKETING

IN THIS CHAPTER

In Chapter 4 we observed some crucial differences between business and consumer marketing. The richest decile (top 10 per cent) of consumers collectively outspend the remaining 90 per cent in very few markets. But the top decile of businesses are utterly dominant in most business markets, and the way they organise, budget and negotiate purchases is generally very different from the way small companies conduct their business. In this chapter we take a look at the special requirements of precision marketing to businesses.

Purchase behaviour is conditioned by the industry sector as well as by the size of the company. Even the purchase of basic commodities such as energy is affected by the nature of the business. A relatively small manufacturing business may consume as much power as a large service business. On the other hand the service company may be a massive telecommunications user.

Size indicators, including capital employed, turnover and number of employees, may be of little value except when comparing like businesses. Furthermore, many large businesses may devolve purchasing of certain commodities to regions, sites or branches. Registered office address data may be useless for marketing purposes. For small businesses it is often hard to collect any business or contact information at all. In some markets, such as the PC and mobile telephone markets, the line between business and consumer customers is blurred.

In business markets the need to chart market penetration is even greater than in consumer markets. Yet there is no complete equivalent to the Register of Electors to make this so easy. Instead, a number of sources must be used.

SOURCES OF INFORMATION

The number of businesses in the UK could be said to equate approximately to the number of Value Added Tax (VAT) registrations. This number excludes those below the VAT threshold (£48,000 turnover at the time of writing) and those organisations that are exempt. This number will vary from year to year but is likely to remain at something over 1.7 million. Only a minority of these are limited companies. Although about 1.3 million limited companies are required to file financial returns at Companies House only about half of them are actively trading. Since most business is conducted on credit, the absence of financial data for over 1 million trading businesses is something of a problem.

The basic reference source that most closely approximates the market universe is telephone directory data, the most useful single source being derived from Yellow Page directories. Companies House data provides far more extensive information about those companies that file returns.

These sources are used by companies that specialise in credit referencing and in constructing business databases. The source data is enhanced by address correction, payment performance data, contact data and so on. Branch data is added to head office data and subsidiaries are attached to parent companies. The difficulties involved are considerable: two unrelated companies may share almost identical business names; one company may trade under different business names. Individual site data may be hard to find. Most business address matching (de-duplication) is performed to a lower level of probability than would be accepted in consumer marketing.

The best solution lies in a combination of third-party bureau data and data collected by the company itself. The precondition for this is enhancement of the company's own data to facilitate matching. Business name and address data that is good enough for an invoice to arrive safely, or a salesperson to find the company, may not be correctly formatted or sufficiently accurate to match against third-party data. If the format is corrected, an outside bureau may well be able to assist in address enhancement. However, there is no substitute for a company-wide commitment to collecting accurate data and correcting inaccurate data. The marketing department may have to make an internal sale on the value of the marketing database to the sales people particularly.

COMPANIES HOUSE DATA

Although companies file their accounts at different times, because not all financial years are the same and some are slow to file their accounts, the data can be enhanced and manipulated to provide very valuable marketing information. Even though the information will be provided for the minority of companies (those that enjoy limited liability) these companies represent the vast majority of purchasing power.

Independent bureaux can provide details of the company's parentage and subsidiaries, trading addresses, directors' names and addresses, number of employees, principal activities and Standard Industrial Classification, of which more below.

The data has been used successfully for profiling and segmentation for both credit and marketing purposes. Indeed, these two purposes may be linked as there is little point in expending selling effort to gain an unacceptable business account. CCN Business Marketing and IBIS have assembled performance indicators for over 550,000 companies that give a good indication of their purchasing power and ability to pay. For all practical purposes, this number can be taken to represent the universe of trading limited companies, although it is much less than the number registered.

In view of the extreme difference between the purchasing power of large and small limited companies, a size indicator is essential. Despite its limitations, number of employees is considered to be the best size indicator for most purposes. Even if it is not comparable across industrial sectors, it certainly provides a useful basis for comparison within a sector. It also permits comparison between sites.

Standard Industrial Classification

First introduced in 1948, the SIC coding system was last revised in 1992. This revision harmonises the UK system with an EU-wide system. Using alphanumeric codes, it breaks business down into Sections, Divisions, Groups and Classes. For one Section, manufacturing industry, there are also 14 Subsections. In some cases Classes are broken down further into Subclasses. In summary the system looks like this:

  17 Sections (single-letter code)
  14 Subsections (two-letter code)
  60 Divisions (two digits)
  222 Groups (three digits)
  503 Classes (four digits)
  142 Subclasses (five digits)

One advantage of adopting this classification for marketing is that it is the same as that used in government statistical reports and, indeed, all EU government statistical reports. Therefore, it makes sense to use the system when undertaking market penetration analysis and when profiling the customer base against the market universe. Furthermore, it is in universal use by the major bureaux, the chief suppliers of credit and prospect data.

THE IMPORTANCE OF TELEPHONE RESEARCH

The quality and comprehensiveness of business data has been increasing quite rapidly and some of the problems noted earlier in this chapter may be receding when you read these words. Bureaux such as Market Location (PrimeFile) and Telephone Data Services (TDS Business File) use telephone research to enhance and update published data to produce high quality 'market universe' contact files. Others, such as CCN, are increasing the volume and quality of credit data available for non-limited companies.

Telephone research enables name and job title data to be gathered for the most commonly contacted functions within the company and this forges a link between basic marketing data and marketing communications data. This does not absolve the marketer from the responsibility for collecting as much relevant and accurate contact data as possible through field sales and telemarketing channels. Third-party data will remain pretty basic. This is a fact of economic life.

SEGMENTATION, PROFILING AND MARKET PENETRATION ANALYSIS

The significant tools for analysis are SIC and company size data, almost certainly overlaid by area data. Most companies operate in sales regions and, if they are sensible, they will construct these regions on postal geography, not vaguely defined areas such as TV transmission areas. Some industries are basically regional and almost all industries are biased geographically. A numerically large industry, business services companies, represents over 27 per cent of the universe of limited companies in the highest area of penetration, defined by postal region, but less than 7 per cent in the lowest area of penetration. When allied to numbers of companies recorded on a market universe database, SIC and company size data can be used to evaluate the potential of a region. They may be used to gauge market penetration by value, not simply by numbers of customers. They can indicate share of customers' spend.

Table 8.1

Size band	Customers	%	Universe	%	Penetration factor
1–9	21	1.6	149,029	58.8	3
10–19	70	5.2	44,500	17.6	30
20–29	209	15.5	32,688	12.9	120
50–99	244	18.1	13,130	5.2	348
100–199	280	20.8	7309	2.9	717
200–499	280	20.8	4689	1.9	1095
500–999	145	10.9	1380	0.5	2160
1000+	98	7.2	613	0.2	3600
	1347		253,338		

Source: Musgrave (1994).

Company size, SIC and area data can be looked at separately to look for patterns in penetration and then brought together. Bringing the dimensions together may explain the patterns. Table 8.1 shows the penetration of a business market universe achieved by an engineering company selling its products to the manufacturing sector. The universe, in this case Market Location's PrimeFile, is broken down by size bands based on number of employees. (This table and Tables 8.2 to 8.4 below are based on actual data from the same case.) The table shows that penetration peaks in companies employing between 100 and 500 people. This may reflect the average size of manufacturing businesses.

			Table 8.2			
SIC Division	**Customers**	**%**	**Universe**	**%**	**Penetration factor**	
Manufacture of:						
20 Wood products	15	1.1	7953	14.3	8	
21 Paper products	55	4.1	11,068	19.9	21	
24 Chemical products	5	0.4	2127	3.8	11	
25 Rubber & plastic	191	14.2	3535	6.3	225	
27 Basic metals	105	7.8	1070	1.9	411	
28 Fabricated metal	211	15.7	6528	11.7	134	
29 Machinery/ equipment	756	56.1	17,266	31.0	181	
31 Electrical machinery	3	0.2	4861	8.7	2	
34 Motor vehicles	6	0.4	1322	2.4	17	
	1347		55,730			

Source: Musgrave (1994).

Table 8.2 shows penetration by the first two digits of the SIC code. This takes the classification down to Division level. The chart shows that all of the company's customers could be classified as belonging to nine of the 23 manufacturing divisions included in the SIC. The highest penetration is in base metals, penetration factor 411, although these customers represent under 8 per cent of the customer base.

Table 8.3

SIC Division	Customers	%	Universe	%	Penetration factor
Manufacture of:					
27.10 Basic iron & steel	4	3.8	113	10.6	36
27.22 Steel tubes	23	21.9	168	15.7	139
27.31 Cold drawing	21	20.0	138	12.9	155
27.34 Wire drawing	7	6.7	229	21.4	31
27.41 Precious metals	10	9.5	150	14.0	68
27.42 Aluminium	26	24.8	203	19.0	131
27.44 Copper	14	13.3	69	6.4	208
	105		1070		

Source: Musgrave (1994).

Table 8.3 breaks down the base metals division into Classes. The highest penetration occurs in copper manufacture but the largest number of customers are engaged in the production of aluminium. Looking at the aluminium customer segment in Table 8.4, we see that size band data is now combined with SIC data. This indicates that the company is dealing towards the top end of the market in terms of size. Even so, there appears to remain ample scope to increase market penetration in the 50-plus employee category.

Table 8.4

27.42 Aluminium production

Size band	Customers	%	Universe	%	Penetration factor
1–9	–	–	58	28.6	–
10–19	1	3.8	50	24.6	15
20–49	4	15.4	41	20.2	76
50–99	6	23.1	24	11.8	196
100–199	6	23.1	16	7.9	296
200–499	5	19.2	11	5.4	356
500–999*	4	15.4	3	1.5	1027
1000+	–	–	–	–	–
	26		203		

* Client database contained one more record than the market universe database in this segment.

Source: Musgrave (1994).

Apparently, this pattern was repeated in other high penetration SIC classes and the case reports that the company was able to refocus its marketing effort as a result of receiving this information.

WHEN IS A BUSINESS NOT A BUSINESS?

In the age of high technology and advanced telecommunications, the distinction between businesses and consumers is becoming blurred. Many people conduct their business from home. Other people, perhaps area sales executives, may purchase small items for business on a credit card account and recharge the expense to their employer. This leads to untidy markets for items such as mobile telephones, faxes, PCs and software.

To begin profiling a customer base by passing it to a business universe database bureau is not always the smartest action to take. Experienced direct marketers are nearly always enthusiasts for 'eyeballing' name and address data. It is surprising how much one can tell by just looking at a few hundred names and addresses. If a large number of the addresses, say one third to one half, appear to be private residences it can be cheaper and more effective to begin by passing the entire file against the Electoral Roll. Software can be written to detect obvious business suffixes such as Ltd, plc, & Co, Associates, Partners and so on. In this way the file can be broken down into Electoral Roll matches, businesses and queries. Further processing can reduce the queries into a manageable number and only the likely businesses passed to the business data bureau for address matching and profiling.

WHO IS RESPONSIBLE FOR BUYING WHAT?

Tracking down buyers, decision-makers, influential end-users and other decision-influencers is a ticklish task. Some decisions may be influenced by consultants. Others may be made in committee. Some may be made at head office, others at individual sites. For large customers and prospects there is no substitute for thorough research using all the communication channels available.

In most cases the database will include name and job title data for comparatively few people, those known to be critically important to the customer relationship. While it is important to have job titles correct, these do not always reflect the individual's precise responsibilities in the expected way. Different job titles may reflect similar responsibilities in different companies. The cost of obtaining data by telephone research and the quality of the information is influenced by the experience, helpfulness and intelligence of the prospect's telephone operators. It can be assisted by asking simple, purposeful questions. For example, it is more effective to ask who is responsible for buying air and rail tickets than to ask for the name of the travel manager. There probably is no travel manager.

For the purposes of managing the contact data, it is better to group people by their relevant role than by their job titles. For example, there may be a buying role, an interested director role and a key end-user role. These people will all be important but will require different communications, offering differing levels of detail, with differing frequency. The communications may variously have to be delivered in person, by telephone and by mail. They will probably need to be delivered or signed by different people. The data on the database should be so organised that it is easy to plan and execute accurately targeted communications.

INDIRECT CUSTOMERS

Some manufacturers of business supplies and equipment deal exclusively through distributors. Others, such as suppliers to the retail trade, will supply direct to large accounts and via wholesalers to small accounts.

The company that is content to leave it all to the distributor or wholesaler, believing that a small expenditure on trade press advertising and trade press relations is sufficient, deserves to fail. It has become essential to build a database of business end-users or indirect accounts.

A company may buy all its stationery through a distributor. The stationery buyer may be under pressure to cut the cost of supplies. To keep the business, the distributor will switch the buyer to a lower quality alternative. The people who use the stationery will never be asked. Unless they complain vigorously, the manufacturer will lose the business. The users will probably never see the manufacturer's trade press advertising. They will never be told why the manufacturer's product is superior. Yet, if the most influential end-user were cultivated by the manufacturer, everyone would gain. The user would gain by using a superior product. This would reflect a more favourable image of the user company, work better or save time. The distributor would gain by continuing to supply a higher margin item. The manufacturer would gain by keeping the business.

The cola manufacturer may generate a lot of business through cash-and-carry wholesalers. Much of this business will be made up of purchases from small retailers who will stock one brand of cola only. To increase distribution and protect existing distribution, it is essential to be able to communicate direct with these retailers. Direct contact permits offers to be made on a discreet basis, unseen by competition. The offers are made on a solus basis before the retailer has driven to the cash and carry. The offers are correctly targeted. An existing stockist will not receive the same offer as a prospective stockist.

If the communication benefits are obvious, the management information benefits should be no less so. Without these databases the stationery and cola manufacturers are marketing into a black hole. They will talk only to intermediaries and cannot see the real market except through market research, and then on a sample basis only. In all probability the information will be received after the damage has been done. Even then, since the manufacturer does not know *which* customers have defected, it is hard to take appropriate action.

The answer to these problems is to build a database of indirectly supplied customers or outlets. This can be done through telephone research. In the case of the cola manufacturer, the research can be combined with a battery of promotional offers appropriate to stockists and non-stockists. These can be personalised and tracked through cash-and-carry redemptions. The whole process may even be self-liquidating – a database for nothing. Unfortunately, it is too late to sell this idea. It has already been used.

THE DATABASE AND INTEGRATED MARKETING – A BRIEF CASE HISTORY

Michael Stevens quotes many interesting case histories in his book *Telemarketing in Action* (1995). One case refers to the UK division of a worldwide air express carrier. The company's integrated marketing strategy dictated that the database must be central to all marketing activities, from marketing planning and sales to customer communication and new business acquisition programmes.

Step one of a four-stage development programme instituted by TDS involved reformatting and deduplicating two customer and prospect files, each of 60,000 names. Previously, some customers had received multiple copies of mailed communications. Step two was to match the new merged file against the TDS Business File of some 1 million businesses. This enabled TDS data to be imported, enhancing the quantity and accuracy of the client's data. It also permitted profiling, using TDS data on company size, SIC and geographic area. The cost was about one-quarter of the cost of original telephone research. Prior to making the investment, it had been demonstrated by testing that TDS telephone research to update contact details could enhance the data quality sufficiently to increase mailing response from 9 to 27 per cent.

Step three involved adding customer value data. This could be compared with potential by using the company size and type data imported from the TDS Business File. The mailing response level increased by 300 per cent over previous experience. A saving of £100,000 was achieved in one year through the elimination of wasted mailings as a result of liquidating duplications and improving address quality.

Step four involved a multi-media customer acquisition programme, using press advertising and mailings devised by Brann Direct Marketing. Mailings were targeted on the basis of matching highest potential customer profiles. The resulting sales leads were qualified by the courier's own in-house telemarketers. The database was also used to exploit cross-selling opportunities (through direct mail and the salesforce) and to undertake a programme of customer-bonding communications. The first three steps took only three months. The entire investment was recovered in 12 months.

Most interestingly, the database was demonstrated to provide a distinct competitive edge. When a competitor was the subject of a takeover bid, the courier was able to target an offer to companies known to be that competitor's customers. The case demonstrates the value of integrating sales force information and customer value data with good market universe data.

TO SUM UP

Customer values and purchasing methods are likely to vary far more widely when the customers are businesses. Furthermore, professional buyers may be more demanding. In fact the buying decision may be a joint effort, the consensus of a decision-maker unit, not all of whose members will have had any contact with the supplier. Inevitably, telephone research will be needed to fill in gaps in the customer information.

A particular advantage that may be enjoyed by the business marketer is the ability to maintain a database that represents the market universe, thus making profiling and penetration analysis more accurate. Classifications used for these purposes include Standard Industrial Classifications (SIC codes), number of employees and region.

9

EXAMPLE OF PROFILING: A COMBINED CONSUMER AND BUSINESS CUSTOMER BASE

IN THIS CHAPTER

The case is based on a real-life example in the cellular (mobile) telephone market. It has been chosen because it illustrates both consumer and business customer profiling and because the data no longer has any commercial value, the analysis work dating back to 1991.

This chapter illustrates an approach to handling name and address data that is known to include both business and consumer addresses. It also illustrates the difficulty of starting from inaccurately captured, badly maintained and incorrectly formatted accounts department data, as opposed to starting from a clean customer name and address file.

The source data was derived from two accounts department files and included records of active, cancelled and suspended customers. The distinction between cancelled and suspended was that the former had ceased to subscribe for their own reasons and the latter were disconnected for non-payment. Although the analysis produced much useful data on the profiles of lapsed accounts, the profile data we will show relates only to active customers.

PLANNING STAGE

The overall objectives of the exercise were *firstly* to clean the existing accounts department files, combining two separate files; *secondly* to profile the customer base and detect the influence of the profile on the propensity to subscribe, pay promptly, remain loyal and spend heavily on calls; *thirdly* to prepare data so that it would be acceptable as customer data for a marketing database. This chapter covers the first step of the sequence needed to reach the three objectives.

The client company had planned to pass the records to a bureau that owned a telephone-researched business market universe database. As the data was likely to include residential address data, the client was asked to print out a sample of a couple of thousand names and addresses. It was obvious from this sample that a high proportion of these were clearly private addresses. Furthermore, many companies could readily be recognised by suffixes such as 'Ltd' or 'Associates'. Finally, it was obvious that there were many formatting errors, with words such as 'for the attention of' appearing in the name field and names or departments appearing in the company field. Starting from poorly formatted data, it is generally easier and cheaper to achieve a high match rate of residential addresses against the Electoral Roll than it is to achieve a high match rate of business addresses against a business market universe database. By appointing a bureau holding the Electoral Roll and asking them to write software to detect all the more commonly recurring business suffixes, it would be possible to create files of known consumers, likely businesses and queries. Likely business addresses and unresolved queries could then be passed to the business database bureau.

ANALYSIS OF RESIDENTIAL CUSTOMERS

After deduplication and matching against the Electoral Roll, 58,403 residential customers could be positively identified. These names and addresses were profiled against CCN Marketing's MOSAIC geodemographic database (1990 edition). At the same time they were profiled against Geo-Persona, a postcode-based lifestyle profiling system extrapolated from data derived from 4 million responding households to CMT's (now Calyx) National Shoppers Survey.

MOSAIC classifications are produced by cluster analysis. Four data sources are used. These are the Electoral Roll, the Postal Address File (PAF), a CCN financial database using a mix of public data and credit activity data, and the census. The Electoral Roll provides information on household composition and, by maintaining historical data, CCN are able to determine length of residence at the address. From PAF it is possible to derive address type data; for example, farms and flats. The CCN financial database records County Court Judgements arising from non-payment of bills and also records incidence of credit applications to credit card companies, banks and so on. Selected census data provides further housing, demographic and socioeconomic data.

MOSAIC describes neighbourhood types, not individuals or households. Because it uses a mixture of census and other data, it can distinguish between postcodes that lie within the smallest census area, which is an enumeration district. There are about ten postcode areas for every enumeration district, or 1.3 million postcode areas in all. The 1990 edition divided neighbourhoods into 58 types within 11 broader families.

Geo-Persona classified households by lifestyle grouping into 21 types within seven broader groups. The number of types quoted for both systems includes one type to cover households that could not be classified. Geo-Persona classifications are descriptive of a set of behaviour patterns.

Table 9.1 shows the breakdown of the 58,403 residential customers by the 11 broader MOSAIC groupings. The descriptions of these are capsules only and are just convenient references. The first column of percentages shows the proportion of customer records classified as belonging to the MOSAIC type. The second column of percentages shows the proportion of all households that belong to the type. The index records the percentage difference between the proportion of customers within the type and the proportion of all households within the type. An index of 100 would show no difference, an index above 100 shows that customers disproportionately belong to that type and an index below 100 shows that customers are under-represented within the type.

Table 9.1 Distribution of customer records by MOSAIC type

Type	Description	Client file %	GB households %	Index
L01	Prosperous pensioners	4.10	3.69	111
L02	Older couples, leafy suburbs	9.22	6.72	137
L03	Inter war semis	10.18	9.48	107
L04	Older communities	14.37	15.35	94
L05	Experimenting singles	12.86	8.08	159
L06	Disadvantaged council tenants	8.97	13.00	69
L07	Older council tenants	4.82	8.99	54
L08	Go-getting council tenants	7.85	8.80	89
L09	Young families with mortgages	17.89	15.19	118
L10	Country dwellers	9.11	9.35	97
L99	Unclassified	0.65	1.35	48

We can see from Table 9.1 that, although nearly 18 per cent of customers live in 'young families with mortgages' neighbourhoods, this type does not have the highest index of market penetration. Both 'experimenting singles' and 'older couples in leafy suburbs' attract higher index scores. We can look within each of these three broad groupings to see if the subdivisions discriminate even more sharply. The results are shown in Tables 9.2, 9.3 and 9.4.

In Table 9.2, we can look within 'leafy suburbs' and see that the average score of 137 was dragged down slightly by Type 06. Type 05 is likely to include many managers who recharge their mobile phone costs to their employer (O/Os are owner occupiers). Types 07 and 08 are likely to include business proprietors and company directors, also charging their telephone costs as a business expense.

Table 9.2 Distribution of customer records within MOSAIC L02
(leafy suburbs)

Type	Description	Client file %	GB households %	Index
2/05	Inter war O/Os, many managers	4.17	2.99	139
2/06	Elite prof/educational suburbs	2.71	2.33	116
2/07	Family enclaves, singles areas	0.81	0.49	165
2/08	Top incomes, mature families	1.53	0.90	170

Table 9.3 Distribution of customer records within MOSAIC L05
(experimenting singles)

Type	Description	Client file %	GB households %	Index
5/19	Flats over shops	1.50	2.17	69
5/20	Singles, financial stress	2.62	1.10	238
5/21	Low status subdivision	2.34	0.95	246
5/22	Owner occupiers, sharing	1.20	0.56	214
5/23	Private flats	2.66	1.76	151
5/24	Bedsits, mobile singles	0.76	0.35	217
5/25	Smart city flats	1.78	1.19	150

Table 9.4 Distribution of customer records within MOSAIC L09
(young families with mortgages)

Type	Description	Client file %	GB households %	Index
9/46	Newest high status areas	0.49	0.30	163
9/47	Suburbs for newly rich	1.68	1.03	163
9/48	Post war O/Os, older children	3.61	2.87	126
9/49	Modern high income estates	1.79	1.68	107
9/50	Modern low cost O/O housing	2.66	2.77	96
9/51	Post '81 houses, first-time buyers	2.22	1.68	132
9/52	Post '81 infill, older suburbs	2.86	2.48	115
9/53	New rural commuter estates	2.58	2.38	108

Table 9.5 Distribution of customer records within Geo-Persona groups

Type	Description	Client file %	GB households %	Index
A	Aesthetes	10.86	7.85	138
B	Materialists	16.59	12.08	137
C	Home makers	24.10	27.29	88
D	Idealists	21.34	21.82	98
E	Sociables	15.62	20.34	77
F	Survivors	7.67	9.03	85
G	Unclassified	3.83	1.61	238

Table 9.6 Distribution of customer records by all 21 Geo-Persona types

Type	Description	Client file %	GB households %	Index
01 B	Golf clubs & Volvos	6.81	4.71	145
02 B	Young affluentials	2.93	1.64	179
03 A	Bon viveurs	3.14	1.81	173
04 B	Achievers	1.96	1.61	122
05 B	New tech-ers	4.88	4.12	118
06 D	Tradition & charity	5.36	4.24	126
07 C	Safe & sensible	7.24	7.26	100
08 C	Craftsmen & homemakers	9.98	11.18	89
09 A	Trinkets & treasures	2.55	1.85	138
10 A	Cultural travellers	5.17	4.19	123
11 E	Carry on camping	1.49	1.53	97
12 D	Health & humanities	4.80	4.57	105
13 D	Wildlife trustees	4.10	3.77	109
14 E	Field & stream	1.84	2.03	91
15 E	Crisps & videos	6.23	9.29	67
16 E	Fads & fashions	3.94	4.12	96
17 C	Home & garden	6.87	8.85	78
18 E	Pubs, pools & bingo	2.11	3.37	63
19 F	Survivors	7.67	9.03	85
20 D	Retired villagers	7.08	9.24	77
21 G	Unclassified	3.83	1.61	238

Looking now at 'experimenting singles' in Table 9.3 we can see that all except one of the subdivisions attracts a high index score. These neighbourhood types occur primarily in inner-city areas and are inhabited by many 'floaters' who may stay at one address for a relatively short time. The more affluent of them will be out and about much of the time. Their mobile phone will not be a car phone but will be carried around, being used at least as much for private calls as for business. Many of them may think it is not worth becoming a regular phone subscriber and some may have left unpaid phone bills at a previous address.

Table 9.4 shows the eight subdivisions of 'young families with mortgages'. Here we can see that two neighbourhood types attract indices of 163, much higher than the average for the group. Houses in these neighbourhoods are occupied by many proprietors of young businesses and successful executives.

In Table 9.5 we see the indices of penetration across the broader Geo-Persona groups. Unhelpfully, Unclassified has the highest index. Groups A and B do not look very exciting with only about 27 per cent of subscribers in approximately 20 per cent of households. Looking inside these groups in Table 9.6 we can see that only 02B and 03A are powerfully discriminatory, although 01B, which overlaps strongly with MOSAIC's leafy suburbs, attracts the moderately high score of 145.

The influence of the CCN Financial Database enabled MOSAIC to outperform Geo-Persona when profiling closed and suspended accounts. It was also more discriminatory between high, medium and low monthly billing customers, almost half of all high spenders falling within the three broad MOSAIC types of maximum penetration. These represented 30 per cent of all households and 40 per cent of customers. None of the indices was so high as to suggest the use of individually addressable media for residential customer acquisition.

BUSINESS CUSTOMER ANALYSIS

The presumed business name part of the file was now passed to the business database bureau. The file still contained many duplicate records, a few incomplete addresses, a vast number of incorrectly formatted records and business names ending in suffixes that suggested it was unlikely that they were limited companies. A total of 33,559 records could be matched with some degree of confidence. The majority of these would still require to be enhanced or corrected. This left a residue of names and addresses that would include good addresses that could not be matched against a market universe database comprising mainly of public and private limited companies. These names and addresses would be of small businesses, partnerships and some institutions not enjoying limited liability status. It would also include records that could be rescued by reformatting to enter the components in their correct fields.

The work of recognising and classifying these names and addresses would be carried out in the next stage of the programme. Meanwhile, it was possible to analyse the part of the file that could be positively identified. Table 9.7 shows the result of profiling the customer data against the broad SIC groups (according to the then latest 1980 edition of the SIC, not the 1992 edition). The resulting index scores reflected the high usage of portable and mobile phones in the construction industry and the mobility of staff in energy and transport.

Table 9.7 Distribution of corporate customer records by industry

SIC group	Industry	Client file %	Total market %	Index
00	Agriculture	0.8	0.9	89
01	Energy	0.7	0.4	175
02	Chemicals	2.8	3.5	80
03	Engineering	13.2	16.1	82
04	Manufacture	11.3	14.5	78
05	Construction	11.4	5.2	219
06	Distribution	23.4	26.2	89
07	Transport	7.4	4.2	176
08	Services	25.0	22.8	110
09	Others	4.0	5.0	80

Table 9.8 shows that the number of employees appears to discriminate sharply between customer and non-customer companies. Table 9.9 shows the distribution of customers within each of three size bands segmented by SIC codes. The columns read downwards. By comparing this table with Table 9.7, we can see that distribution and construction customer companies were somewhat disproportionately likely to be small. Distribution companies included small wholesalers and retailers. Service sector companies were dominant in the large company size band. The probable explanation of the high penetration of 'Others' in the large size band was the incidence of hospitals and municipal organisations.

Further analyses showed the distribution of disconnected customers by SIC and size, the distribution of customers by region and by SIC and size within region. Finally, customers were grouped by number of telephones and by revenue band. Although handset numbers and revenue increased with size, it became obvious that many larger companies were using more than one cellular telephone provider. The incidence of multiple telephone usage was too small for all the figures to be treated as statistically significant. Nevertheless, a general pattern was observed that suggested the client's share of customer was quite low in respect of larger companies. This reflected a behaviour pattern of allowing executives to choose their own telephone and to have accounts invoiced by their chosen supplier to the company. The picture was complicated by the fact that many customer agreements were negotiated by appointed dealers. These people merely sold telephones and arranged servicing. They were not responsible for airtime billing.

Table 9.8 Distribution of corporate customer records by size band (number of employees)

Size code	Employees	Client file %	Total market %	Index
AA	1–19	32.1	58.5	55
AB	20–49	25.8	20.3	127
AC	50–99	16.8	9.3	181
AD	100–199	11.2	5.8	193
AE	200–499	8.5	3.7	229
AF	500–999	3.0	1.2	250
AG	1000 +	2.7	1.2	225

Table 9.9 SIC profiles of small, medium and large corporate customer records

Industry	Small (1–49) %	Medium (50–199) %	Large (200 +) %
Agriculture	0.80	0.85	0.80
Energy	0.35	0.85	2.50
Chemicals	2.20	3.15	4.70
Engineering	12.10	15.15	12.60
Manufacture	9.05	15.20	10.50
Construction	**13.35**	10.15	5.10
Distribution	**27.55**	19.55	11.10
Transport	8.20	8.30	2.90
Services	23.50	23.30	**35.80**
Others	2.90	3.10	13.90

WHAT WAS THE DATA REALLY SAYING?

In looking at the consumer profile data you, the reader, may have been struck by the fact that penetration and usership peaked in neighbourhoods occupied substantially by a floating population. It is possible to ring up a large telephone bill very quickly and the thought that occurred immediately was that this distortion in the profile might reflect poor credit control. This was indeed the case. There were many unpaid accounts and these were distributed disproportionately within inner-city areas. The company's dealers were taking on too much bad business and the company's credit vetting procedures were too lax to prevent this. This led to a tightening of credit control and was one consideration in a decision to rationalise the dealer network.

The problems revealed by the analysis of company data were even more severe and their solution was potentially a great deal more profitable. The analysis of cancelled and suspended accounts by size of company revealed a surprising number of suspensions (for non-payment) among larger companies. In fact larger companies were the most likely to default. The technical explanation for this was that larger companies are generally reluctant to sign direct debiting mandates and, because the bills were due for settlement within 15 days, a late payment could result in automatic suspension. To the marketing people, the data at last gave much-needed evidence of poor service. The fact was that companies were being forced to stop paying as their only means of drawing attention to poor service standards. A can of worms was opened. A search of correspondence files revealed examples of ignored customer requests and broken promises by dealers or within the company. A service overhaul was put into immediate effect.

Another market segment

It was decided to recognise larger companies as a separate market segment and improve the terms, service offer and call-charge analysis data available to large users. These companies' service requirements would be met directly in every case, whether or not they had purchased their telephones through a dealership.

The revised terms were aimed at encouraging larger users to consolidate their mobile telephone contracts with one supplier in exchange for vastly improved service (for example, replacement of faulty telephones within one hour) and superior call-charge reporting by individual user. The corporate sales team was refocused on the target market of larger companies, particularly service companies.

The analysis and further investigation of accounts and service department records gave impetus to a greatly improved service offer to both large and small users. Data from the analysis was used to predict sales and service workloads and the reduced number of dealers required to operate within a tiered sales and service structure catering differently for large, medium and small users.

Although the problems should have been detected much sooner, they are not uncommon in businesses enjoying explosive growth. In this case, hard data was used to expose weaknesses of which there was already anecdotal evidence. The data proved its value in pinpointing credit control and service weaknesses even before the process of building a customer marketing database had begun. The marketing database was later used as a vehicle for conducting satisfaction research among the entire universe of customers.

CONCLUSION

Before undertaking expensive file processing work it is a good idea to pause for thought. In this case the client company sought a second opinion before commissioning a business database bureau to convert the accounts department files and match them against a market universe database.

It wasn't difficult to guess that many of the accounts would be held at private addresses. Although the client did not know how many, it was a simple matter to answer a request for a sample printout of the name and address data. There is no substitute for looking at a sample of data. This revealed that data was inconsistently formatted and that there were empty fields within the customer records. Furthermore, it revealed that a good many genuine business accounts were held by non-limited companies. By the time processing began we had some inkling of the extent of the problem and, therefore, of the likely time and cost involved in producing a usable file.

Even though the data from the first attempt was incomplete, there was sufficient information to provoke actions that went far beyond the original intention of producing a file to permit customer analysis and facilitate addressable customer communications. The data could not by itself demonstrate that accounts were being lost through poor service. It could suggest, however, that the behaviour of larger companies looked odd and required investigation. This illustrates the importance of summary data, permitting comparison of behaviour by different customer segments. Incidentally, it also emphasises the need to maintain close links between marketing and customer service. Although the company would have got round to improving its customer service sooner or later, analysis made possible by the file processing work gave impetus to ensuring that it was sooner, not later.

TO SUM UP

Had the company established a customer database from the outset, summary data would have drawn attention to credit control and service weaknesses. It would also have pinpointed the customer segments most adversely affected and made possible a cost:benefit analysis of improved administration and customer service. The return on the database investment would have been recouped many times over even if the database had never been used for customer communications. Finally, it would have ensured that the bills were correctly addressed.

10

DATA FOR INTERNATIONAL MARKETING

IN THIS CHAPTER

For the multi-national company there are few problems. The philosophy of 'think global, act local' works in a direct marketing context. In most cases, multinationals still replicate nearly all functions in each national market and, although this may change, it will have little practical effect at an executional level. In this chapter we examine the situation of the smaller company originating personal marketing communications and fulfilling orders from one office.

The multinational recognises that there is little to be gained by continually reinventing the wheel but individual organisations vary in the degree to which they are prescriptive. Where advertising production is a major item and market situations are sufficiently similar, adaptations may be used in many markets.

The same applies to direct mail for customer acquisition. In some cases, this is bulked up, produced in several languages in one production run and distributed through one post office. In these and a few other cases, a master customer database may be held centrally with on-line access by marketing users at different locations. Apart from bulk production and postage savings, there are few economies of scale available and most companies are likely to maintain separate customer databases in each market where they operate. Usually there will be a company-wide standard for customer information, data management, customer service and contact procedures.

Our main concern in this chapter is not for the multinational but for the smaller exporter, the company that has no choice but to conduct its marketing effort from one centre. Direct marketing, as a method of distribution, opens up major opportunities for the exporter. To all intents and purposes, the EU will become the domestic market but the opportunities extend far beyond the EU. Direct mail is relatively simple to manage on an international basis and this will often be the preferred medium for customer acquisition.

MARKETING AND PERSONAL DATA

We have already referred in Chapter 8 to the harmonisation of industrial classifications within the European Union. The relevant standard is set by NACE Rev. 1 (Nomenclature générale des Activités économiques dans les Communautés Européennes). Standards for the obtaining, processing and use of computerised personal data for marketing purposes are also harmonised. We refer to personal data protection in Chapter 11.

At the time of writing, use of personal data within the public domain is still permitted. This includes data from sources which there is a statutory duty to publish. In the UK, the Register of Electors falls within this category and is the primary reference source. Telephone directories must be published but telephone subscribers may opt to go ex-directory. Shareholders' registers must be published. In Europe's major car markets, Germany and France, car manufacturers and distributors can access competitive model ownership data. This is because the register of car owners is within the public domain. In Sweden, census data is available at household level, not by enumeration districts containing an average of about 150 households, the smallest areas for which British census data is released. The threat that the use of all this information for marketing purposes would be outlawed was lifted, at least for the time being, in 1995.

The international list market

As a reasonable generalisation, it could be said that the availability and quality of data is quite high in Northern Europe but rather less so in Southern and outlying Europe. In Eastern Europe, data sources are hard to come by but direct mail responsiveness has been very high as markets have become freed from restriction. Elsewhere, the direct marketer must contend with huge variations.

Fortunately, an international list market grew up many years ago. This was primarily through the influence, demands and persistence of American publishers such as Time Life, Reader's Digest, Newsweek, Fortune and McGraw-Hill. Most of the best lists available are lists that are the by-product of someone else's business. The market was developed more quickly through the far-sighted willingness of publishers to exchange lists for mutual benefit. Since these early times the market for such lists has expanded, improving the variety of lists available for both consumer and business marketing. There are still very great differences between the technical quality of the best and worst lists the international marketer may use. Most overseas lists can be accessed through UK-based list brokers. Advice can also be sought from local direct marketing associations. The Direct Marketing Association (UK) has close links with overseas associations.

MANAGING INTERNATIONAL ADDRESS DATA

This is generally best left to one of the small number of bureaux that specialise in international address management. System and support software designed to handle UK customer names and addresses is not up to the job. The same bureau can be used to manage data about established customers and to process files bought in for customer acquisition. The bureau will weed out completely unacceptable addresses and correct others. This will not be done to quite the same standard as it would within the UK because PAF (the UK Postal Address File) cannot be used as a reference tool.

An overseas name and address will not usually be expressed in the same sequence as a UK name and address. Therefore, international address management software has to recognise valid address formats for each market. For example, in the UK, your title and name would appear on the first line of your business address. Your job title would appear on the second line and your company's name on the third. In Austria, your company's name would appear on the first line and your own title and name would appear on line three.

A typical UK address might appear in this sequence:

23	High	Street
A	B	C

In France the order could be ACB or it could be CBA. It could not be ABC. In Germany, B and C could be combined as one word. In Belgium, the same title and address could be expressed perfectly correctly in two different languages. *Previnairestraat* is the same street as *Rue de la Previnaire*. *Bergen* is the same town as *Mons*. The postman knows this but your software will not. It will fail to deduplicate the two versions of the same address.

To address its customers correctly a company must not abbreviate their names. UK address management software will do this when it meets a name with too many characters in it. There is no acceptable short form of *Srta Anna Maria Delgardez-Miguel Millornia-Lugaretta*'s surname. This includes family names which it would be bad form to drop, giving offence to one or other branch of her family.

A further problem is that somewhere in the world a postcode or place name change occurs almost every week. International address management and processing requires specialised software, technical skills and information sources that few companies can afford in-house.

HOW TO TARGET WITHOUT RESEARCH DATA

You may recall from the example of Mrs Emily Smith in Chapter 6 how much can be derived from a title, name and address. In many overseas markets there may be little else to go on, but it is surprising how effective selection on such a simple basis can be. Thanks to the generosity of the London-based bureau, Printronic International, and its clients we can look at a few examples.

Within each list of acceptable names and addresses, there are individuals whose propensity to respond or buy will be much greater than that of others. This enables the direct marketer to extract the gems from lists it would otherwise be uneconomic to use and discard the dross from the better lists. These selections can be made in the same processing run that is removing undeliverable mailing addresses and deduplicating the files.

What a job title can tell us

For a company marketing specialised computer software of value to both academics and commercial users, 50 distinct job titles were recognised, each of them in the local language. By comparing the responder base with the mailing base, it was discovered that the 'best' job title was 15 times as likely to respond as the worst.

Job title	Response index
Professor	300
Manager	39
Computer job title	20

Recognising company types

In the same case, 25 different company or institution types were recognised in all the relevant languages. Below are four examples:

Group	Response index
School	163
Engineering company	154
University	134
Bank	41

Looking at the dimensions of job title and type of organisation separately introduces an element of double counting: an engineering company is unlikely to employ many professors. Therefore, the variables were combined into one response score model. This produced a response score range from 42 to 200. In other words, the best combination of job title and organisation was approximately five times as responsive as the worst. This would almost certainly be a greater difference than that between the best and the worst list used. Therefore, some names should be dropped even from the best list and weaker lists could be rescued by being more selective.

Using a model of this sort, it is possible to predict the overall gains that can be made. The software company marketed to both business and consumer addresses. The projected gain from business records was 157 per cent and from consumer records 138 per cent, near enough two-and-a-half times the response rate that would result from using the lists unedited.

Selling in English

A peculiarity of direct mail as a medium is that it can also be used to sell English language products in foreign language markets. Books, magazines and recordings in English can find a niche market in many countries. It was this niche market that prompted some American publishers to help develop international mailing list rental. Sophisticated international address management software can recognise English-sounding names when they crop up in overseas lists. Even when proven successful lists are used, these names will usually be more responsive than presumed local names. In a mailing analysis for an international bookseller, marketing in 191 countries, it was found that English-sounding names were 47 per cent more likely to respond in non-English speaking markets and 9 per cent more likely to respond in English-speaking markets.

Compulsive responders

Niche market names frequently recur in rented lists. Naturally, they are deduplicated if they appear on two or more lists rented for the same mailing. However, this fact is recorded. Names that recur frequently do so because they are responsive. For the same bookseller, the following response index was produced:

Name found	Response index
On one list	95
On two lists	178
On three or more lists	249

By retaining a full record of each mailing, the same names can be spotted on lists to be used for subsequent mailings. The same principle applies to cross-selling within an established customer base: it is easier to sell a third product to people who have already bought two products than it is to sell a second product to people who have bought only one.

Before we leave this subject, it is worthwhile to record that people are generally less insular in small markets. They are often more used to new influences from abroad and are more willing to buy direct from overseas suppliers. It is generally much harder to export manufactured products and services to big markets such as Germany and the USA than to export them to countries which are less self-sufficient. New Zealand is said to be one of the most competitive markets in the world because it imports almost everything except wool, butter and wine. Direct marketing can empower the smaller company to export to many markets. The total size of each market is not important. What matters is the market's receptiveness to the exporter's offer.

TO SUM UP

Using direct mail, it is possible to undertake rudimentary targeting quite satisfactorily without market reference data. Furthermore it is practicable to undertake the activity out of one centre. The selection process can be executed while a mailing is being produced and the mailing can be produced in various languages simultaneously, quoting prices in different currencies and making whatever other variations are called for. International address management and production are specialised activities. Only a few bureaux have the resources to do the job properly. Nevertheless, direct mail is one of the easiest media to use internationally.

You will find more information about marketing communications in Part Four.

11

MARKET RESEARCH, VOLUNTEERED DATA AND PRIVACY ISSUES

IN THIS CHAPTER

The customer database is, or should be, the heart of the marketing information network if we are to undertake integrated marketing successfully. But now we'll look at the important things it *can't* tell us. We consider other sources of marketing information, looking particularly at how our customer data can be used to improve the quality of our marketing research. Finally, we consider the need to protect personal data.

Nearly all companies operate within a competitive environment. Although the database may reveal transactional information, it can't tell us about the business our customers choose to award to our competitors, either direct competitors or indirect competitors. In short it doesn't tell us where the rest of their money goes.

Neither does it reveal any information about the trading environment. It does not describe trends in the economic situation, or in business and consumer confidence, or social and demographic changes. It cannot tell us that there is an explosive growth in the market for widgets unless we already sell them.

Finally, it does not yield up much information about the reasons why people make the choices they do or suggest how their preferences are likely to change in the future. To find all we need to know, we may need to undertake desk research, exterior macromodelling, panel research, qualitative research and *ad hoc* quantification surveys.

Although the database does not give us all this information, it can help us in our quest for it. It can provide us with excellent data for market research sampling. It can also be used to capture information volunteered by customers on a less formal basis.

I won't attempt to describe the role of market research in business. Other authors are better able to do that. Nevertheless, I can explain how a customer database should be used, firstly, to provide information that would otherwise have to be gathered through research and, secondly, to make research cheaper, more relevant and simpler. We'll begin by summarising the areas in which the database has rendered sample survey market research obsolete.

WHERE THE DATABASE WINS

The database is a vastly superior information provider in the following areas:

- present number of customers and trends in this population;
- profile of customers and changes in this profile;
- purchase behaviour of customers and trends;
- patterns of behaviour indicating degree of customer loyalty and changes of habit;
- customer response to marketing or service communications;
- customer response to new products, price changes and new terms;
- response by matched samples of customers to product, price, offer, terms, communications or service tests;
- profitability of customer relationships;
- return on marketing investments;
- determining the relative effect on behaviour of each variable when more than one change occurs at a time.

The data retrieved from the customer database covers the universe of customers, not a sample. The numbers are bigger and not subject, except in the case of tests, to sampling error. When samples are selected they are perfectly random. Thus sampling error is reduced and the limits of confidence can be calculated.

The data gives information about each customer. Except in the case of tests, no extrapolations from sample data need to be made. The false assumptions required for sample survey extrapolations – such as all 25–34 age band BC1 male car owners are the same – become obsolete. Even when profiling data is used, its significance is checked against actual purchase behaviour on a continuous basis.

The shortcomings of quota samples

In sharp contrast to this happy situation, most market research sampling is on a quota basis because this is cheaper than random sampling. Quota samples are based on false assumptions about the homogeneous nature of the populations of artificially defined market segments. Even if this were not the case, sample selection is biased by difficulty of contact. People who are not on foot in the street or difficult to find at home will be under-represented in the sample.

But the problem of *who* is asked to answer sample survey questions is often less serious than the problem of *what* they are asked. The research interview places the respondent in an artificial situation. The respondent may be asked to recall items of past behaviour or experiences. Anyone who has seen a group of accident wit-nesses contradict each other will be aware of the difficulty in doing this. Less reli-ably still, the respondent may be asked a series of hypothetical questions about their future buying intentions. By the time the resulting data is in the hands of a marketing decision-maker, the database could have reported the results of a live test producing real data about actual purchases. If this were not enough, a bonus is that a live test produces revenue. It may even, unlike buying intentions research, produce an immediate profit.

The database can provide data in a continuous stream. The data can be interro-gated at any time without a cost penalty. The research manager does not need to second guess what every decision-maker may want to know. The information is always accessible to any enquiry. The research manager is not committed to any specific method of segmentation. The customer population can be segmented more meaningfully into behavioural groups, customers' purchase behaviour determining their classification. Customer migrations from one behavioural seg-ment to another can be tracked.

Finally, the database reports in a way that is meaningful to managers. It gives bottom-line profit results and projections. It reports in a way that is directly related to the business objectives. It reports what customers do, not what they say. It reports the return on marketing investments.

SUPERIOR SAMPLING FOR RESEARCH

A serious problem with sample research studies is that the population of estab-lished customers within the sample is often too small to permit detailed sub-sample analysis and it is expensive to correct this. The fact is that almost the entire profit of most companies is derived from established customers. Their buying behaviour is vastly more influential than the buying behaviour of the market at large. That's why Toyota used their database for research in preference to select-ing random samples of motorists. Remember the quote from *The Machine that Changed the World* in Chapter 1?

The database enables the researcher to weight the subsample of established cus-tomers. (By *weight* we mean increase the size of the subsample so that statisti-cally significant results are produced from it.) The researcher can also create subsets of customers representing differing purchase patterns and lengths of rela-tionship. Furthermore, the behaviour of responding customers can be tracked sub-sequently. This allows the validity of, for example, buying intentions research to be checked. The interpretation of future survey results can then take into account the inevitable discrepancies between what people say and what they eventually do.

Less obviously, perhaps, the database can also assist in the sampling of non-customers. Non-customers include people who are very likely to become customers, people who are fairly likely to become customers and people who are never likely to become customers. The last group is often the largest but there is no point in sampling them. The superior profiling offered by the database enables external samples to be selected more precisely.

WHAT ARE THEY BUYING FROM COMPETITORS?

Although the database provides a continuous flow of information about customer purchases it fails to provide any information about the purchases they make elsewhere. Analysis of customer purchase patterns can reveal indications of disloyalty. For example, an interruption in the regular pattern of a customer's purchases may indicate that the customer is giving a competitor a try. Depending on the result of this, the customer may divide future purchases, return to the fold or migrate to the competitor's customer base. Such information is extremely useful because it allows appropriate action to be taken in individual cases, even when the customer base can be counted in millions.

Equally, inferences can be drawn by matching purchase data to profile data. If the majority of customers within a segment spend £300 to £400 but a substantial minority spend £150 to £200, it may be assumed that the low spend customers are dividing their business fairly evenly between two suppliers. Although data of this sort does not provide factual evidence of disloyalty, it will often provide an inference that is sufficiently accurate for well targeted action to be taken.

When panel research is essential

In some cases, the information derived from the database may be enough. However, in two cases at least, it will not. Firstly, we may be interested in the customers we don't have. Secondly, our customers may be choosing from a whole portfolio of brands or suppliers and, to increase our competitiveness, we must understand much more about their behaviour.

In either of these cases we will probably need panel data. Like the customer database, a research panel provides a continuing, if not actually continuous, stream of transactional data. To all intents and purposes it is a miniature customer database, except that it includes competitors' customers as well. Panel respondents provide information through pantry checks or other reporting methods on their purchases within a specific product group. If we are lucky we may operate within a market where such research is syndicated. If not, and that is the more usual circumstance, we may have to set up our own panel.

The database enables a panel to be established far more cheaply than would otherwise be possible. If our primary interest is *share of customer*, the panel sample can be drawn entirely from the customer database. This will reflect the entry of new customers and also customer defections. If we also need to know about non-customers' purchases, the database will enable us to weight the sub-sample of established customers correctly, without undue expense.

If we are able to buy in syndicated research, we can use the database as a check on the accuracy of the data produced about our own customers. We may even be able to have people who are on our database flagged on the research company's panel. There are precedents for this. It is particularly useful in the fmcg field because it is impossible in this field to maintain full transactional data for people on the database.

The use of panel research increases our understanding of how our customers behave. It enables us to improve our behavioural modelling so that we draw more accurate inferences from our database information flow. Instead of having to assume that our low spend customers are spreading their purchases around, we can check our assumption with the research sample. We can see what alternative choices they are making and may undertake further research, again using the database for sampling, to find out the reasons for their choices.

SAMPLE SELECTION

The customer contact data on our database facilitates all contacts with research respondents, whether for qualitative or quantitative studies and however these studies are conducted, whether face to face, in groups, by post or by telephone.

Telephone research has proved to be a most cost-effective way of deriving information because it is the cheapest method of establishing an interview dialogue. In theory, it is less subject to sample distortion than postal research. Sample distortion occurs through non-responses. It is rare for postal studies to achieve response rates much in excess of 50 per cent. This invariably leaves the question: 'How do non-respondents differ from respondents?'

Unfortunately, a large segment of the population has chosen to go ex-directory. This creates another source of sample distortion, about 40 per cent of potential respondents being excluded because they cannot be contacted. These same people may have released their telephone number to businesses they deal with, thus reducing the potential for sample distortion. Information on the database allows samples to be constructed in a way that is relevant to the object of the research: If the research study is designed to discover reasons for customer defections, only defecting customers need be contacted. If it is designed to discover why some customers use product A but not product B, then the sample can be created at random from within the appropriate customer segment.

In industrial market research it is often difficult to discover exactly who to interview. Again, the contact data on the database can be used to locate potential respondents who are directly concerned with the research topic.

SOFT DATA AND QUALITATIVE RESEARCH

It is often said that direct marketing data reveals an astonishing amount about how people behave but almost nothing at all about the reasons for their behaviour.

This is something of an over-simplification. If we test offering a sample of customers a £10 discount and check their behaviour against that of a matched sample of customers who were offered no discount, the result of the test may tell us all we need to know. The resulting data will be more reliable than anything we could have discovered from research. The result will tell us about what people do, not what they say. It will not only tell us whether our customers respond to discounts but also how many extra sales will result and whether that is enough to make the offer profitable. It may even tell us what kind of people the extra responders are, enabling us to target the offer appropriately instead of wasting money by offering the discount to everyone.

Accurate and significant though test information is, it does not tell us all we need to know about what kind of people our customers are, their attitudes to us or how they go about making choices. Without this sort of information, our databank will be very clinical, full of stimulus and response data but giving us no clues about how to forge a mutually satisfactory business relationship. It's one thing to know what treatment to give the patient, it's another to adopt a confidence-inspiring bedside manner.

Some years back, a rather old-fashioned mail order company trading in home furnishings tested the offer of a gift to encourage customers to recommend their friends to use the service. Such offers are a standby device in mail order, usually providing the cheapest source of new customers. In this case the test flopped. A number of customers wrote angrily to explain why. They had been trading with the company for years and had always recommended it to their friends without being bribed. They considered the offer to be insulting. With a better understanding of their customers and of its image among established customers, the company might well have avoided this mistake.

Customer beliefs, attitudes and circumstances

Customers are more than the sum of various items of behaviour. Their behaviour stems from a set of beliefs, attitudes and circumstances. The way we embark on a dialogue, how we express our ideas, even the words we choose are all important in shaping a customer relationship that will be mutually satisfactory.

We may be collecting a wealth of attitudinal data informally through customer contact, for example at a call centre or through sales staff, but we may also need more formally gathered and interpreted information. Most often, qualitative research to gather this information will have a highly specific objective. It may be designed to gauge reactions to a new product. Nevertheless, it can still be productive of insights that are more generally applicable.

Some direct marketers use qualitative research in conjunction with testing. This most often occurs in the case of direct mail tests. It can advance the learning curve by helping to explain why A outpulled B in an A/B split-run test. By discovering more about recipients' reactions to each mailing, it is often possible to find good features in the losing direct mail shot that can be incorporated within the winning direct mail shot. There may also be features missing from both mailings that could have been included with benefit to the response. The winning mailing can then be enhanced before rolling out, although the modified version will almost certainly be retested first.

This is a useful but narrowly defined function of marketing communications research. The integrated marketer must gather soft data on the establishment and maintenance of a consistent image through all media of communication. Otherwise how is the company to know the contribution, positive or negative, of the individual components that make up its marketing communications mix? An example of communications research is advertising tracking studies. These studies are designed to monitor recall of advertising and its effect on brand awareness, product knowledge and image. Such studies would be greatly assisted – and made a practical possibility for smaller advertisers – if sample selection reflected the importance of established customers. The use of unweighted samples lends artificiality to these studies, giving disproportionate credence to the views of people who will have little or no influence on future profitability.

Advertising is only one component of a whole battery of influences that contribute to a company's image. For example, the image of British Gas will certainly be affected by both its corporate and product advertising, including promotional or customer information leaflets enclosed with the gas bill.

But it will also be affected by media response to its initiatives, such as overseas investments, directors' bonuses or salary hikes, closure of sales and service centres and any unfortunate gas explosions that may occur. It will be subject to external pressures, perhaps from regulatory authorities or consumer groups. Finally, in its customers' eyes, its image will be affected by the size and accuracy of their gas bill, by how quickly the phone was answered when they last called for service, by the helpfulness of call centre staff, by the response, attitude and quality of service engineers and by the assistance received when last choosing (or deciding against) a new gas appliance.

It is, or should be, the responsibility of marketing to monitor the effect of all these influences and, when necessary, to take or propose corrective action. Thus the integrated marketer must track the total effect of communications and customer dealings. It is not enough to take the hard transactional measurements that have proved so successful in direct marketing. In taking soft, attitudinal measurements, it is the views of customers on the database that are critical because it is the customers who are the profit providers.

VOLUNTEERED DATA

Thus far we have been discussing formally conducted market research. However, customer contact permits less formal information gathering. The line between the type of study that would meet with the approval of the Market Research Society and less rigorously conducted enquiries can become blurred.

One of the most significant blurring influences is that of the so-called lifestyle surveys, in which massive numbers of lengthy postal survey questionnaires are distributed in product packages, in magazines, by door-to-door distribution or by direct mail. Responses to these questionnaires are induced by the promise of money-off coupons and prize draw participation. Some questions are sponsored by individual companies, some response data is sold on an exclusive basis and the majority of the information is used to rent lists of potential customers to direct mail users. The respondents are informed of this intention and may opt out of being mailed. This is a perfectly legitimate activity that produces huge volumes of useful personal data. However, it should not be confused with market research, the latter being a confidential process in which the identities of respondents are not disclosed.

What is research and what is promotion?

The ownership of a customer database permits companies to undertake various enquiries among their customers that may or may not be conducted to ordinary market research standards. But what is research and what is promotion?

If an independent research company undertakes a satisfaction survey within a sample of a company's customers, that is clearly research. But what if the company conducts its own satisfaction survey, mailing postal questionnaires to its entire customer base? Perhaps the questionnaires are coded or personalised so that the identity of each responder is known. Perhaps an inducement is offered to respond. Perhaps the motive for sending the questionnaire is more closely related to establishing a caring image than to producing actionable answers. This has clearly crossed the line between research and promotion.

Again, there is nothing wrong with this. Provided it is transparently clear to respondents that their identities will be known at the time their answers are analysed, and that the answers are acted upon to their advantage, everyone gains. It is not customer research in any terms acceptable to a professional market research person but it is a mutually beneficial activity for the company and its customers.

Listening in to customers' calls

A further source of information is inbound telephone calls from customers. These may be to make enquiries, ask advice and place orders. The company has a responsibility to check the quality of call handling and, to do this, managers will listen to recordings of a sample of the conversations. While the primary purpose of this is to facilitate staff training, the recordings can also be used to gain insights into customers' concerns, the way they wish to be treated and the way they express their wishes.

This is akin to a form of qualitative research but is not research in any formal sense. The customers do not know their conversations are being recorded, they do not constitute a formally selected sample and the results are not reported in any formal way. This is not research, it is fly-on-the-wall observation.

However, an increasing number of organisations are using information gained from calls in a more formal and organised way. Customers are asked specific questions, for example about house purchase intentions, contemplated major purchases or insurance renewal dates. In these cases it is transparent to the customer why the questions are being asked. Such information can be used by banks and building societies, allowing them to contact customers with a relevant offer at the appropriate time. In some cases, both inbound and outbound telemarketing staff are briefed to request information to fill in blank fields in the customer contact data that they can see on screen while they talk.

WHY THE DATABASE WON'T KILL OFF FORMAL RESEARCH

Some of the more assertive direct marketing database enthusiasts have suggested that the days of formal market research are numbered. It is certainly true that the database has overtaken the need for research into customer behaviour and customer profiling. It is also true that much customer information, actionable at an individual customer level, can be gathered informally. Finally, qualitative research can often be more meaningfully quantified through live testing than through quantification studies.

Yet, far from obviating the need for research, the database makes hitherto impracticable studies (because of their sampling difficulties) perfectly feasible. There will always be a need for independently gathered information on a strictly confidential basis. Paradoxically, the database may foster research projects for two reasons. Firstly, it can make research studies cheaper to conduct with more precise and relevant sampling. Secondly, the database creates a thirst for greater customer knowledge. The more we know about *how* customers behave the more we want to know *why*. We cannot use a customer database effectively to build customer relationships unless we exhibit some customer understanding at a human level.

PERSONAL DATA AND THE PROTECTION OF PRIVACY

Any organisation that data captures personal information for commercial purposes falls within the scope of data protection legislation and must register as a keeper of personal data. A name and address with no supporting detail is enough to constitute personal data.

The harmonisation of personal data protection across the European Union has caused a number of changes over the years and the direction of these changes has not always been easy to predict. These changes have not come to a halt at the time of writing and it is therefore more useful to discuss the principles guiding legislation, which are not likely to change, than the detail, which is.

The most important aims of personal data protection are to ensure the fair obtaining and fair processing of data. What is meant by obtaining? An example will help. If you are in London and stroll down Oxford Street you may decide to call into Selfridges, the department store. You may buy a greetings card for cash and disappear, unknown, back into Oxford Street. On the other hand, you may be rather taken by their Persian rugs and ask for one to be delivered. Somebody may write your name on a delivery note and your name may never be transferred to a computer system. Alternatively, it may be transferred to such a system. If you applied for a Selfridges credit card, it certainly would be. As soon as you give your name, providing it is later transferred to a computer system, Selfridges have obtained your data.

There is now nothing to stop Selfridges from direct mailing you as a customer. You would not be surprised by this and might even be quite pleased you were not forgotten. What you would not expect would be to receive an invitation to shop with Freemans' catalogue by telephone or pop into a Sears Group shoe store to take advantage of their spring sale. Selfridges is owned by the Sears Group and so, until recently, was Freemans. But you could not be expected to know that or to anticipate your name would be passed on to these companies.

Within the principles of data protection legislation, your data would have been unfairly obtained.

A timely warning

To avoid penalties under the legislation, Selfridges (if they intended to pass your personal data on) would have to warn you of this intention. You would have the opportunity to opt out of allowing them to use your data (probably by ticking a box on a form) or to refuse to give your name and walk out.

Under the EU Data Protection Directive (1995) it would be permissible for Selfridges to warn you of their intentions later and give you the option to prevent them from using your name at that time. However, they must not use your name except within their own business until you have been given the opportunity to refuse permission. There is no particular significance to my choice of Selfridges in this example, of course.

Fair processing

What is meant by fair processing? As with fair obtaining, the principle of transparency applies. A company you deal with may add to your personal data other information, perhaps obtained from a different source, to build up more information about you than you could reasonably anticipate. If you had known they intended to do this you might have been reluctant to give them your information. This would be unfair processing. For some time it seemed likely that all profiling, even the mere attachment of, say, a MOSAIC code to your address data would fall foul of the legislation.

The 1995 Directive provided that profiling could not be defined as unfair unless it had 'legal effects' or 'significantly affected' the data subject. At the time of writing it appears likely that the use of information which there is a statutory duty to publish, such as the Electoral Roll and shareholders' registers, will not be restricted for individually addressable marketing communications. This might change. It could be considered inconsistent with the broad principle that information you give for one purpose should not be used for another purpose without your consent.

Many companies have adopted their own data protection policies, more stringent than legislation has required. For example, it is commonplace for companies to give their own customers the opportunity to opt out of receiving any marketing communications from them. Virtually all customer information systems allow for the deletion of customers' names from any list that is to be used for direct mail or telemarketing. In addition there is a national Mailing Preference Service and an equivalent used by telemarketing organisations, allowing consumers to have their names deleted from many large companies' lists just by writing to one address.

TO SUM UP

In this chapter we have seen that our view of our customer relationships would be somewhat introspective if it were formed purely from what the database told us. We need to know what share of our customer's wallet is being gobbled up by competition so that we can improve our competitive strategy.

We also need to know more about why our customers behave the way they do. What do they think of us? For example, how do they position us as a supplier compared with our competitors?

Far from killing off conventional market research, the database can help make it more accurate and useful, particularly through improved sampling. We may also supplement our more formally acquired research and database information through volunteered customer information.

We concluded by taking a brief, lay view of data protection and its regulation.

PART THREE

HOW TO INTEGRATE DIRECT MARKETING

THE HENLEY COLLEGE LIBRARY

12

PLANNING FOR DIRECT MARKETING

IN THIS CHAPTER

Marketing communications are like the tip of the iceberg we can see. They are the visible or audible expression of a marketing plan. Direct marketing communications are frequently directed by mail or telephone and may often be tactical, perhaps featuring short-term promotions or other specific offers.

This has led to confusion about the role of direct marketing. It has been a recurring complaint from the direct marketing fraternity that managers view direct marketing as tactical, nothing more than a form of personalised sales promotion.

Yet, as we have seen, the collection, manipulation and exploitation of information about individual customers or end-users is central to a company's ability to adopt true customer focus. A strategic plan that disregards this ability is doomed to failure. In this chapter we consider the extent to which our enhanced customer knowledge informs planning.

In Figure 12.1 we display a conventional strategic planning model that would cover a period of not less than three years. The steps shown in this model form a logical planning sequence. The model is affected by our marketing database analysis in content rather than shape. Thus we need not quarrel with the main headers. However, in Chapter 5 we began a discussion of customer marketing objectives and strategy. This is central to the planning process. In a way it always has been. The only differences are that the microchip has empowered us to consider customers at a micro, not just a macro, level and, even more importantly, to study the dynamics of customer relationships. So how does this affect our plan?

HOW SUPERIOR CUSTOMER KNOWLEDGE AFFECTS THE PLAN

Functions and scope

This part of the plan deals with the company's customer and market orientation, looking towards the future. It will answer the question: 'What business are we in?'

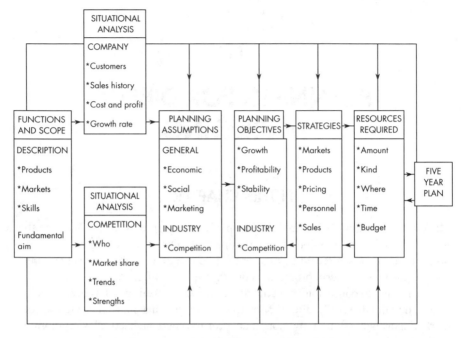

Figure 12.1 A strategic planning model
(Source: *The Practitioner's Guide to Direct Marketing*, 1992)

It will define the requirements, both financial and ethical, of stakeholders. It will describe the long-term objectives and strategy of the business. It will state the company's mission. It will include a description of the company's markets, its customer base within those markets, its products and its capabilities.

The long-term strategy of the business will usually be described as a competitive strategy. The competitive strategy describes the means by which a company seeks to build and maintain a sustainable competitive advantage. According to Michael Porter (1980) there are only three generic choices. These are *cost leadership*, *focus* and *differentiation*. Cost leadership differs from the other two choices in that only one company can be the lowest cost producer in any market. A focus strategy depends on defining a specific market segment and aiming to meet the needs of that segment more precisely and profitably than the competition. A differentiation strategy implies aiming at a broader market but creating brand preference through a differentiated product, service, offer or image. The next stages of the planning process must follow from this strategy and the competitive situational analysis will be used to show whether competitive advantage can be sustained.

But is our competitive strategy real or are we deceiving ourselves? The customer database can provide information that will help to confirm the validity of a competitive strategy or suggest change. This is because the database portrays the dynamics of customer relationships, distinguishes between profitable and unprofitable relationships and describes how profitable customers differ from unprofitable customers.

Experience shows that many companies aiming at broad market segments are in practice deriving almost the whole of their profit from much narrower segments. Their marketing effort would be better directed if they were to recognise what their customers (and non-customers) were telling them. Furthermore, almost the whole of the profit generated by a company in any one year is derived from customers gained in previous years. Measurement of the customer gains and losses arising from present strategy is essential to checking the robustness of the strategy and to forecasting future profitability. Conventional market research methods are sometimes too slow and almost always too imprecise to provide the right quality of planning information.

At this planning stage we use our customer information to check the logic of the strategy.

Situational analysis and planning assumptions

In the model we are using (Figure 12.1) the situational analysis comprises two parts. The first part is a review of the company's present position and the second part is a review of the competitive environment. Looking at the captions you can readily imagine how knowledge of the value and dynamics of customer relationships can add enormously to the quality of the analysis. For example:

- the rate of customer gains and losses and trend data;

- relative profitability of new customers and lost customers;

- causes of customer gains and losses;

- success rate in uptrading customers;

- success rate in cross-selling other lines to customers;

- role of each product in customer acquisition and retention.

The last item on our list, the *role of each product*, may need a little explanation. Some products, credit cards being an example, are good door-openers. They attract new customers and can create cross-selling opportunities for higher profit products such as personal loans. Naturally, if we look only at the direct profit contribution of each product, we may jump to the wrong conclusion as to their relative values. If we reversed their roles, both products might become loss-making. Only an analysis of the dynamics of customer behaviour will allow us to value the introductory role of the credit card correctly.

Other products may be useful in prolonging customer relationships. Again the database can help us to value this. (We return to the roles of products in Chapter 14.)

Without going laboriously through each caption in Figure 12.1, how can we summarise the difference in our approach to planning?

Valuation of customer base

The direct marketer sees *customers* as the source of profit and *products* as the means by which customer-profit can be generated. No direct marketer would prepare a profit projection for a new product without having calculated the sales volume that could be generated from established customers. That is because cross-selling is generally cheaper than selling to new customers.

Thus the direct marketer is looking firstly at revenue streams from established customers and secondly at revenue streams arising from growing the customer base. *It is absolutely critical to the company's competitive position that its return on customer acquisition is superior to that of its competitors.* The competitive part of the *situational* analysis (Figure 12.1) should attempt to draw comparisons.

How can the company increase its return on customer acquisition?

- Reduce its acquisition cost per new customer.

- Increase its share of customer by uptrading.

- Increase its share of customer by cross-selling.

- Reduce the loss-rate of customers.

It follows that the company must undertake an analysis of its return on acquiring each new customer and identify:

1) The productivity of each acquisition source.

2) The productivity of each method of increasing customer values.

The analysis will show what would happen to the business if no marketing expenditures were undertaken. In direct marketing, expenditures are shown correctly as the cause of sales volume, not as the consequence of sales volume. The latter is all too often the case in old-fashioned, conventional marketing. Thus each marketing investment must show a return. Customer acquisition may be a loss-making activity in the short term but, providing that an acceptable rate of return is produced, it may nevertheless be a sound investment. In this context, the customer base is seen as an asset. Possibly the accountants may eventually get round to capitalising this and giving substance to goodwill in the balance sheet.

Critical success factors

The penultimate output from the situational analysis (Figure 12.1) will usually be a SWOT analysis (a brief description of strengths, weaknesses, opportunities and threats). This analysis will be more useful if the critical success factors have been predefined. For example, customer retention rate may be a critical success factor. Each critical success factor may be weighted so that its relative importance can be compared with other critical success factors. Scores against each factor should be allocated. Finally, competitive scores against each factor should be allocated. Although this process will involve guesswork, it does at least provide a more disciplined framework for a SWOT analysis. You will appreciate that the SWOT can be more precise and profit-related by being given the direct marketing treatment. Direct marketing methodology removes the need for many of the woolly, qualitative measurements that are so resented by senior managers from non-marketing backgrounds.

This hard-nosed planning approach should be also adopted for the planning assumptions.

Feeling the heat

This was the title of a paper published in 1995 by two American business school professors, Jag Sheth and Raj Sisodia. The paper refers to specific causes of profit leakage and poor marketing accountability that are readily curable by any company with a fully functional customer database. For example:

- Management focuses too much of the marketing arsenal on getting new customers; in most companies, keeping the customers is somebody else's job. In many industries … customer 'churn' has become a major drain on marketing resources and company profitability.

- There is an enormous degree of cross-subsidisation across accounts [customers] in marketing; a few highly profitable accounts often hide the inefficiency in serving the rest. Such a marketing system is highly vulnerable to bypass or cherry-picking.

- Many marketing phenomena are still not accurately measurable. Without reliable measurement. meaningful improvements in efficiency levels are extremely difficult to achieve. Marketing is beginning to resemble manufacturing in 'pre-quality' days. Whereas the TQM philosophy resolved many of manufacturing's problems, a similar change still awaits in marketing.

Incidentally, it was cross-subsidisation that opened the door to the now dominant *direct writers* of motor insurance and paved the way for successful low-interest credit cards. Both of these are examples of cherry-picking. A company that fails to optimise its customer values, fails to spot that its best customers are getting a bad deal and fails to quantify the value of its marketing investments cannot possibly remain competitive.

Planning objectives

A business needs only one objective and this objective should be capable of being described in one short sentence that includes a number, such as £5 million pre-tax profit. However, there should be stages within a three-year plan, so there might be three numbers.

Without descending into strategy, the objective may also be prescriptive to some degree. This prescription may follow from the mission statement or the long-term corporate objective. Perhaps the former requires the company never to lose a profitable customer through failure to resolve a complaint. Perhaps the long-term objective of the business is to take ownership of the market for widgets. In that case the objective for the planning period may refer to an increase in customer retention and an increase in market share. Neither of these is a financial objective but both are capable of quantification and both have financial implications.

The marketing objective is separate from the overall business objective. A company with more than one business objective will lack direction. However, there will nearly always be more than one marketing objective and, most often, there will be more than one kind of objective. The objectives will not always be financial but should always be measurable. A good marketing planning objective is SMART – specific, measurable, aspirational, realistic and timed.

Table 12.1 Five criteria for setting sound objectives

1.	Ensure objectives focus on results
2.	Establish measures against each objective (return on investment, turnover, % market share, etc)
3.	Where possible have a single theme for each objective
4.	Ensure resources are realistic
5.	Ensure marketing objectives are integral to corporate goals and objectives

Source: The Practitioner's Guide to Direct Marketing, 1992

Table 12.1 suggests five criteria for setting sound objectives. Financial objectives should be displayed separately from other objectives and should be ranked. Commonly, companies will set a profit objective, a net cash flow objective and a market share objective. The last may be the least significant. Market share gains can be achieved in a variety of ways, not all of them profitable. It is possible, for example, to increase market share by wholesale price-cutting. It is often more profitable to increase market share by reducing customer defections than by increasing the number of new customers. It may be more profitable still to increase the ongoing value of customers' purchases. The widespread use of customer databases fosters the notion of setting a share of customer objective. A 10 per cent share of market gained from a 25 per cent market penetration will usually be more profitable than a 10 per cent share from 50 per cent of the market.

The direct marketing view is that customer marketing objectives should take precedence over product marketing objectives. A product is simply a device for maximising revenue streams derived from customers. A product may do this either directly or indirectly: directly by generating high net revenues in its own right; indirectly by attracting new business leading to cross-sales opportunities. That is, after all, the principle of a grocery market loss-leader.

Strategies

The situational analysis tells us where we are, the objectives tell us where we want to be within a given timeframe and strategy tells us how to get there. There will be exactly the same number of strategies as objectives; that is, only one strategy for each objective. The purpose of the strategy is to surmount or side-step the obstacles in the way of achieving the objective it supports.

The nature of a strategy is that it is:

- theoretical;

- descriptive;

- general;

- a guideline.

The fact that only one strategy is required for each objective does not preclude consideration of alternatives. Indeed, there is no reason why alternative strategies cannot be tested either theoretically (usually through a combination of marketing research and statistical modelling) or on the ground, by developing operational plans for each alternative and test marketing. However, a strategy is by definition a way of achieving a three or more year objective. Testing on the ground generally takes some time (though not three years) and competitive pressures often preclude the luxury of live testing.

There may be some debate as to what is strategic and what is purely tactical. It would be a strategic decision for a PC manufacturer to disband a dealer network and market directly to customers. It would be a tactical decision to sell the PC as part of a bundle including software and peripherals, as opposed to selling it on its own. The former decision would be almost impossible to test (except theoretically) while the latter could be tested with ease. Furthermore, the tactic of selling a bundle could be retested periodically and changed readily when customer response dictated this.

Although there can be only one strategy for each objective, there can be a number of tactics for each strategy. Figure 12.2 illustrates the point. The tactics may be alternatives and may be reduced to one after testing. On the other hand they may work in parallel, being used in combination or in different situations. Tactics are:

- operational;

- specific;

- detailed.

They form part of the action or operational plan covering a period of one year or less. This plan is not part of the model in Figure 12.1.

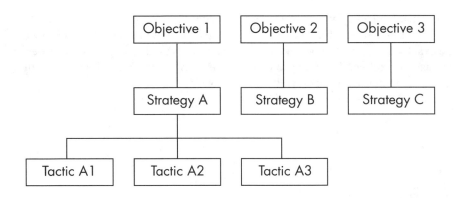

Figure 12.2 Objectives, strategies and tactics – the essential differences

Resources

An important function of a stated strategy is that it highlights the need for resources. It may well involve a change in existing organisational resources, not simply an amount of money. Any change must be detailed in the resources statement. This will include both the cost and time involved in implementing the change.

The ability to collect and use customer information to the customer's and company's advantage has become a critical success factor, greatly affecting a company's competitiveness. The use of information technology, purpose-designed call centres to provide customer service and the provision of customer helplines are all ways of establishing competitive advantage and are of vital interest to marketers. It is, however, a mistake to assume that the optimum answer to providing customer service is always to strive for perfection regardless of cost. The optimum answer may be different for different customers, the level for highly profitable customers being higher than for less profitable customers. The information derived from the database can be used to suggest appropriate service levels and, if necessary, to differentiate between different groups of customers.

IMPLEMENTATION AND THE MARKETING MIX (UP)

Strategies are theoretical. Nothing is achieved until the strategy is implemented. The strategist cannot afford to stand aloof from the action or operational plan because implementation must be monitored and controlled. The operational plan brings together the different elements of the marketing mix to offer the customer or prospect an irresistible proposition.

The concept of the marketing mix was evolved by N.H. Bordon in 1965. Bordon's mix consisted of 12 elements. This was simplified to four elements by E.J. McCarthy, the four Ps we know today. However, McCarthy's four Ps (Product, Price, Place and Promotion) include, as subsections, all of Bordon's 12 elements and are therefore less clear if more memorable. Since then, Booms and Bitner came up with the seven Ps for service product marketers in 1981. This adds People, Process and Physical Evidence. All great fun but not much help to those tasked with preparing the plan. You will find a more extensive discussion of the marketing mix in Chapter 6 of Paul Fifield's *Marketing Strategy*.

Most companies have set financial objectives based on what the stakeholders want to achieve rather than on a realistic assessment of what it will cost (in innovation, time and money) to arrive at any specific goal. The result is often a sales forecast that is not only higher or lower than the optimum but is also inherently unreliable. This is what Schultz, Tannenbaum and Lauterborn (1993) call inside-out planning. Direct marketers have never done this or, at least, never admit to having done this. Direct marketers plan outside-in. They work out what it will cost, using their back data and forecasting models as a guide, to achieve any given volume of sales and cut off their plan at the optimum level.

Schultz, Tannenbaum and Lauterborn (1993) point out that outside-in planning can just as well be applied to an integrated marketing plan. In Figure 12.3 we see a diagrammatic representation of an integrated marketing planning model. The product could be a cooking oil or a margarine. The plan is set within a strategic framework and is driven by data derived from a database of own- and competitive-brand users. Separate objectives have been set against three target groups: loyal users, competitive users and switchers who are not brand loyal. These objectives would be expressed in value terms as well as words and the size of each target group should be detailed. The number of objectives dictates the number of strategies. Since not everyone in the market has had their personal details data-captured, the plan has to recognise this, setting objectives against both users and non-users who are unknown to the company.

The plan illustrates how information from the database suggests a strategic approach that is much more precise and less wasteful than, say, the indiscriminate distribution of money-off coupons against a background of mass media advertising. The overall aim is to build customer loyalty and usage by giving customers a stream of ideas about how they can use the product, also associating the brand with good cookery in the process. The plan will allow occasional and non-users

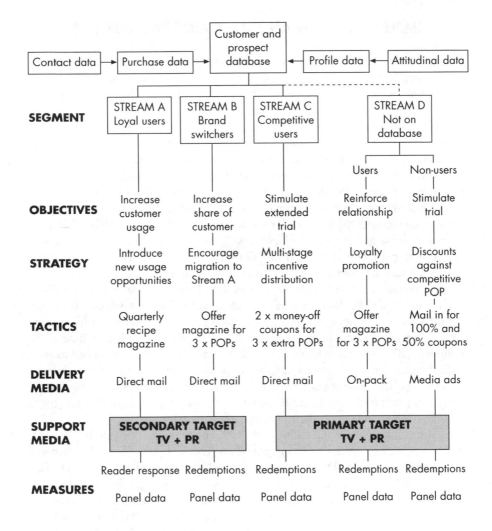

Figure 12.3 Example of an integrated marketing planning model

NB: Reader response will be checked by *ad hoc* reader surveys. Consumer panel data will be supplied with database names as subsample.
POP is an abreviation of 'proof of purchase'.

to graduate to this programme.

An achievement target can be set against each stream of customers, using information derived from the database as a planning tool. It will be much more difficult to achieve significant usage gains among unidentified customers and prospects. Therefore, lower achievement targets will be set and the per capita marketing spend will also be lower. The abbreviation 'POP' stands for proof of purchase, which may be a wrapper, a bottle top or a label.

In practice the plan might be more complex than shown. There are three reasons for this: firstly, the plan might distinguish between heavy and lighter users; secondly, more than one tactical idea might be tried against each strategy; thirdly, the manufacturer would have a range of products and there would probably be a cross-selling objective, enabling part of the cost to be recovered from incremental other-brand sales. The magazine might be an ideal vehicle for introducing other products in recipes or within serving suggestions.

Media ads are used to target competitive-brand users not on the database. These ads offer a coupon to 100 per cent of the purchase value on production of competitive-brand proof of purchase. A second 50 per cent off coupon can then be sent to redeemers together with the offer of the recipe magazine for three further proofs of purchase. The offer can be tightly close-dated to avoid stimulating competitive brand purchase.

Support media activity can be coordinated. TV ads can feature the same well-known cookery writer used to supply recipes for the quarterly magazine. PR can feature recipes from the magazine and, although the brand would not usually be identified in press featuring, the association of the featured cookery writer with the brand can be well established. The result is a fully integrated campaign with customer marketing objectives differentiated by segment. The campaign theme is capable of interesting extensions, for example in provoking some dialogue between the company and its customers. At the most basic level questionnaires could accompany direct mail delivered proof of purchase offers, adding to the depth of customer information. Beyond this, magazine readers could be invited to submit recipes for inclusion, write in with cookery tips and so on. A cookery advice line might be set up, possibly with calls charged at premium rate. The effect of this fully integrated campaign would be to forge a strong identification of the brand with quality cooking, thus raising its perceived quality and establishing non-price based preference.

In Chapter 14 we will consider the operational plan and the management of its implementation in greater depth.

TO SUM UP

Our ability to record and measure interactions with customers enables us to banish the presumptions about cause and effect and the vague generalisations about customer behaviour that have bedevilled marketing planning.

Without changing the basic planning framework, we can set up customer marketing objectives in parallel to product marketing objectives. Because it is generally more profitable to maximise business by maximising customer values rather than by maximising product market shares, our customer objectives will usually take precedence.

This change is not just theoretical, it has practical effects. For example, in the United States, 3M redeveloped its information systems so that any one of its formerly specialist salespeople could sell any one of its 60,000 products to any given customer. A 1994 study among 165 US companies by Marketing Metrics showed that 53 per cent of marketing budgets were spent on customer retention and only 47 per cent on acquisition, reversing the proportions from 1991.

The tracking of customer relationships in the database enables the marketing planner to forecast the future more accurately and to spot trends or sudden changes of behaviour more quickly. Planning derived from direct marketing is outside-in planning. It is based on the reality of what previous customer behaviour suggests is achievable, not the pipe dreams of stakeholders. We'll take another look at outside-in planning in the next chapter.

13

ROI-DRIVEN MARKETING

IN THIS CHAPTER

The sole justification for any marketing activity is to meet a specified objective. Direct marketers like to ensure that each objective has a numeric value, although the objective will generally be expressed in words, not just numbers.

In this chapter we encounter zero-based budgeting and a battery of direct marketing-derived measurements, remarking that the less obviously measurable elements of an integrated marketing effort should be isolated and tested as often as possible. Marketing is too costly and influential to escape the cost-effectiveness disciplines that are applied to other aspects of business performance.

A few years ago, I met the marketing director of a large importer of German cars. He wanted to know how much it would cost, in direct marketing expense, to create the sale of one car through his dealer network. When I told him that my best guess would place the cost in the region of £200, he was greatly unimpressed. He pointed out that it cost only £80 in advertising to sell a car. What he should have said was that he spent £80 on advertising for every car he sold. He had apparently never worked out how many cars he would sell without any advertising at all. Yet about 60 per cent of his sales were from repeat business and a fair proportion of the 'conquest' sales were made by dealers who recovered only part of their selling expense from the company. A smaller number of sales was generated from negotiation with companies who ran fleets of cars for executives and salespeople. I was astonished that such a highly intelligent man had never thought to cost his advertising against incremental sales; that is, the sales he would fail to make without any advertising.

It is not simple to make such a calculation but it is necessary to attempt it. Otherwise there can be no way of arriving at the optimum budget for any marketing activity. The integrated marketer will use a mix of both directly measurable and less easily measurable activities. Often it is necessary to calculate the payback on less easily measured activities by guesswork. Even so, it is better to make the guess than avoid the problem. In fast-moving consumer goods markets, it is possible to measure the immediate effect of advertising by resting it for a period. But there is also a longer-term effect that still requires an element of guesswork. By withdrawing advertising permanently, market share will fall to a point at which the brand is delisted by retailers, so losing distribution and, therefore, sales indirectly caused by advertising.

If my German car importer withdrew all advertising, dealers would soon begin to find it harder to sell both new and second-hand cars and would be forced to discount more heavily. The importer would start to lose good dealerships. His fleet customers would begin to notice an increase in depreciation because second-hand values would suffer. Some of his loyal individual buyers would be tempted away by competitive marketing activity. Over a period of time the loss caused by withdrawal of advertising would escalate.

It is not a difficult decision to continue advertising in these circumstances. What is difficult is to allocate the optimum financial resource to it. This requires a mixture of measurement, calculation, competitive analysis and good judgement. Direct marketing method focuses attention on the payoff, the return on investment. It also focuses attention on the importance of measurement. By doing these things, it leads to greater clarity of thought and superior decision-making.

RETURN ON INVESTMENT IS EVERYTHING – ALMOST

Most companies think of marketing as an expense. A budget for marketing activities is often calculated as a percentage of the turnover derived from a sales forecast. This forecast may be made independently of any consideration of proposed marketing activity. It is as if the management were saying we'll sell £10 million worth of widgets so we can afford to spend £200,000 on marketing activities. Yet the only justification for the £200,000 is the sales that could not be achieved without spending it.

Direct marketers begin their planning the other way around. They start by calculating how many sales can be made for nothing, then how many can be made for very little and continue until it ceases to be profitable to make any more sales. This is the only sensible way to construct a marketing budget yet, at the time of writing, most companies do not actually budget this way. As we discovered in the last chapter, the direct marketing way is what Schultz, Tannenbaum and Lauterborn (1993) have called outside-in planning.

To practise outside-in planning, it is essential to begin with an analysis of the business that can be derived from the established customer base. That is because it is cheaper to make sales to established customers than it is to acquire new customers or recover lost customers. It is not possible to complete this analysis accurately without a customer database.

Outside-in planning: making the cheapest sales first

If we return to our example of the motor engineers from the first chapter, we can see how they could undertake their analysis. Their system tells them how many routine services they have undertaken in the past year, when each car is due for its next service, what type of service it will be and, therefore, what it will cost. Their records will also show the ratio of repairs and replacement parts business to service business.

Now they need to make a calculation of customer loss rate (through changes of car, address and other defections) to arrive at the value of sales to be derived from the small cost of sending out service reminders. This will give them a clear picture of how much business can be generated at minimal expense, where it will come from and when to expect it.

Their next cheapest sales will be derived from telephoning customers who have not responded to service reminders. Telephoning will reduce customer defections arising from forgetfulness, minor dissatisfaction and change of car. It will also enable the motor engineers to delete gone-aways from their customer file. In the event that they miscalculate their return on telephoning customers, they can change the emphasis on this activity as their results experience dictates.

Before even thinking about targeting new customers, they might then consider how they can maximise recommendations from their current customers. They might decide to make this easier for customers, for example by asking customers for the names and addresses of any friends they could write to.

Where to start looking for new business

Only when all their ideas for generating business through their customer base were exhausted should they consider new customer acquisition. Even at this stage they can use the database. They can start by revisiting the *prospect file* and prioritise new customer targeting by *probability*. Some people who responded to give information on when their next service was due will, for one reason or another, not have become customers yet. These people are more likely to become customers than those who did not respond to the first 'mailing'. Why?

Firstly, their approximate service date is known so they can be contacted at the right time. Secondly, the very fact that they responded demonstrates interest. Therefore, the return from contacting this group is likely to be greater than from any other group of potential new customers. However, it is unlikely there will be enough of them to meet the sales target. Therefore, it is also necessary to revisit the *suspect file* and plan to recontact non-responding (presumed) Renault and BMW owners within the catchment area. Renault and BMW owners are more likely to provide service work than owners of other makes.

If we now assume that the desired business expansion rate demands broadening out the targeting, our motor engineers can consider non-Renault/BMW owners who live within a short radius of their garage and the preferred make owners who live farther afield. They no longer have time to get on their bikes but they can reach motorists cheaply from within the catchment area by arranging a leaflet distribution.

By referring to the database, they can calculate their response rate from Renault and BMW owners by postcode. This will enable them to prioritise postcodes for their leaflet distribution and will provide a basis for calculating potential response. They may decide that non-preferred make owners are, say, five times less likely to respond. On this assumption they can generate a marketing cost-per-service estimate.

ROI outside the database

By now, they will have had the benefit of a few months' exposure in local directories. Because they always ask new customers how they found out about the service, they will have a good appreciation of what directory advertising is worth and will make their decision to renew or withdraw accordingly. Directories may provide the cheapest solution to targeting preferred make owners from outside the immediate catchment area.

The resulting sales calculation may or may not provide enough business. If not, the probability is that some weeks or months will be predicted to be quieter than others. Reference to previous results will indicate the time lag between promotion and business and this can be used in planning. Now, more speculative activities will be considered, for example hiring a student on vacation to tour streets farther afield and identify potential Renault and BMW owners. Results from previous activity will again provide some basis for pre-calculating the likely cost of deriving this additional business. If it costs £3 to bring in a tightly selected prospect, it might cost between £10 and £15 to secure business from a less well targeted prospect. This assumption will be live-tested.

Activities for which it is impossible to make any realistic forecast of return will be left until last. These might include using slack time to give free trial services to local companies or offering a service to a local newspaper in exchange for a review.

This is a simple demonstration of outside-in planning, starting with the cheapest sales to make and working outwards to those that are likely to prove more costly or to represent more of a gamble. We can represent this process as a target, starting with repeat business in the centre and working outwards until we reach a sales forecast that takes us to full capacity or until it is marginally unprofitable to continue. The target is shown in Figure 13.1.

It is impossible to argue against the logic of this planning method. Indeed, most companies selling indirectly to their end-users through retail outlets or distributors will construct their sales targets using a similar method. However, they will do this by estimating sales through each sales channel instead of to each segment of potential customers. When it comes to budgeting for marketing communications, the logic will all too often be discarded.

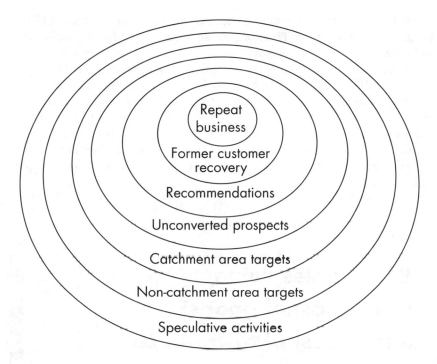

Figure 13.1 ROI-driven planning

ZERO-BASED BUDGETING

Our motor engineers correctly allocated the lowest priority to the least easily quantifiable investments. Yet most large companies allocate resource by precedent. Expenditure on advertising, most often the largest expense, may be decided on the basis of what was spent last year. It will not be the same as last year, some ratio being applied to allow for media cost inflation or a projected sales increase or decrease, but there will be a clear relationship. This means that planning never improves, the assumption being that former managers were gifted with superior wisdom. Most often the precedent was set by an assertion that it would cost £X to achieve the desired impact in the marketplace. Thus an unsound budgeting method is perpetuated, rendering the business less competitive and slower to change than it need be.

The solution is to sweep away precedent and employ *zero-based budgeting*. Zero-based budgeting is the process by which every investment is given equal consideration. Each potential expenditure is accorded priority according to its forecast return on investment, whether this return is direct or indirect. An example of indirect return is the use of advertising in order to maintain retail distribution. Often, the expenditure needed to deliver indirect benefits will be less than the actual expenditure. Therefore, the additional expenditure must be justified by the direct returns it can produce.

As its name implies, the starting assumption for zero-based budgeting is that some sales will be achieved without any marketing expenditure at all. Thus every marketing expenditure must be justified by what it can add during the budgeting period. This does not mean it must necessarily add to profit within the period. Some expenditures may be justified by what they pay back over a longer period. For example, the cost of new customer acquisition may be amortised over a period longer than one year, the projected lifetime value of the customer being an important consideration.

£   **Sales value**

less   **Cost of goods**

less   **Cost of distribution**

less   **Required profit margin (£)**

= AMC

AMC = Allowable marketing cost or 'marketing allowable'

Figure 13.2 Calculating contribution: the allowable marketing cost

It is common practice to budget for an allowable marketing cost. The allowable marketing cost is the amount that can be spent on marketing activity while preserving the required profit margin. The formula is shown in Figure 13.2. Sticking to this formula allows a company to maintain cost control. It was just such a formula that enabled the German car importer to tell me that he spent £80 per unit sale on advertising. Direct marketers prefer, quite correctly, to think in terms of the allowable per *marginal* sale. They recognise that some sales will be made at little or no cost, some at about average cost and some at above average cost. The question is: *How far above average is an acceptable cost?* Another way of putting it is: *At what point would it be more profitable to do something else with the money?* Whatever this point is will determine the ultimate marketing expenditure. Usually, the actual amount spent will be less than the ultimate because it is prudent to recognise that forecasts are never absolutely correct.

How to set a marketing budget

You will readily see that budgeting for an allowable per marginal sale is zero-based budgeting. There is no pre-set limit to the marketing budget unless this is imposed by the constraints of cash flow and available liquid funds. Only in this way can sales be maximised. Figure 13.3 shows three ways to set a marketing budget. The first way, working to a pre-set budget independently from the sales actually achieved during a given year, is the least effective but the most common. It is most common because it makes life easier for the accountants. It treats marketing as an expense instead of treating marketing as the way to make sales.

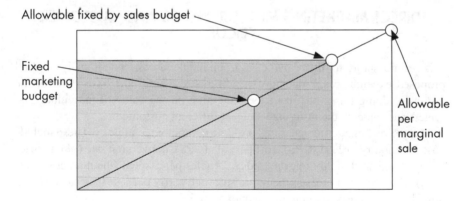

Figure 13.3 Budgeting to maximise profit: setting a marketing allowable for the marginal sale maximises profit

Working to an allowable per marginal sale means making constant adjustments as results justify change. Furthermore, not all marketing objectives are as simple as maximising unit sales. The objective might be to achieve the optimum new customer inflow or the optimum revenue per customer. The results of many activities are hard to forecast accurately and some activities may not pay back within any given year. These complications enforce a degree of conservatism that inhibits the aggressive pursuit of a marketing allowable per marginal sale policy. Nevertheless, the principle is correct even if the practice may be less than ultimately enterprising.

The case of the magazine publisher

An elegantly simple illustration of allowing marketing activity to be driven by its marginal utility is provided by magazine publishers. I was working on a series of direct mailings to *Newsweek International* subscribers inviting them to renew their subscriptions. There were ten invitations in all. This is a number that provokes traditionally trained marketers to assume the magazine people are a few brain cells short of a set. After all, what is there left to say to someone who has refused nine previous invitations?

Actually, that was my problem because ten was the logical number. Nine would have been one too few and eleven one too many. The tenth mailing secured renewed subscriptions at a marginally lower cost than a 'cold' mailing brought in new subscribers. The cost of obtaining new subscribers set the marginally acceptable cost of securing a renewal. Only the analysis of results permitted by accountable direct marketing activity would enable a marketer to make what seems such an eccentric, but in fact profitable, decision.

DIRECT MARKETING MEASUREMENTS AND CUSTOMER FOCUS

It is second nature to direct marketers to undertake a cost:benefit analysis of all proposed expenditures, reducing expenditures to a unit cost basis. One of the virtues of doing this is that it focuses attention on the value of individual customers and, indeed, the differing values of different customers.

Many direct marketing measures pre-date computer technology. These include cost per enquiry or lead (CPE), cost per sale (CPS), conversion rate (of enquiries to sales) and, still highly relevant today, £s sales per £ spent (the marketing cost ratio). These simpler measurements are still used partly because they can be taken quickly, giving early warning of the unexpected.

The advent of modern information technology has led to vastly superior measurement of ongoing *customer values* rather than just the cost of sales. This is not a new idea in direct marketing but ongoing values were not always so easy to measure. Businesses such as book clubs and continuity series marketers (of everything from cookery cards to collectibles) always measured the lifetime value of customers and the word *stamina* was often used in expressing the number of purchases a customer would make before dropping out.

In more complex businesses, for example home shopping catalogue trading, it was much harder to track customer values except in terms of averages. This made it very difficult to evaluate the true worth of each source of new business or to calculate lifetime customer value (LTV).

Now that it is possible, if not always easy, to keep track of customer values, it has become more feasible to compare returns on alternative marketing expenditures. At one time it was almost impossible to compare the return on spending money to increase business from established customers with the return on spending it to recruit new customers.

This could lead to overemphasis on customer recruitment because it produced a more easily quantifiable immediate gain. Even now, many businesses are still beset with this problem because they lack customers' transactional history. Thus precedent rules. The different activities are considered entirely separately, each working within expenditure budgets jealously fenced off by interested parties. This is no way to undertake integrated marketing.

Effectiveness versus efficiency

In Figure 13.4 we reduce measures of effectiveness and efficiency to the simplest possible level. Yet some of the most difficult decisions for marketing management are in making the choice between the most effective strategy and the most efficient, for they are often not the same. The most effective strategy is the one that generates the most business, maximises new customer gains or generates the highest customer values. The most efficient strategy produces the best return on marketing investment.

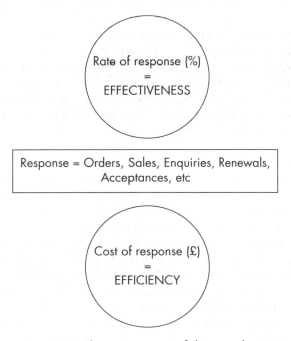

Rate of response (%)
=
EFFECTIVENESS

Response = Orders, Sales, Enquiries, Renewals, Acceptances, etc

Cost of response (£)
=
EFFICIENCY

Figure 13.4 The measurement of direct marketingt

A company that pursues effectiveness at the expense of efficiency may over-stretch itself and get into financial difficulties. A company that always opts for the most efficient solution may decline in share of customer and share of market because its competitors are more enterprising.

The information and disciplines derived from direct marketing enable the marketer to make the best informed and most rational choices. In our example of the motor engineers we can see that they were prepared to invest more effort to minimise customer losses than to target potential customers from outside the immediate catchment area. They were prepared to telephone potentially lost customers personally. Yet they might spend only a small amount on local directory advertising to reach more distant potential customers.

For the cheapest source of custom they pursued the most *effective* course of action. For the most expensive source of custom they pursued the most *efficient* course of action. In each case their actions were determined by the potential return on investment. This would be correct assuming that the whole of the first activity would produce a better return than any of the last activity.

Rate of return versus final payback

Direct marketing measures set the limit on acceptable marketing ratios. The most effective strategy may be pursued, even if it fails to pay back within a year, providing that it is expected to produce an eventual yield that justifies the investment.

Sometimes the strategy that produces the highest eventual return on investment does not produce the fastest return. A simple example would be the offer of deferred payment terms on refrigerators or other white goods. Sales will be increased by this offer but cash flow will be slowed and bad debts incurred, making the short-term position look pretty bleak. It may be difficult to optimise the balance between effectiveness and efficiency when the rate of return from alternative investments is different.

Suppose that a company makes an offer to customers who have been inactive for some time. Response is such that the company breaks even on the promotion. Thus some customer relationships have been salvaged at, apparently, no cost. Now suppose the same company spends money on new customer acquisition and makes a loss on the first orders received.

On the face of it, the customer retention promotion looks a much better investment than the acquisition promotion. But direct marketers look beneath the surface by using the test and control procedure. If we take the customer retention promotion apart, we can see that many of the customers would have been retained without any promotion. Some of these customers would have ordered goods at full price but, instead, the retention promotion allowed them to order at a discount. The lost margin on these orders is a concealed cost of the promotion.

Making a true comparison

Direct marketing test and control procedure demands that a matched sample of customers would not receive the promotion. Thus the incremental value of the promotion can now be measured, because the effect of *not* undertaking it is known. There is now a true basis for making a comparison between the two investments. It is possible, although not very likely, that the new business investment produces a better immediate return on investment. In Table 13.1 we see the return is actually the same. Yet, without using the test and control procedure, it would have appeared that the retention strategy was profitable, while the new business strategy was loss-making. Actually, both strategies make an immediate loss, each costing £2 for every £1 gained.

Table 13.1 Comparison of acquisition and retention investments

Activity	Customer acquisition	Customer retention test	Control group
Target group size	100,000	20,000	20,000
Orders received	2,000	2,000	1,000
Total order value	£50,000	£42,500	£25,000
Margin on orders	£25,000	£17,500	£12,500
Marketing cost	£50,000	£10,000	Nil
Profit/loss	–£25,000	+£7,500	+£12,500
Extra orders gained	2,000	1,000	Nil
Extra margin gained	£25,000	£5,000	Nil
Marketing costs per £ margin gained	£2	£2	Nil

NB: The net gains from the retention activity are derived from comparing the results with the control group in the right-hand column. The order value and margin on orders is reduced by a 15 per cent discount offered in the retention test.

Table 13.2 Extended comparison of acquisition and retention investments

	New customers	Incrementally retained customers
Net cost of first orders	£25,000	£5,000
Customers gained	2,000	1,000
Subsequent order value	£150,000	£60,000
Margin on orders	£75,000	£30,000
£s margin per £ cost	£3	£6

NB: The lower average value of retained customers arises from this population being composed of potential defectors or low order frequency customers.

Longer-term measurement will reveal whether the values of customers reactivated by discounting are sufficient for the retention strategy to produce the higher eventual return (see Table 13.2). Even if they were not, the retention strategy would produce a quicker payback. Obviously enough, if the eventual returns are equal, rapidly generated cash flows are more valuable than slowly generated cashflows and the value of money now, as opposed to money later, will be taken into account. However, a counterbalancing factor that would need to be considered in this example is the risk of building up dependency on discounting.

Applying direct marketing disciplines within integrated marketing

Direct marketing test and control procedures are easy to apply when each marketing investment is designed to produce a specific and measurable return. Thus they can be applied to direct response advertising, telemarketing, direct mail, sales calling, sales promotion, sales agents, dealerships and so on. Yet the principle can, and should be, applied to less directly measurable activities such as the advertising with which we started this chapter.

If the main advertising medium is terrestrial TV, there is no rule to say that the medium cannot be used in different weights in two regions and rested in a third. Database or consumer panel data can then be used to track any changes in sales performance resulting from these variations to the media advertising weightings. If it is desired to run satellite TV advertising, there is no reason why satellite homes cannot be identified on a consumer panel or the database and their purchase behaviour measured.

Direct marketers measure the effect of background advertising on their direct response activities. For example, although Direct Line Insurance TV commercials may carry a response mechanism, they most often refer the viewer to Yellow Pages and Thomson Directory advertising. The payback of TV is evaluated on the basis of indirect, not just direct, response. Reader's Digest have used TV in short bursts specifically to support prize draw subscription promotions delivered by direct mail. There is no reason why any advertiser using sales promotion or customer direct mail cannot use the test and control procedure to gain a better understanding of the impact of background advertising on direct response marketing communications.

The more rigorous disciplines derived from direct marketing should be preferred to the artificial measures produced by, for example, advertising tracking studies. The latter can have the effect of distorting advertising content because of their preoccupation with measuring its effect on people not within the immediate target market. This tends to favour advertising that we remember for its own sake, rather like the bad accompanist who tries to upstage the singer. Advertising has no intrinsic value. It is a means to an end. Its contribution to that end must be isolated and measured.

TO SUM UP

From the early days direct marketers were fastidious about measuring and recording the results of their marketing expenditure decisions. When they could, they would measure the staying power of their customers and thus derive lifetime value measurements.

Cheap computing power made this type of measurement a practical possibility for many, more complex businesses with less tidy customer relationships. The value of most marketing investments can be assessed, even though some element of guesswork may have to be included. Where there is less emphasis on quantification, there is more wastage. In marketing, the unwatched kettle never boils.

This outside-in planning approach leads to zero-based budgeting in which money is allotted to the activities that produce the best predicted return and continues to be allocated for as long as these activities justify their star billing.

From reading the brief case histories in Chapter 21, you will see how the Range Rover case appears to reflect this philosophy more closely than the Audi case, although both are evidently success stories. The Range Rover people appear to have been more confident about meeting the bulk of their sales target from people who had bought or seriously considered Range Rover before. This would enable the database to play a central role, affecting their targeting and reducing their costs.

14

HOW TO MAKE ACTION PLANS AND MANAGE PROJECTS

IN THIS CHAPTER

In many of the standard marketing texts, discussion starts with the product. Excitingly simple ideas, such as product lifecycles and the Boston Matrix are introduced. The latter categorises products into stars, question marks, cash cows and dogs according to the market growth rate and the market share of each product.

In this chapter we see that the principles of direct marketing do not necessitate discarding these ideas altogether but, rather, they add another dimension. Customer-based marketing forces us to allocate roles to products beyond their turnover, profit and cash contributions. These roles can be defined in terms of what they contribute to the start, the development and the maintenance of profitable customer relationships. We recognise customers as being the source of profit and products as being devices to gain and maintain customers' business. Thus product marketing objectives are subservient to customer marketing objectives.

Because most of our near-future profit will arise from customers we already have, this puts a different slant on the Boston Matrix. It is not share of the whole market we should use to categorise products, it is share of our customers' contributions. A declining brand may be very important to, for example, a minority of our most profitable customers. We withdraw this product at our peril unless we have pre-sold a superior alternative.

In looking at our product portfolio, we do not look first at the whole market to spot gaps. Rather, we look first at those of our customers' needs we are unable to meet. Each need we fail to meet drives customers into the arms of our competitors. Thus, more usefully than defining products as stars, question marks, cash cows and dogs, we may define their roles as *new business getters*, *customer uptraders* and *relationship maintainers*. Their value in fulfilling these roles will have a direct bearing on the marketing investment they attract. We may choose to take a loss on a new business getter if our main concern is its effectiveness at starting new customer relationships.

We recognise that our profitability depends on the levels of customer dependency and customer commitment we can achieve. The greater the contribution gained from established customers, the higher the gearing on our new business investment. The planning process we suggest is akin to the Toyota example quoted in Chapter 1. The role of each product in our portfolio will be determined in advance of preparing the product sales and contribution forecasts. Of course, because we are direct marketers we reserve the right to change our minds about these roles as the hard evidence of response and sales data may suggest.

THE PROCESS OF PLANNING

Planning is the first of four stages which form a loop. The second stage is *implementation*, the third is *monitoring* and the fourth is *control*. Planning is deciding what to do and how to do it, implementation is doing it, monitoring is measuring the result and control is taking whatever actions the result suggests. This takes us back to planning for the next period of activity.

The planning period for the action plan will never be longer than one year and may be shorter. For example, if we were marketing holidays we would usually plan the summer and winter holiday marketing programmes separately. The planning process will refer back to the strategic plan, following its guidelines. Unlike the strategic plan, the action plan will be operational, specific and detailed.

This chapter began with a reference to products. Product planning may be seen as a strategic process, nothing to do with action plans. This is not the case. Where a lengthy and expensive product development cycle is involved, product development decisions are certainly taken at a strategic level. But the roles of individual products may change rapidly and every product must be fitted into a detailed action plan for each period. For example, a bank may base its customer development strategy around introducing an instant access savings account to current account holders. But the precise terms and features of the account may be changed very quickly and the marketing effort may be increased or reduced according to its current competitiveness or the need to attract funds.

The planning process for all marketing activity follows broadly the same steps and this chapter will highlight the extra considerations that bear on planning and project management when the marketer can forecast and measure the results on a customer-by-customer basis. The purpose of the plan is to bring together the different elements of the marketing mix into an irresistible combination.

Format of the plan

The plan must contain the elements listed below, preferably in the same order.

- *Objectives*. Each objective will be in the form of a quantifiable target. There will invariably be volume, value and margin objectives. The volume target will not necessarily be a unit sales figure. It could be number of active customers. This part of the plan will include references to results for the current and previous period.

- *Strategies.* Each objective will have its supporting strategy. There will be only one strategy per objective.

- *Subordinate objectives.* These are objectives for component parts of the business or market segments. They should include reference to acquisition, retention and customer values, not simply to product targets or market shares. They should be quantifiable and capable of totalling up the overall objective.

- *Subordinate strategies.* This is a guideline indicating how each subordinate objective will be met.

- *Tactics.* These are the means by which each subordinate strategy will be implemented. There may be more than one tactical idea for each strategy. These alternatives may be pruned or added to in discussion with those involved with implementation. They may be further altered as a result of research or may be tested during implementation.

- *Summary of planned activities.* This gives a capsule description and sets a budget allocation for each planned activity. It may include activities by sales channel as well as centrally driven product launches, marketing communications and promotions.

- *Contingency plan.* This includes all key planning assumptions including the basis of forecasts and their likely error range. The plan should provide an outline plan of action in the event of failure to meet forecasts.

- *Forecast results and financial ratios.* This includes turnover, gross margin, finance costs, marketing costs and operating costs. The ratios show return on sales and return on capital employed. There may also be additional key performance measures if these are relevant to the objectives, for example market share, average customer value, number of active customers, etc.

- *Activity schedule.* This shows the timing for each planned activity and the lead times allowed for the detailed planning and preparation of each activity.

The plan should be written in sufficient detail to act as a briefing document to members of the team responsible for its execution.

Some special considerations for direct marketing

So far we have avoided using the word *campaign*. Traditional marketers like this word, probably because of its macho imagery, and its use has spilled over into modern integrated and direct marketing. There is nothing wrong with this; indeed, the idea of a campaign suggests concentrating the combined efforts of a group of forces to achieve a specified objective. However, in the highly accountable world of direct marketing, each single event within the campaign assumes some importance.

It is self-evident that a direct response advertising campaign comprises a series of events. Each advertisement is not simply part of a whole but provides hard response evidence of its individual contribution. Similarly, each person in a sales team and each sales call has a result. Each telemarketer and each telephone conversation has a result. Direct marketing brings marketing communications into line with other marketing activities, making individual components fully accountable (see Figure 14.1).

Each 'event' within a campaign has its own independent value...

...an event can be isolated and included (or excluded) according to its own unique worth

---

...a campaign may comprise hundreds of events.

Figure 14.1 Events not campaigns

Naturally, it may not always be practicable to saddle activities such as brand-building advertising with the burden of accounting for the value of every single advertisement. However, the integrated marketer will want to make as much of the marketing activity as measurable as possible so that tactical changes can be incorporated while the campaign is running. Doing so also ensures that future campaigns will be planned and their results forecast with greater accuracy.

The discipline of forecasting – aggregating events

Figure 14.2 illustrates the discipline of forecasting. Direct marketers see the campaign result as the aggregate of hundreds, or thousands, of individual skirmishes. The forecast gains in accuracy because of this. It is easier to predict the outcome of 1000 events to within 5 per cent or so than the outcome of one event. That is because the statistical base for doing so is sounder and because the mistakes, with luck, should help to cancel each other out. There will be swings and roundabouts, although not necessarily in equal numbers.

Each 'event' has its own forecast

Budget is **aggregate of events**

Forecasts **based on past results**

Need to compare **forecast vs actual**

Explanation of variances

Figure 14.2 The discipline of forecasting

Naturally, this makes planning an integrated or direct marketing campaign somewhat more laborious than old-fashioned marketing, but much of the additional effort is delegated to computers and, more particularly, to predictive models.

Generating test drives from an integrated campaign

We can use the example of generating test drive requests for car dealer franchises to illustrate how a campaign can be broken down into a very large number of events. Our background advertising campaign may be on TV and, although its primary purpose is not to generate sales leads, the use of a telephone response mechanism will provoke enquiries.

From back data it is possible to arrive at a relationship between the number of TV rating points (TVRs) and the number of previous responses. This relationship may be different by spot length, day part and channel. Thus, instead of generating a single forecast of response, we may actually generate 20 or more.

From our previous experience we can also forecast the quality of response, grading enquiries into time-wasters, longer-term leads and immediate sales opportunities. Our telemarketing team will be briefed on the information we seek to classify enquiries and will make the test drive offer only when that is appropriate. Thus there will be different test drive and conversion rate estimates according to this classification.

We may also run loose inserts in a range of magazines. Let's say these make the direct offer of a test drive in exchange for the respondent's volunteered information about current car ownership and intended purchase date. There will be a separate forecast of response, test drives and conversion to sales for each magazine.

Furthermore, we may also decide to test an incentive and a change of copy. These tests will be executed by means of split-runs in several of the magazines and will each be the subject of their own response and conversion rate forecasts. Thus there could be one hundred or more separate forecasts for this one part of the campaign. We may run several of these loose insert campaigns in the course of a year.

Naturally, we will probably send direct mail invitations to previous enquirers. The file will be segmented according to our predictions of the responsiveness of the various names on it. For example, our scoring may indicate that factors such as recency of previous enquiries, models owned, drive-time from nearest dealer and declared purchase intentions are indicative of response rate, likelihood of test drive and likelihood of conversion to sale. At the simplest level, the file may be divided into deciles (ten equal parts), each with its own estimates. However, we are certain to run tests within this part of the campaign too, and each test within each cell will attract its own forecasts.

Already, the number of events is in the hundreds for a very simple campaign for one model in one period of the year. In practice, we would have begun our planning with a forecast of the effect of contacting current owners, prioritising those whose cars were estimated to be due for replacement. If we have sufficient back data to do so, we may also estimate lead distribution and conversion rate by dealership, adding hundreds more variables. The more we put in the pot, the more precise our final forecast will be, providing, of course, that the quality of the data used for analysis is up to scratch.

We can see from this example that not all the events will produce the same type of result. Some will produce financial results such as sales value, others won't. There is no direct financial benefit in providing test drives. However, since the number of eventual sales will bear some relationship to the number of test drives, it is worth measuring both numbers. By doing so and by comparing the results with previous campaigns, we can use this information diagnostically. Did we persuade enough people to take test drives? Were enough test drivers persuaded to buy?

We can also appreciate that an event is the aggregate of a series of components, for example the product, the targeting, the offer, the message and the timing. Measuring the results of hundreds of events helps to isolate the value of the individual components.

Our planning must recognise our intention to record and monitor the contributions of individual events so that we can ensure we have the information system to do this.

MANAGING PROJECTS OR CAMPAIGNS

The project is kick-started by the action plan we have discussed. The three main tools of project management are:

1) the project file;

2) the campaign schedule;

3) the activity schedule.

The *project file* will usually include these components:

- the campaign marketing plan (including budget);

- a list of team members and their responsibilities;

- briefing forms for team members and suppliers;

- timetables for the campaign and its preparation;

- descriptions of materials to be produced (including identifying codes);

- a description of events (including identifying codes);

- authorisation for the project;

- a forecast of results.

At the time when the project file is opened it will often not be possible to include full details of materials or events because these may need to await the creation of a media plan. The forecast may therefore be a provisional one. The project file remains open until the campaign has been completed and will be updated as the information becomes available.

The *campaign schedule* outlines:

- what events are planned;

- the materials needed;

- the timing of events;

- the costs;

- the forecast results;

- any uncommitted reserve.

If the campaign or project is planned to coincide with other marketing activity, perhaps for other products, a clash schedule may need to be produced to identify potential conflicts of timing and targeting.

The *activity schedule* describes the actions required to make the campaign happen:

- shows what has to be produced (eg radio commercials, mailing packages);

- identifies interdependent actions;

- allocates time for the completion of actions;

- isolates the critical path (identifies potential bottlenecks);

- shows the status of the project today;

- displays any slippage and revises allowed timings accordingly.

The activity schedule will most often be devised and maintained with the help of a standard management software tool such as Gantt or PERT. An example of a Gantt chart (named after the originator, Henry L.Gantt) is shown in Figure 14.3. This shows which tasks must be completed before dependent tasks can be started. These critical tasks, the ones on which others depend, are identified by the use of capital letters on the chart.

ID	5 days per symbol	02	06	10	17	21	26	03	04	08	13
ID	Task name	Dec96	Jan97	Feb	Mar	Apr	May	Jun	Aug	Sep	Oct
001	Define market	X_____
002	Campaign plan	XXXX_____
003	Produce brief	_X_____
004	Agency response	_XXX_____
005	Agree strategy	_XX_____
006	Confirm budget	__X_____
007	Go/no go	__M_____
008	Contact strategy	__X_____
010	Media plan	__xx>>>>_____
014	Determine lists	__xx>>>>_____
012	Creative work	__XXXX_____
021	Plan fulfilment	__xx_____
009	Do selections	__xx_____
015	Order lists	___xx_____
011	Order media	___xxxxxxxxx>_____
013	Creative submit	___X_____
016	Creative agreed	____M_____
017	Copy/artwork	____XXXX_____
018	Copy/art agreed	____M_____
019	Pack finalised	____XX_____
020	Production begin	_____M_____
022	Printing	_____XXXX_____
023	Lasering	_____XX_____
024	Packs made up	_____XXX_____
028	Ads appear	_____m_____
025	Mailing begins	_____XX_____
026	Fulfilment	_____XXXXXXXXXXXXXXXXXX_____
027	Campaign close	_____X_____

| xxx | non critical | m | milestone | >>> | float/delay |
| XXX | critical | M | critical milestone | XXX | final delay |

Figure 14.3 Example of a Gantt chart

The PERT chart (Figure 14.4) shows the interdependence of tasks in a form that is easier to follow when several tasks may depend on the completion of a critical single task. The more complex the project, the more useful PERT is likely to be.

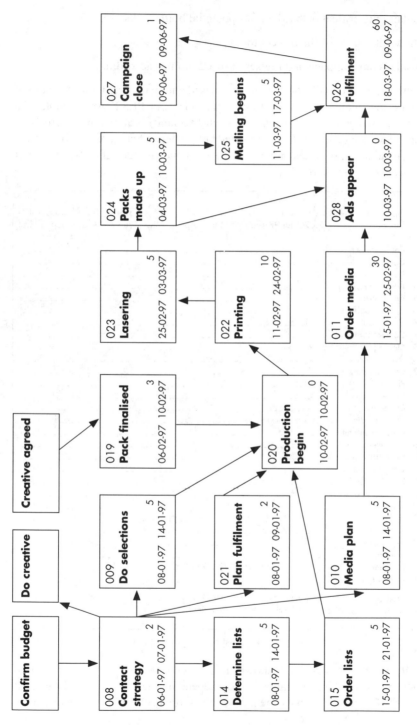

Figure 14.4 Example of a PERT chart

A PERT chart can be used to identify and display the critical path, that is the time required for completion of the lengthiest chain of interdependent tasks.

These aids are useful. However, the important features of an activity schedule are, firstly, that it allows sufficient time for completion and approval of the tasks and, secondly, that it is kept up to date.

Once a campaign is running, its status will continue to be reported. In the case of a direct marketing campaign or any integrated campaign in which results can be tracked through response, sales and so on, the primary status report will always be results based. This will show progress towards the forecast result. Clearly, the more up-to-date the report, the more useful it is in provoking timely corrective action, should this be required. Today, such results are often available on-screen and may change minute by minute, particularly if enquiries or orders are flowing into a call centre. The most sophisticated operators will sometimes break their forecasts down into daily segments so that the actual results can be compared against forecast on a day-to-day basis.

Acting on immediate results

Very often the first measurable effect of a campaign is to provoke enquiries, sales following after an interval. In these cases, adjustments to the plan will be made on the basis of enquiry performance alone, it being assumed that the conversion of enquiries to sales will remain at the percentage originally forecast. The most common adjustment made will be to media selection, advertising space in specific media being booked, cancelled or renegotiated according to results in those media. However, the campaign may also include creative or offer tests and the results of these, too, will be acted upon as quickly as possible.

Monitoring is, we can see, an ongoing process and we do not wait until we plan the next campaign to digest the lessons of current activity and modify our plans. If we have sufficient evidence to suggest logical and reasonable changes now, we will act on it without delay. Such changes may be fairly limited, of course, and the full effect of the campaign cannot be known until all the results, in terms of immediate business (and, possibly, changes to customer attitudes and retention rates), have been received and analysed.

TO SUM UP

In direct marketing, we see product marketing objectives as being subservient to customer marketing objectives (or ought to). This changes the way we view and value products. Withdrawal of a less profitable product could drive customers into the arms of competitors.

We also view campaigns differently because we are capable of using individual events as the building bricks for campaign forecasts, monitoring and control.

Planning is the first of four stages that form a loop. The four stages are planning, implementation, monitoring and control.

The format of the plan is unaffected by our forecasting method. The objective and strategy still sit above subordinate objectives, strategies and tactics. The plan also includes a summary of planned activities, a contingency plan, the forecast results and a schedule.

The process of project management is aided by three tools: the project file, the campaign schedule and the activity schedule. The project file describes the plan, the needs and the team. The campaign schedule shows the events and their projected results. The activity schedule shows what has to be done by when.

PART FOUR

DIRECT MARKETING COMMUNICATIONS

THE HENLEY COLLEGE LIBRARY

15

HOW MARKETING COMMUNICATIONS WORK

IN THIS CHAPTER

Is there a right way to do advertising? Probably not. Certainly not, if we label all marketing communications as advertising.

What has a full-page advertisement for a book club got in common with an instant coffee TV commercial? Or a Visa card symbol in a shop window?

Labelling all these things as advertising doesn't make them all the same. The task set for each advertisement is different. The task determines what each advertisement says, the way it looks, where it appears and the impression it attempts to make on us. The crucial question is: what do we want the audience to think or do? From *The Economist* and Audi cases in Chapter 21 we can see that different tasks may be awarded to different elements of the same integrated campaign. This imposes an additional task: to ensure that each element reinforces the others without compromising its own effectiveness.

In this chapter we examine how marketing communications work together and independently.

While running a direct marketing agency, I had a client who couldn't understand why our ads, which were designed to generate leads for his salesforce, were completely different from the almost surrealistic cigarette ads he so admired. The cigarette ads contained no contact information, no logo and, except for the government health warning, no words at all. Reasoned argument would silence him for a while but the subject kept coming up. I hope he felt better when he gave up smoking. I certainly did.

Guided by results, direct marketers soon formulated ideas about advertising that seemed to conflict with mainstream advertising theory:

- Even though it is mostly designed to provoke enquiries, direct response advertising usually contains more information than other advertising.

- Conventionally, it was believed that advertising had a cumulative effect, yet repeated direct response ads produced diminishing returns.

- Successful direct response ads apparently made no attempt to widen the target market. Their messages were addressed solely to the predisposed.

These differences have always been explained by the very different task that is set for direct response advertising. However, we suggest that the way direct response advertising's contribution is measured may be even more influential. The fact is that there is a degree of artificiality and imprecision in the measurement of advertising effectiveness. Now, many of the conventional axioms of advertising are being challenged.

The idea that we react positively only to messages that are relevant has long been accepted in direct marketing.

As direct marketers, we are primarily interested in persuading people – who were already predisposed in our favour – to act now. Like political canvassers, we have learned it pays better to mobilise our voters than argue with those whose votes will probably be cast in favour of our opponents. Our experience (of results) has taught us that appeals which really motivate genuine prospects will always beat messages that try to interest everyone. It has taught us that throwing money at the problem makes no difference to this. Relevance is everything.

WHY REPETITION DOESN'T GUARANTEE RECEPTION

In the heyday of mass media it was most often supposed that advertising effectiveness was largely a product of advertising weight. The assumption was that constant repetition embedded the advertiser's message in the long-term memory of the receiver.

The fragmentation of media audiences and the escalating cost of media coverage have forced advertisers to think again. Few, if any, advertisers can afford to match the media exposure commonly achieved in the 1960s and 1970s. Even when sheer weight of advertising was widely equated with effectiveness, direct response advertisers were dubious about this assumption. Their experience was that the first exposure of a message was often the most effective and that constant repetition produced rapidly diminishing returns.

Most messages are rejected

The fact is that we are all the recipients of many more messages than we can process and store. Therefore we have learned how to select messages that appear pertinent and easy to absorb. Since we are destined to reject the majority of the messages we receive, the correct targeting of messages is more important than their frequency. However, the messages themselves must also signal their pertinence to us very clearly. They need not be pertinent in a strictly economic, practical or logical way, of course. They may simply appeal to our sense of humour or to our imagination in some other way.

Messages that we are willing to process must fit into a system we have already built. This has simplified elaborate ideas into easily understood concepts. For example, a whole system of communications technology, such as a cellular telephone network, is transformed into a simple concept, say a device that makes us easy to reach. Our system wants to categorise concepts, so the cellular telephone may be categorised with other devices that make us easy to reach, like a fax machine, or with other items we use when travelling, like a laptop computer.

A message which gains our interest artificially, perhaps because it features a well-known personality, runs a risk of not being processed for inclusion in our long-term memory or of being mis-filed in the wrong category. Most of us can recall hilarious commercials for long-forgotten products.

Is Heinz soup or is soup Heinz?

When we recall a category, there will be a few attributes or associations that spring to mind. Thus, if the category is soup, there may be top-of-mind associations such as quick, warming and nourishing.

Below this top level, the network of associations will increase and may include types such as home-made, canned and packet soup, and commoner ingredients such as tomato. Beneath this second level there will generally be a third level, perhaps including condensed soup, cold soup recipes and various brands. Clearly, the more closely we position a brand to the top level, the more likely we are to buy it.

A dominant brand, such as Heinz, is likely to be positioned at the second level by a large number of consumers and possibly at the top level by some. Smart advertising people are quick to claim the credit for this. But, while advertising may have played a considerable part in such top-of-mind awareness, it is more likely that a combination of factors have been at work. These include experience of the product range, its association with the most popular flavour (tomato), its dominance at the point of purchase, the logo and so on. The more consistent the impression delivered by all the ways in which the brand communicates or interacts with us, the higher up it will appear in our memory's retrieval system. This is the primary justification for integrated marketing communications.

FORMING BRAND PREFERENCES – IMAGE MATCHING

For many simple commodities, we are not interested in absorbing more information than a few snippets gained from half remembered impressions and possibly inaccurate inferences. At this level we are satisfied to form our brand preferences, generally preferring the familiar to the unfamiliar. We may have one preferred brand and a short portfolio of acceptable substitutes. Only if we have a heightened interest in the category, or we are making what we see as an important purchase, do we want to be bothered with more facts.

This process is sometimes referred to as *image matching* (see Figure 15.1). We become aware of and form preferences for products or brands that match our desired self-image or just appeal to us for reasons we don't attempt to rationalise. These brands form our initial shortlist, even when we make a lengthily considered purchase.

Figure 15.1 Buying decisions – stages in selection

For product categories in which most people are willing to make their purchase decisions on the basis of image matching alone, there may seem no justification for direct marketing communications. Indeed, this would have been the majority view until relatively recently. Yet even the most ubiquitous product category is in reality made up of a number of segments or niche markets.

Direct marketing and special relevance

Buyers of soups will include people who are interested in low-calorie products, people who want vegetarian products, people who are adventurous in their choice of recipes, people who are interested in nutritional information and people who are willing to collect labels for a future benefit.

All of these people will have (at least temporarily) a heightened interest in the category. Many will readily trade some personal information for better product information, recipe ideas or special offers. The act of beginning a dialogue with the manufacturer of a brand will raise that brand to the second or top level in the category's hierarchy, provided that the delivered impression is consistent with expectations and the experience is satisfactory.

It is hard for any brand to retain a substantial market share profitably unless it is represented in the various small segments that make up much of the market and appeals selectively to minority groups of consumers. It is more effective and is becoming less costly to do this than to strive for dominance by the saturation of a single communications medium, such as terrestrial TV, with a single message. By targeting specialised communications to people who are interested, the brand avoids its messages being filtered out. It avoids diminishing returns, but only if there is a strong, consistent element in the various messages it delivers.

CONSIDERED PURCHASES – FACT MATCHING

For many products, particularly in durables and commercial markets, the buying decision process is more complex. Image matching is simply the first stage in a filtering process. Figure 15.1 displays a typical sequence. Although awareness and image matching are shown sequentially, the image matching process will generally begin as we first become aware of a product. Its pack, an advertisement, a press story, its parent (corporate) brand, a recommendation or another message will transmit a signal which we will either discard or use to position the product in some way.

If we are embarking on a carefully considered purchase we will start to collect information, primarily about the products that match up to our image requirements. Any product we have rejected at image-match stage will stay rejected. Products we first become aware of at this *fact matching* stage may also be at a strong disadvantage. We have learned of them at the wrong stage and we may see them as unwelcome intruders.

The way we collect information may be quite haphazard or fairly well organised. The more critical or interesting the purchase, and the closer the intended purchase date, the greater the effort we are prepared to make. To a major extent our research method will be affected by our prior knowledge of information sources. If we intend to buy a car there are magazines tailor-made to provide some or all of what we want to know. If we need motor insurance, we probably know we can find brokers' or insurers' telephone numbers in Yellow Pages or Thomsons Directories. We know holidays are advertised in the classified sections of newspapers and may even know that teletext is a good source of information about cheap flights. In many cases we will know people who have had to make a similar purchase decision and may ask their advice. If we are making a business purchase, the consultative process may be formalised to some degree and we may be required to request a set number of quotes.

Direct dialogue improves the odds

Of course, the user of integrated marketing communications can influence the way we collect information and encourage us to enquire about as few alternatives as possible. This is done by offering further information in advertising, perhaps using an 0800 telephone number or a coupon, to make it easy to request the information. If we are not at fact matching stage yet we won't bother to enquire, of course, but the advertising may still work on us at image-match level.

Because advertisers have recognised the importance of moving prospective buyers effortlessly into the fact matching stage, there has been a massive growth in the number of advertisements carrying response mechanisms. The offer of information not only increases the chances of staying on the prospect's shortlist, it permits the advertiser to control the presentation of the facts. These can now be presented in a style and tone that reflects the imagery of the original advertising. Furthermore, the prospect has identified him or herself to the advertiser, possibly volunteering relevant personal information in the process. Now the advertiser can remain in touch and encourage the prospect to advance to the next stage.

For example, the car advertiser will ask enquirers requesting a brochure, cassette or other offer: *When do you intend to buy a new car? What car do you own at present?* The answers will affect the number, timing and content of future communications from the advertiser.

The fact that the advertiser now has a list of prospects also enables the marketing people to gather information to track the movement of this population towards a purchase and discover, through research, the causes of conversion and defection. This is another example of using a database to undertake superior research sampling.

At the time of writing it must be said that the majority of advertisers fail to do this and many appear not to check the efficiency of their own post room. It is by no means uncommon for prospects to be kept waiting for two weeks or more after requesting a brochure or some other information. We will return to this theme in Chapter 20.

Correctly used, direct marketing communications guide the prospect towards a favourable purchasing decision, adding enormously to the power of the integrated marketer's armoury. The influence of person-to-person communication is immense. Now, probably for the first time, the prospect is actually experiencing dealing with the advertiser. When it goes wrong this influence becomes destructive. It therefore requires careful attention to detail to ensure that service quality is maintained and the prospect will want to move to the next stage.

DEALER SELECTION

When the purchase is completed face to face, the prospect will usually visit a dealer or a branch. The careful advertiser will have made finding the dealer simple. The information sent at fact matching stage will have included a dealer list or, better still, a personalised invitation to visit a specific dealer. Often, when the process is protracted, as in the case of a long-contemplated car purchase, a separate invitation may come directly from the dealer.

This improves the odds of winning the prospect's custom, especially if the competition has been less thoughtful. It also creates a better impression than does a trawl through the local newspaper for dealer ads, most of which will offer inelegantly expressed second-hand car deals. Again, the aim is to make communications consistent with the impression delivered by the advertising that provoked the original enquiry. However, the personal nature of the invitation medium can be used to advantage. Using information supplied by the prospect, the test drive invitation can refer to the specific model in which the enquirer has expressed interest.

We are still referring to Figure 15.1 and we are now at the third level.

TRIAL PURCHASE OR TEST DRIVE

This next stage may take various forms. In the case of a consumable product, a trial purchase may be made. In the case of a car, this stage would usually consist of a test drive. In some cases, the prospect may even have the use of the product for a day or two. A mail order trial purchase may be on free approval for up to 30 days. Depending on the importance of the purchase and satisfaction with the trial experience, the prospect may make an immediate or deferred decision and may or may not try alternatives. Clearly, the deferred decision-maker should receive a follow-up call.

The offer of a trial of a suitable kind reduces the prospect's risk and can make the purchase a more pleasant, less anxious process. It helps to maximise conversion from the enquiry stage and may even increase the number of enquiries if its availability is advertised. If all goes well, the prospect will become a customer. As a customer, first impressions of experiencing the product and any after-sales service will usually prove crucial, although customers who are satisfied after making a complaint will often prove more loyal than the average of all customers.

TRUNCATED PURCHASE DECISIONS

The model shown in Figure 15.1 is illustrative and does not describe the sequence of every considered purchase decision. For example, the retailer or supplier may be selected before the products are shortlisted. The brand imagery of a store such as John Lewis may be much stronger than that of most of the products it stocks. Many of the products may be unbranded or be own-label, as in the case of Marks & Spencer.

The best direct marketers are highly proficient when it comes to provoking truncated purchase decisions, taking direct mail or press advertising readers from ignorance of the advertiser to a purchase decision in one, albeit lengthy, communication. In some cases the value of the purchase may be in hundreds, occasionally thousands, of pounds.

This type of marketing communication (a one-step or one-stage sell) will attempt to deal with every significant sales objection, provide independent testimony of the value of what is being offered and make some kind of trial offer. It deliberately apes the process we have described. The respondent will often refer to the communication again and again before making a purchase decision. For this reason, most one-step advertising appears in newspapers, magazines or direct mail. However, TV is also used, mainly for lower priced items.

Indeed, most examples of this type of communication are for moderately priced items, such as women's outerwear, magazine subscriptions or books. However, expensive collectables, financial service products and holidays are also offered in this way. Increasingly, business products are sold through one-step communications.

THE ESSENCE OF DIRECT COMMUNICATIONS

We have remarked that many advertisements, the majority in many media, offer the reader, listener or viewer the opportunity to respond. This does not necessarily qualify them to be considered as direct marketing communications. The response mechanism may be seen as a service to the audience, allowing those who have entered the fact-matching stage to request more detailed information. However, the performance of the advertising is not judged solely or mainly by the quantity and quality of the response it produces.

Direct marketing communications are different. They are different in being aimed at those who have entered, or are willing to enter, a purchase window. An enquiry-generating advertisement may be aimed at list-builders, people who have begun to take an interest in fact matching within a specific product category, and/or active shoppers, those who are in the immediate market for the advertised product.

Thus the language course direct marketer does not advertise the value of learning another language but targets only the readers already convinced of this. Instead, the direct marketer advertises a simpler, quicker, cheaper or more modern way to learn. The direct marketer's advertisements are measured purely by the quantity and quality of enquiries they produce. Advertisements targeted primarily at active shoppers almost invariably pull in more business than advertisements designed to have a broader appeal.

Figure 15.2 shows a breakdown of those recalling seeing financial ads in national newspapers. Of the 31 per cent of research respondents claiming to recall seeing any financial ad, 9 per cent had no interest, 17 per cent were browsing without an active interest, 4 per cent were list builders (beginning to collect facts in a more organised way) and under 1 per cent were actively shopping for a specific product or solution. Obviously, these percentages would be significantly different for different product groups and in different media.

They might also be affected by season; for example, holiday advertising might attract more active shoppers in January than in May.

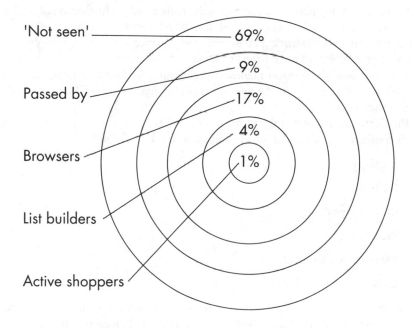

'Not seen' — 69%

9%

Passed by — 17%

4%

Browsers — 1%

List builders

Active shoppers

Figure 15.2 How readers react to financial ads
(Source: Lowe Howard-Spink, 1990)

General advertising is usually assessed on its ability to provoke a comparatively mild reaction from a large segment of its audience. Direct response advertising is measured against its ability to provoke a very strong reaction, in fact action, from a small segment of its audience. What gets measured gets done.

● The first of three salient characteristics of direct marketing communications is that they are addressed solely to those in or close to the immediate target market.

- The second is that their aim is to provoke a response in the form of an enquiry or order.

- The third is that each communication is justified by its individual performance, expressed financially, not by its contribution to a complete campaign.

Direct response provides marketing information

Direct marketing uses a variety of advertising performance measures and these will be covered in the following chapters. The measures that matter are financial. Two common examples are cost per order and advertising ratio. The latter means the cost of advertising expressed as a percentage of the sales value. Ultimately, however, we are concerned with the return on advertising investment. This will be shown over varying periods according to the nature and sophistication of the business. For example, only immediate sales may be taken into account. On the other hand, the return on advertising investment may be measured against the projected lifetime profitability of the customer inflow.

Because each of the direct marketer's messages produces a specific and measurable reaction, it adds to the total of available marketing information. It does this in two ways.

Firstly, the result helps to describe the *effectiveness* of the communication and each component will be examined independently. For example:

- the targeting;

- the offer;

- the message content;

- the timing;

- the creative treatment;

- the size, length or format of the ad.

Secondly, because individuals respond to our ads, they tell us more about themselves. Perhaps all we knew about these individuals before was that they were readers of *The Daily Telegraph*. Now they transfer from being *suspects*, people who were theoretically in the target market, to being *prospects* or *customers*.

In future they may expect to hear from us through the mail or, possibly, by telephone, although they will also continue to be exposed to media advertising. At the time of responding, the new prospect or customer may have volunteered personal information and, in any event, a name, address and postcode provides valuable information, as we discussed in Chapter 5. Most important of all are the facts of the response, the form the response took and the timing of the response.

The purposeful definitions of direct marketing

Figure 15.3 shows how response data helps direct marketers to use purposeful definitions to describe target markets, seeking to differentiate between suspects, prospects and customers. Another way to look at this is that the direct marketer attempts to track people by their buying stage, distinguishing between image matchers, fact matchers, trialists and the more committed customers.

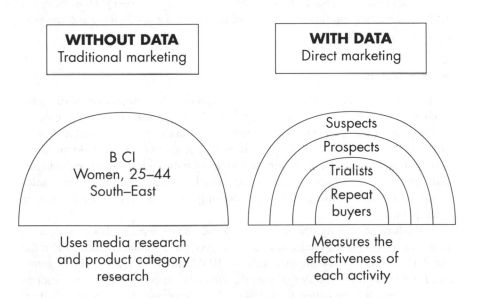

WITHOUT DATA
Traditional marketing

WITH DATA
Direct marketing

B CI
Women, 25–44
South–East

Suspects
Prospects
Trialists
Repeat
buyers

Uses media research
and product category
research

Measures the
effectiveness of
each activity

Figure 15.3 Response data helps to define target markets

The most appropriate media and messages are chosen to perform the right task at the right time. The identified customer or prospect is recognised as a known individual. Meanwhile, information about the source of the prospect's enquiry or the customer's business is fed back into media planning and buying, so that advertising is targeted and negotiated by results, not by theory.

ACQUISITION AND RETENTION

You will remember, no doubt, that when we plan direct marketing communications we think of return on investment.

Market segments are prioritised by potential yield, that is the return on marketing communications investment. Thus established customers are likely to be accorded a higher priority than new business. This causes the planner to think about acquisition and retention as distinct tasks.

The conventional advertising media planner does not usually make this distinction although the role of advertising may be quite different for an established brand in a mature market than it is for a new brand in a dynamic market. It is in the nature of public media that they are not very efficient in reaching established customers (unless the customer base is very large) and, in any event, they do not permit the customer to be recognised and given special treatment. Thus the direct marketer generally prefers to reserve public media for acquisition and use personal media for retention.

Retention media

Table 15.1 lists commonly used retention media. As interactive media gain ground, more office, home and store-based electronic vehicles will be used to permit multi-media personal communications for both acquisition and retention. These vehicles are capable of approximating genuine customer dialogue more closely than direct mail, their immediacy being more akin to the telephone but with important additions. These include touch screen information and order options, moving and still pictures and, possibly, printouts for later reference or redemption.

At the time of writing, the Internet is already being used in this way as are a variety of in-store multi-media devices. However, the eventual combination of the telephone, the personal computer with CD-ROM and the TV offers the opportunity for interaction in a way that puts the customer in control, able to extract as little or as much information as is desired. To what extent the somewhat impersonal nature of the new media may slow down their acceptance remains to be seen. As with all new media, they will almost certainly add to the available choices, not supplant existing media.

PRIORITISING COMMUNICATIONS – AN EXAMPLE

Before getting down to the allocation of resources by individual media, the direct marketer will look at the relative contributions of the main sources of business. Table 15.2 shows the result of making a first rough budget allocation in a hypothetical mail order business with 100,000 customers. The company could be selling anything from plants and garden supplies to clothes or books.

Looking at the profit and loss figures in the right-hand column, we can see the company could have made almost 95 per cent of the projected profit just by concentrating on established customers. However, the result of doing this would be to ensure a shrinkage of the business each year. Therefore, the company is prepared to invest in more speculative activities, even taking a small loss on new business.

Table 15.1 Direct marketing retention media

Catalogues

Magalogues

Newspapers/bulletins

Mailings
  – single-product
  – multi-product

Enclosures
  – statements
  – parcels

Telemarketing
  – outbound
  – inbound

Miscellaneous
  – birthday cards
  – thank you notes
  – invitations, etc

Table 15.2 Prioritising communications: financial priority

Target group	Rough sales forecast	First expend forecast	Cost to sale (%)	Gross profit (@ 20% margin)	Profit/ loss
Customers	£5m	£200k	4%	£1m	+£800k
Lapsed customers	£750k	£75k	10%	£150k	+£75k
Unconverted enquirers	£350k	£52.5k	15%	£70k	+£17.5k
New business	£1m	£250k	25%	£200k	−£50k
Total	£7.1m	£577.5k	9.5%	£1.42m	+£842.5k

Lapsed customers (the second row, reading down) are people who have ordered in the past but not from any of this year's catalogues. Unconverted enquirers (in the third row) are people who have phoned or sent for catalogues within, say, the last 12 months, but have failed to order any merchandise.

Populating the customer base

In Table 15.3 we see the forecast effect of this first rough budget proposal on the number of enquiries and orders received. The plan should increase the active customer base by 7000 or 7 per cent. Just to replace the inevitable losses of established customers 30,000 new or recovered buyers are needed.

Table 15.3 Prioritising communications: by population

Target group	Total size	Number of enquiries	Number of orderers	Gain/ loss
Customers	100,000	–	70,000	(–30,000)
Lapsed customers	90,000	18,000	12,000	+12,000
Unconverted enquirers	60,000	12,000	5,000	+5,000
New business	7,000,000	50,000	20,000	+20,000
Total customers			107,000	**+7,000**

If the customer loss rate is moving upwards, naturally the company will be concerned about this and will be undertaking research-based initiatives to rectify the situation. (See Chapter 19 for more on this.) Meanwhile, we can assume for the sake of this example that the board has set an objective of 15 per cent customer growth and a gross profit contribution of 11 per cent.

The first attempt at the budget produced 11.9 per cent gross profit but on only a 7 per cent growth rate. A model will now be produced to show the effect on profit of securing 15 per cent growth. We can see the result of this in Table 15.4 next to the words 'Second forecast'.

Table 15.4 Prioritising communications: modelling

	Growth rate	Gross profit
Objective	15.0%	11.0%
First forecast	7.0%	11.9%
Second forecast	if 15.0%	then 10.0%
Third forecast	or 11.0%	to hit 11.0%

This model has caused the projected profit to fall to 10 per cent. Now a third model must be produced to show the maximum growth achievable without falling below the Board's 11 per cent profit requirement. This is captioned 'Third forecast'.

Ideas for increasing business

In devising the second and third models, the marketing people will have considered various options for increasing business from each market segment. For example, it will very likely be more profitable to improve the offers made to customers and enquirers than to spend more on advertising.

Table 15.5 illustrates actions that might have been considered. For each action, a separate forecast would be made and the actions producing the highest forecast return on investment would have been chosen. It will be obvious that the more controlled testing experience the company has, the more likely it is to make the right choices.

Table 15.5 Actions to improve growth rates

Customers	Offer a price reduction or free gift to non-ordering customers
Lapsed customers	Mail non-responders again with new offer
Unconverted enquirers	Increase value of offer against first order
New business	Increase coverage and/or frequency of advertising – increase value of offer

This is a simple example of outside-in planning (see Chapter 12) but the principle can be applied, using assumptions, regional tests or econometric models, to marketing budgets that include non-direct response elements.

TO SUM UP

Marketing communications, even when appearing in the same media, may be allocated different tasks. The integrated marketer seeks to ensure, firstly, that each communication performs its task effectively and efficiently and, secondly, that each is instantly recognised as belonging to the same brand, adding to the brand's desirability.

We have looked at two ways of dividing marketing marketing communications into broad groups. The first way was to distinguish between awareness and response communications. The former are designed to increase awareness and assist image matching, enabling prospective customers to associate a brand with a category and a self-image. The latter are designed to provoke a direct response, either by capitalising on established brand awareness or by acting independently of any other influence. Direct response communications may be used at any stage in the buying decision process.

Although awareness communications may carry a response mechanism and response communications may be supportive of the brand image, they should each be so planned and designed as to fulfil their roles effectively.

The second way in which we divided marketing communications was between those that are tasked with acquiring customers and those that are tasked with retaining customers. The latter make use of addressable media, such as the telephone or direct mail, but a great deal of media advertising is also intended to influence established customers. The precise role of any direct marketing communication is always clear and the remaining chapters will continue to draw a distinction between acquisition and retention.

Direct marketing communications work when they are clearly relevant to the interests of those people who receive them. To a great extent, this may well be true of all marketing communications.

Direct marketing communications are (a) addressed solely to those in or close to the immediate target market, (b) with the aim of provoking a response in the form of an enquiry or order, and are (c) justified by their individual performances, expressed financially, not by their contribution to a complete campaign.

The response element in direct marketing communications gives each one a marketing information value as well as a potential financial value. Each acquisition communication adds to our knowledge of what works, but it also introduces us to potential customers who we can now recognise as individuals.

The information produced by direct marketing communications allows us to prioritise investments on an entirely rational basis. The example of a mail order business was used to illustrate this.

16

DIRECT RESPONSE: ATTRACTING NEW CUSTOMERS

IN THIS CHAPTER

The last chapter drew a distinction between customer acquisition communications and customer retention communications. While it might not always be clear whether general advertising is aimed at increasing market penetration or share of customer, direct marketing communications leave no doubt about their intentions.

This chapter discusses customer acquisition only. In particular, it describes the six success factors that are crucial to direct response. As everyone who creates direct response ads knows, these are:

- the product;

- the targeting;

- the offer;

- the format of the ad;

- the creative execution;

- the timing.

The last chapter referred, briefly, to the three salient features that make direct marketing communications special. More briefly still: *direct marketing communications are devised to secure a response from immediate potential buyers and their effect is measured individually in financial terms.*

This description makes it clear that we are not discussing the whole gamut of marketing communications, not even all the communications we may use to pull in new customers. In Figure 16.1 we see potential buying influences that may be left to act independently or will, ideally, be coordinated within an integrated marketing communications plan.

PURE DIRECT MARKETING

If integrated marketing is the ideal, it is nevertheless possible to spend 100 per

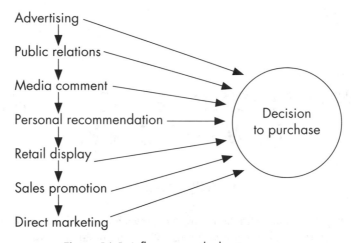

Figure 16.1 Influences on the buying process

cent of the customer acquisition budget on direct marketing communications and achieve considerable success, even market leadership. For years I worked on two brands, Encyclopaedia Britannica and Linguaphone, which were not just the market leaders but also the best known brands in their categories. Yet neither spent a penny on advertising that was not justified by the direct sales it created.

Companies relying solely on direct response advertising most often use direct marketing as the only sales channel, completing all transactions by telephone, by mail or by other remote means. Many services are sold this way: for example, motor insurance, low-cost flights and tickets for concerts or other events. Sometimes manufactured products are also sold exclusively on a direct basis, for example computers, clothing and curtains.

The role of direct marketing communications within the mix will depend on whether it makes most sense to buy direct or, if not, how much information the buyer needs or wants to collect before arriving at a purchase decision.

Anyone contemplating spending thousands of pounds on a luxury cruise will eagerly collect information about cruises and will value the information received. Potentially, there is a substantial role here for direct marketing communications. On the other hand, the same person will place a much lower valuation on information about a hair shampoo and conditioner. Probably only a free sample offer or 50p coupon will be powerful enough to provoke a response and such expensive devices will be used with restraint, possibly only when a new product is launched.

WHY PEOPLE RESPOND – AND WHY THEY DON'T

In an earlier book, *Advertising That Pulls Response* (1990), I advanced the view that 'people respond to advertisements only when the immediate gain in responding exceeds the risk or cost of responding by an acceptable margin, and it appears easy to respond'. Thus far more people will respond to an offer of free information about a product than will order the same product direct from any advertisement. The product is the same but the risk:reward equation is different.

This is not to imply that all two- or multi-step response mechanisms produce superior results to one-step ('buy now') mechanisms. Sooner or later, the potential customer has to make a buying decision and that involves raising the risk and reward stakes. If the buying decision is to be made remotely, it may actually be more efficient to truncate the process and to try to secure an order immediately. The marketer will attempt to work out whether one-step or two-step offers will be more effective (see Table 16.1) but only live testing of each offer will produce the definitive answer.

Table 16.1 Making the choice between one-step and multi-step

- How expensive is the product?
- Does the product need explanation?
- Is it a complex product/service?
- How important is the need for reassurance?
- Will the customer require a demonstration?
- Will a trial be needed?
- Have prospects already been identified?
- Is the product/service difficult to distribute?
- Must intermediaries be consulted?
- How are competitive products offered?

QUANTITY OR QUALITY?

Clearly, the marketer does not want to be deluged with enquiries of doubtful value. These enquiries must be satisfied and simply represent a cost until sales have been made, customers won and the potential value of the prospects established. On the other hand, any attempt to qualify enquiries will usually cost something in lost sales; some potential buyers will be weeded out along with the 'tyre-kickers' when the marketer plays hard to get.

One-step versus two-step test example

If we sell women's outerwear by mail and telephone order, we can test selling a garment off the page in a magazine against soliciting catalogue requests. Let's assume our one-step ad produces 100 orders for a £60 coat at a cost of £20 per order. For each £1 invested in advertising we have pulled in £3 worth of orders.

On the other hand, our two-step ad, because we are reducing the responder's risk, produces 1000 catalogue requests at a cost of £2 each. If 10 per cent of our new potential customers order, we will have the same number of customers at the same advertising cost-per-sale as in the one-step example. So it's a draw, isn't it? No, wait. It cost £1 to send out each catalogue and we used up ten catalogues to get one order, so our total two-step cost per order is not £20 but £30.

In practice, tests of this sort never work out quite so simply. The two-step approach is likely to increase both the number and average value of orders. It will increase the number because the one-step offer would discourage a few genuine potential customers along with the tyre-kicking catalogue collectors. Furthermore, a complete catalogue offers more choice. It will increase the average value of the orders because some people will buy more than one item.

Many more differences of greater subtlety may emerge, not all of them immediately. For example, the one-step customers will be sent a catalogue with their goods and may order from this. Some of the unconverted enquiries from the two-step population may be converted later when the new catalogue comes out. The two ordering populations may exhibit a different propensity to return garments for a refund or a different propensity to recommend friends to buy from the catalogue. Finally, one population may be more loyal than the other.

Adjusting the risk:reward equation

Most users of direct marketing communications do not have a choice of one- or two-step approaches, but it is still possible to make adjustments to the offer so as to increase either the quantity or the quality of response. The one-step advertiser can adjust the risk:reward equation by offering a free trial (see Table 16.2). The two-step advertiser can adjust response upwards or downwards by a whole series of initiatives to increase response or improve quality, as in Table 16.3.

Table 16.2 When free approval makes good sense

- High selling price
- High margins
- Low returns
- Low bad debt risk
- Lifetime value of customer
- More profitable?
- More customers?
- Cash flow no problem
- Admin costs affordable

Table 16.3 Tactics to optimise response rates

Increase response	Improve quality
0800 or Freepost facility	Enquirer pays for call or post
Offer small gift for response	Request telephone number
Use loose inserts in magazine	Use only space advertising
Use 'mail responsive' mailing lists	Use list of people qualified by job title or personal wealth
Depict free brochure	Offer 'further information'
Offer sample or cassette	Ask for personal data
Emphasise reply device	Ask respondent to state which of alternative products is of interest

SUCCESS FACTORS

Although theories and fashions in advertising have come and gone, there has long been widespread agreement about what makes direct marketing communications successful. The direct marketer's ability to test variables individually allows the success factors to be exposed and evaluated independently of each other. You can see a table pretty much like Table 16.4 in any book about direct marketing communications or direct response advertising that has been written in the last 50 years. Not only will the list of success factors be the same, but the items will appear in the same order. The fact is that repeated tests tend to support a particular pecking order of variables in terms of their relative influence.

Table 16.4 Success factors

- Product
- Targeting
- Offer
- Format
- Copy
- Timing

This does not mean that the experience of every direct marketer always supports this league table of influence. For example, timing may be crucial for a highly seasonal product and move up the table in consequence. Furthermore, the best-to-worst range for each variable is immense. The result is that, within any campaign, the best-to-worst range for creative treatments, say, can easily exceed that for targeting.

To bring some perspective into this we might say we would generally expect the best creative treatment to be 50–100 per cent better than the worst. We might expect the best medium to be 200–300 per cent more efficient than the worst. However, we can adopt our best creative treatment throughout the campaign. Unless our campaign is a small one, we can't put all our ads in the best medium. By medium, I mean individual publication, mailing list, radio station or whatever.

THE PRODUCT

Still on Table 16.4, the *product* means the complete package of product, price and any added-value features. We therefore have the freedom to change the product considerably without altering its basic specification. For example, we could offer a computer with software or on its own. We could offer it with a modem or a printer. We might even offer to tailor the product to the precise requirements of the customer.

Direct marketing enables us to test the effect of product variations on response, on sales and, therefore, on marketing costs. Although direct marketers concede that this is potentially the most important success factor, products are seldom tested because product decisions are usually made by people who are ignorant of direct marketing and its scientific methods. The exceptions most often run businesses that depend on direct marketing as their only sales channel.

TARGETING

Targeting is considered at a number of levels. The first level is the choice of media group, for example national newspapers, TV or direct mail. The second level (within these three groups) is the individual medium, for example, the *Daily Mirror*, Central TV or Country Holidays customers. The third level (within these three media) is within-medium, for example early right-hand page, afternoon or visitors to Devon and Cornwall.

Notice that we do not consider size of space or length of commercial here. These are not targeting decisions. They are considered under *format*.

We will be discussing the media of direct marketing in the next chapter.

THE OFFER

By *offer* we mean any feature not built into the product package that can be added to provoke a greater response level. It might be a sample, a gift or indeed anything from a prize draw entry to a buy now, pay later finance scheme.

Just as American business is dominated by lawyers and, as a consequence, US corporations spend enormous sums of time and money on litigation, so British business is dominated by accountants who are preoccupied with avoiding the risks that are the stuff of enterprise. I have never met an accountant who made money for a business until he or she stopped thinking like an accountant.

What brings this small digression on is that the most common mistake in direct marketing (and any other form of marketing) is fostered by a desire to avoid risk. This mistake is to get the risk:reward equation wrong. You will remember that I have said the reward for responding to an advertisement must exceed the risk or cost by an acceptable margin or the audience will simply dismiss the offer as insufficiently attractive. Beyond changing the product (whose ownership is the eventual reward) the only way to tilt the odds in the would-be respondent's favour is for the advertiser to accept more of the cost or more of the risk.

How to sell almost anything direct

Almost anything can be sold by direct response, even by a company previously unknown to the new customer. It simply requires the promoter to make the risk:reward equation sufficiently attractive.

Until the late 1970s it was widely supposed that life and general insurance could only be sold by a determined salesperson. After all, here were extremely low-interest products whose purchase depended on pricking the conscience of the prospect. Yet, by the mid-1980s, many millions of pounds were paid in premiums as a result of direct response ads and mailings. Figure 16.2 shows why.

Direct marketing has created huge markets for books, music collections, videos, outdoor clothing, collectables, magazine subscriptions and many other products simply by adjusting the odds in the consumer's favour. Direct marketing has turned the markets for motor and household insurance and for personal credit on their heads. Direct marketing has provoked current bank account customers (the most loyal customers of all) to switch accounts.

In every case, the success of direct marketing has involved altering the risk:reward equation in the customer's favour. Since the purpose of this activity is not to make an immediate profit, but to maximise the resulting revenue stream, it is entirely logical for the direct marketer to turn the customer acquisition offer into a visible and attractive competitive advantage. The initial offer must help to over-come the inertia that prevents the customer from making the all-important first purchase. After that, inertia may help to sustain the customer relationship.

'To be accepted you must first answer the following list of questions truthfully. We shall then check with your doctor and may also ask for a medical.'

'You will be guaranteed acceptance if you answer the 3 simple questions satisfactorily.'

'You are guaranteed to be accepted if you can answer "NO" to the 4 simple health questions.'

'Not necessary to answer these health questions.'

'We will pay your first month's contributions – up to £50.'

'Free cover for up to 3 months.'

'Send for your quotation today, even if your policy has 6 months to run.'

Figure 16.2 How insurance became a direct-sell phenomenon

Free approval

The simplest way in which direct marketing companies have adjusted the risk–reward balance in the customer's favour has been through free approval. An invoice arrives with the goods and the customer is required to return the goods or to pay the invoice within a specified period. Of course, some customers default. But the supplier benefits by attracting many more orders. Furthermore, the supplier builds a list of customers who have previously honoured their obligations and are likely to do so again.

In the case of two-step offers, the more powerful the offer to respond, the stronger must be the subsequent offer to purchase. That is because the average quality of response will be lower. The payback comes from securing the initial enquiries for less advertising cost and from converting more of them with a compelling offer. By doing these things the advertiser is reducing a fixed cost (advertising) in favour of paying by results.

The variable costs that may be increased are bad debts (free approval), gifts for responding or purchasing, enquiry handling costs, cost of funding postage on returned goods, financing of slowed cash flow and administration expenses associated with invoicing and chasing payments. Like almost everything connected with direct marketing, the offer is susceptible to testing and refinement until the ideal formula (for the moment) is found. Chapter 18 discusses testing.

Prize draws and competitions

One type of offer does not replace a fixed cost with a variable one. That is the prize draw or competition. A prize draw fund is fixed but the same fund may be used to cover a whole year of response generation. The cost may be as low as 10p per response and it is therefore an attractive vehicle for the advertiser. Prize draw entries cannot be conditional on purchase if they are to avoid being classified as illegal lotteries. Only contests involving skill and judgement may be conditional.

Although the offers associated with direct marketing are derived from the use of direct marketing as the sole sales channel, they are equally relevant to other situations. The offer features strongly as a device for overcoming the inertia that gets in the way of response. Offers are the more powerful when they carry a closing date, especially if the closing date is near and specific, not 'reply within 15 days'.

FORMATS

Format describes the physical or temporal attributes of the advertisement, for example the length of the commercial, the size of the ad, the number, size and shape of pieces in the mailing package, and so on.

Small advertisements are better than big advertisements. The most efficient press advertisement format ever devised is probably the classified ad. Much the same applies to TV. If you can convey your message clearly in a ten-second TV commercial, this will usually be the most efficient length even though longer commercials are not *pro rata* but are far cheaper on a per-second basis.

My agency first demonstrated this for AA motor insurance in the early 1980s when conventional thinking was that a direct response commercial had to be at least 60 and preferably 120 seconds in length. The length should always be the minimum needed to allow the viewer to understand and act on the message. This might well be 120 seconds if the viewer has to understand an offer, find it absolutely compelling and order the product from a remembered telephone number or simplified postal address.

If, on the other hand, someone who has just received their motor insurance renewal request wants to know how they can get a competitive quote from the AA, all they want and need to know is the telephone number. Incidentally, saying and showing the number simultaneously (or anything else you need people to remember) is crucial. You can do this in ten seconds.

Even if small is less beautiful, it is more efficient

Space ads do not produce response in proportion to their size either. A good formula to use for forecasting if you have no back data is the square root formula. As a rough average, response will increase by the square root of the increase in size. Thus an ad that is doubled in size will pull, say, about 40 per cent more response (see Figure 16.3). If it does much better, then the original size was smaller than the optimum and something important was having to be left out. If it pulls no more response at all, it may be worth trying a space that is smaller than the regular space as this may already be too large.

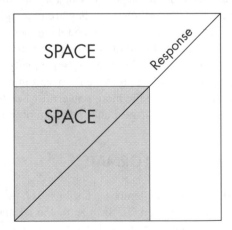

Figure 16.3 Diminishing returns of size and space

A critical difference between press and broadcast media is the amount of information that can be conveyed in a small advertisement. It is not difficult to pack 120 words into a tiny space but the same number of words takes 60 seconds to say at newsreader speed. Print advertising is much more efficient for long messages, complex messages and messages that may need to be referred to later or by someone else.

Many one-step messages require long explanation and/or detailed illustration.

Loose and tipped-on inserts

Inserts, both loose and tipped-on (ie spot-gummed) to the page, are important devices for maximising impulse response and also for breaking away from the format constraints of space advertising. Inserts can range from simple postcards to mini mailing packs; they can include involvement devices such as peel-off tokens, stamps or scratch-'n'-sniff panels. They can increase response exponentially without incurring an increased cost-per-response penalty (see Figure 16.4).

Mailing packages

The most expensive-looking mailing packages are seldom the most efficient. On the other hand, one-piece mailers requiring the recipient to tear along a gummed strip to read the message are seldom the most efficient either. The most important item in almost any mailing pack is the letter, the piece that reinforces the personal nature of the medium. On the whole, the more this looks like a conventional letter the better. Many mailings would benefit by the removal of the main leaflet or brochure. This may make no contribution at all. It is often there simply because no one has had the wit to test leaving it out. Sometimes pictures help, sometimes not.

CREATIVE

Creative denotes words, sound and pictures. Many direct marketing communications are designed around the response device. Although this may seem rather mechanical, a direct response vehicle is wasteful unless it makes it easy to give an intelligible response. More than this, it must also make responding *appear* easy. It is absolutely essential to begin by considering how people will respond when writing radio and TV commercials. Listeners can't see the response device and viewers can't see it unless it is already on screen. Warning would-be responders that a phone number or response address is coming up nearly always increases response.

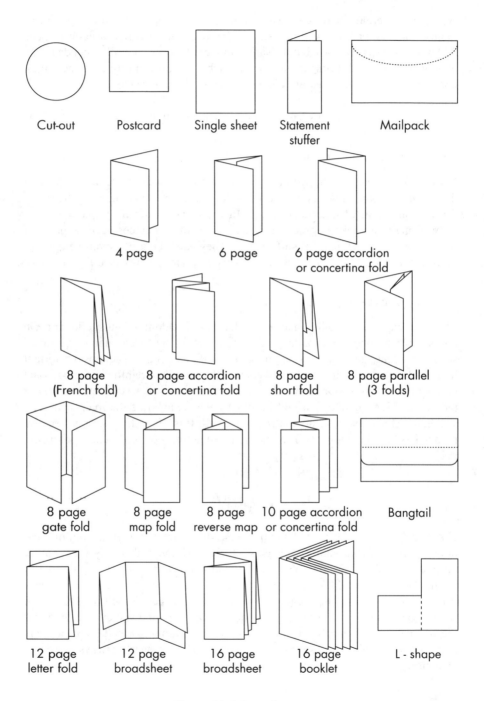

Cut-out   Postcard   Single sheet   Statement stuffer   Mailpack

4 page   6 page   6 page accordion or concertina fold

8 page (French fold)   8 page accordion or concertina fold   8 page short fold   8 page parallel (3 folds)

8 page gate fold   8 page map fold   8 page reverse map   10 page accordion or concertina fold   Bangtail

12 page letter fold   12 page broadsheet   16 page broadsheet   16 page booklet   L - shape

Figure 16.4 Insert formats

AIDA – not just an opera

Although the old AIDA formula is out of fashion in general advertising, it still appears relevant to direct response, most particularly one-step response communications as these are most likely to present something akin to a reasoned case for purchase. The preferred version in direct marketing is AIDCA: *Attention, Interest, Desire, Conviction, Action.*

Attention is generally gained by an appeal to self-interest or (often in the case of fund-raising) a pretty unsubtle tug at the heartstrings. On the whole it pays to be direct and, by gaining attention through an appeal to self-interest, we make it easier to develop interest in what we have to offer quickly – our message is simple and clear.

An appeal to self-interest is not necessarily the immediate statement of a benefit. For example, the letter from your bank that starts 'I only wish I could offer our Gold Card to every customer' is not yet stating a benefit but is attempting to flatter, begin a promise of exclusivity and suggest powerful benefits in a few words.

In the last chapter we referred to the stages of awareness, image matching, fact matching, dealer matching, trial and purchase. A study of some of the best cold direct mail packages will show how these attempt to truncate this process while also following the AIDCA principle. These direct mail packs invite the recipient to match his or her desired self-image with that of the product, often before attempting any logical explanation of why the product is beneficial in any practical way.

Two-step, enquiry-generating communications need not always develop an argument for responding. On the whole, long copy works for one-step direct response because it must overcome every objection to responding. We are back to the risk and reward equation. We may need no persuasion to send for a free holiday brochure but quite a lot to request a visit from a replacement window salesperson.

It is sometimes possible to tell enquirers too much. If their curiosity is satisfied, they are less likely to respond. Long copy tends (although not invariably) to qualify enquiries, not increase them. The Racing Green advertisement in Figure 16.5, seeking catalogue requests, offers an image match (the association of picture and branding says it all) and is designed around the reply telephone number and coupon. The ad is stripped to the bare essentials and commands attention from the right readers.

The purpose of any direct marketing communication is to make a small minority of those who are exposed to it feel so strongly about it that they must respond. This is quite different to most advertising messages. It is a mistake to be bland or attract the wrong people's attention through cleverness. Involvement with the message is only likely to lead to action if that involvement is purposeful. A direct appeal to self-interest, a seductive argument and a generous offer are the essentials. If you look at *The Economist* case in Chapter 21 you will see that Evans Hunt

Figure 16.5 Racing Green advertisement
(Reproduced by kind permission of Racing Green)

Scott's sharp headlines, which connected with other advertising and assisted image matching, were to the point, either stressing savings or free delivery.

TIMING

Timing can refer to season but also to day of week or time of day. Timing in a seasonal sense is a difficult topic on which to generalise, as so much depends on the individual product or market.

For non-seasonal products, the best periods are often early January and early September, perhaps because these are times when we are most likely to forget about the holidays and get down to serious matters. Response tends to fall back gradually after the January peak but July is usually the worst of the summer months, not August. Response often plummets again late in November and December is likely to be the worst month of the year. There appears little difference between consumer and business markets in this general pattern.

We are more responsive early in the week, newspaper ads appearing on Monday and Tuesday usually outpulling ads appearing on other days. The main exceptions are products for which the media owners have created specific market places for their own purposes, for example ads for personal finance and travel mostly appear at weekends.

The best TV slots for response tend to be daytime, but other neglected time segments can also be good. On the whole, peak time is to be avoided unless there is some compelling reason for using it. It has long been the experience of direct response time buyers that wallpaper programming, in which the viewer is not really involved, is preferable. No one wants to interrupt their favourite viewing to dial an 0800 number.

Drive-time is a heavily demanded period by radio advertisers who want to increase their cumulative audience coverage but, again, this is not a favourite for direct response advertisers. Who is going to pull into a lay-by and dial an 0800 number on their car phone?

This discussion of timing leads us into the media of direct marketing and that is our topic for Chapter 17.

TO SUM UP

In this chapter we have reviewed long-held beliefs about what makes direct marketing communications work. Although what is called the marketing literacy of consumers and business buyers keeps increasing, this will not affect the principles, only the style of communications.

We do well to remember the word 'direct' in deciding how to talk with our potential customers. Our aim is to maximise the intake of the right kind of customers and this means engaging their interest for the right reasons.

The need for clarity helps to focus attention on the strength of our proposition. If this forces us to take a long, critical look at our product package and our promotional offer, all the better. Clever formats and good creative work will not save a weak proposition.

The precise style of our communication will depend on whether it capitalises on a powerful brand identity established by other means or whether it is stand-alone direct marketing. In the former case it will work better if it recalls aspects of the established brand personality. In the latter case it can help to create brand awareness but it must be measured against its ability to pull in paying customers.

Although I have admitted the usual pecking order of success factors – the product, the targeting, the offer, the format, the creative and the timing – doesn't always hold good, it is not a bad order in which to consider your alternatives nine times out of ten. Disciplined direct marketers test the most important things first. Testing is discussed in Chapter 18.

17

MEDIA PLANNING FOR DIRECT RESPONSE

IN THIS CHAPTER

Here we are still hungry for new business. Despite our preference for one-to-one customer relationships, when it comes to fishing for new customers we have no particular brief for angling rather than trawling. Thus we have no predilection for the addressable media, direct mail or the telephone, which are the primary media of direct marketing. Our media selection will be governed by the value we are offered for our money. As always, our aim is to maximise the return on our investment.

Direct response advertising plans evolve. They change constantly as fresh empirical evidence replaces older evidence or rational judgements. No grand design will be ruined by making changes, the overall plan being neither more nor less than the sum of its components.

It is crucial to grasp the three fundamental differences between media planning for direct response and conventional media planning. These differences are described at the beginning of the chapter.

DIFFERENCES IN MEDIA PLANNING

Traditional media planning is partly qualitative but depends largely on black-and-white market definitions, for example: 'All 25–34-year-old females are in the target market and are of equal value; all not conforming to this definition are outside the target market and have no value.'

From such a definition, a series of models will be built to show which combination of media delivers the best combination of coverage and frequency for a given sum of money. In practice, some models may be more sophisticated because weights may have been allotted to different market segments in an attempt to represent their relative value. Direct response planning is fundamentally different from this in three distinct ways.

- *The first difference* is that it is based on extrapolations from past results. That is to say, it depends on an assumption that history will repeat itself unless the circumstances are known to have changed.

- *The second difference* is that, instead of attempting to reach a target market with optimal coverage and frequency, the attempt is to allocate financial resource by spending money first where we think it will produce the biggest return, then working outwards from this ideal until it's unprofitable to continue or we run out of money. Little or no account may have been taken of market coverage, frequency, cost per thousand audience or any of the other factors that preoccupy the traditional planner.

- *The third difference* is that each single press insertion or TV transmission is an event in its own right, required to justify its cost by a directly produced return.

USING MEDIA AUDIENCE RESEARCH

Despite these differences, the intelligent direct marketer uses media audience research for three reasons.

Firstly, the relationship between (a) cost of coverage, (b) audience profile and (c) response is important because it provides two points of comparison (a) and (b) between previously used media and so far untried media. To some degree, (c) will be related to (a) and (b), two factors whose values can only be established by reference to research.

We should distinguish here between primary readership and total readership, the former including only the buyer of the newspaper or the person to whom the mailing was addressed, not pass-on readership. Some planners believe secondary readers are of lower value; that is, are less likely to respond.

The second way media audience research helps is in measurement of coverage and frequency. Efficient direct response requires a minimum of duplicated coverage. High coverage, low frequency plans are more productive.

Figure 17.1 shows the effect of adding three additional media to the first one selected. By adding the numbers in the solid part of each column, we reach 80 per cent. This would be the total coverage of the four media if their readerships did not overlap. Because they do overlap, the cumulative coverage is only 50 per cent and the average frequency is 1.6 (80 divided by 50). Average frequency means the number of times the average readers could see an advertisement. It does not mean the actual number of times readers see ads.

Research makes it possible to estimate overlaps, or duplications, like this. The general aim is to maximise coverage at the expense of frequency to avoid the onset of diminishing returns – the number of prospective customers who will respond the first time they see the message is greater than the number of prospective customers who need to see the message three times (or four times) before they

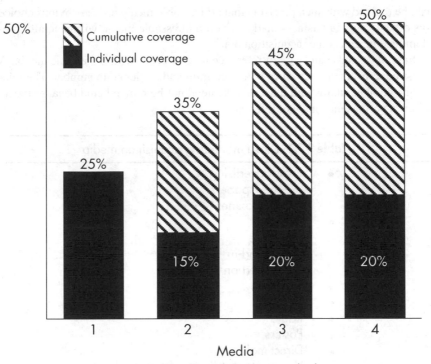

Figure 17.1 The effect of duplicate readerships

will respond. However, the attempt to extend coverage may itself be thwarted if it necessitates the use of additional, less efficient, media.

Finally, media audience research data is used to assess the campaign plan from a pure advertising standpoint. By this, we mean its potential contribution to brand awareness or other objectives. By adding to coverage or frequency within an integrated campaign, the direct response activity may offer a bonus over and above the enquiries or sales directly attributable to it.

MEDIA GROUPINGS

Table 17.1 shows the main groups of media that are used for customer acquisition. In terms of response effectiveness, these media differ greatly.

Addressable media (the telephone and direct mail) are a great deal more effective than non-addressable media. Of the non-addressable media, those which make it easiest to respond are the most effective. By effectiveness we mean response rate, not cost of response. Ineffective media are generally cheaper per thousand audience reached than effective media. Thus, unless the target market can be defined with such precision that addressable media are the obvious choice (as often occurs in business markets) non-addressable media will generally predominate in a customer acquisition plan.

Ease of response and ease of reference tend to occur within the same media. A press advertisement may carry both a coupon and a telephone number. The telephone number, along with other details, need not be remembered because the ad offers a permanent source of reference.

Table 17.1 Direct marketing acquisition media

- Press advertising
  - newspapers
  - magazines
- Inserts
  - loose
  - bound-in
  - tipped-on
- Television
- Teletext
- Radio
- Posters
- Direct mail
- Household distribution (door-to-door)
- Third-party enclosures
- Telephone
- Other interactive media

Media that can't be used for reference

Broadcast media might offer a choice of response methods but they cannot offer a permanent source of reference to the telephone number or address. For this reason, radio and TV are often used as support media, cross-referring to another medium such as Yellow Pages or teletext.

Used as direct response vehicles in their own right, commercials are often either ultra short (say, ten seconds), being used as the equivalent of a very small press space, such as 5 or 10 centimetre double column, or ultra long (at least 60 seconds), this being the only way to communicate as much information as a typical direct response press advertisement. Outdoor advertising sometimes carries a response telephone number but is almost always used as a support medium.

Where the money goes

A very large proportion of all direct response expenditure goes on conventional space advertising in the press – national newspapers, consumer magazines and business magazines.

Regional press media usually perform poorly for direct response unless the advertiser is local or the ad is in the form of a loose insert. Space advertising is a low cost way of conveying and requesting information. The targeting and effectiveness advantages of other media and formats are often insufficient to outweigh this cost advantage. However, most large direct response advertisers employ a mix of media and formats partly to offset potentially diminishing returns from over-use of any media type and partly for insurance – for no obvious reason the relative performances of different media types and formats fluctuate between campaigns.

A rule-of-thumb effectiveness ranking is given in Figure 17.2. This more or less plays back the cost differentials. Since media have to compete with each other, the cost of securing a convertible response from any two media is likely to be much the same on average, though not necessarily so in any one particular case.

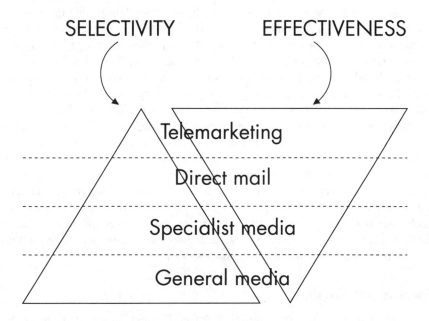

Figure 17.2 Broad distinctions between the main media groups

OFFSETTING DIMINISHING RETURNS

Does advertising on a low budget have any effect on awareness of the product or its image? It's certainly hard to measure. This has created the impression that advertising has a cumulative effect and, therefore, offers economies of scale. This impression has always appeared false to direct marketers. Indeed, the reverse appears to be true if we use as evidence the hard facts of actual response, rather than the soft evidence of marketing research.

Bigger isn't better

In Chapter 16 I pointed out that large space advertisements and long commercials are generally less efficient than small space advertisements and short commercials. The caveat was that this is only true to the extent that the small advertisement or short commercial is the optimum size or length. By optimum, I mean sufficient to offer the audience enough understandable information to act on the message. Clearly, if small is better than big, this is one respect in which advertising offers dis-economies of scale.

Frequency isn't the answer

A second respect in which advertising threatens us with diminishing returns is in frequency. The first or second advertisement in a closely-packed series within one medium will usually prove to be the most effective, all other things being equal. Figure 17.3 makes the point graphically. But what is closely packed? In the case of a rapidly self-renewing market, like motor insurance, a frequency of more than one ad a week will not generally produce diminishing returns. In the case of a once-in-a-lifetime purchase, for example the full *Oxford English Dictionary*, a frequency of four advertisements a year may be enough to provoke diminishing returns. This is most likely to be the case if the market is small in unit terms.

The need to avoid excessive frequency is the reason why direct marketers like to avoid media plans that contain a high degree of duplicated coverage as in Figure 17.1. In direct mail, where both the effectiveness and the cost per contact are high, duplicated coverage is avoided by deduplicating mailing lists against each other. In Chapter 21 we see that over 70 per cent of the recipients of a Martell mailing recalled receiving it. Duplication in this circumstance would be ineffective for the advertiser and irritating to the recipient.

Formats with firepower

One way in which advertisers attempt to offset diminishing returns from excessive frequency is to use high-performance formats, such as tip-ons (inserts spot-gummed to a page ad) and loose inserts. These will often pull much higher

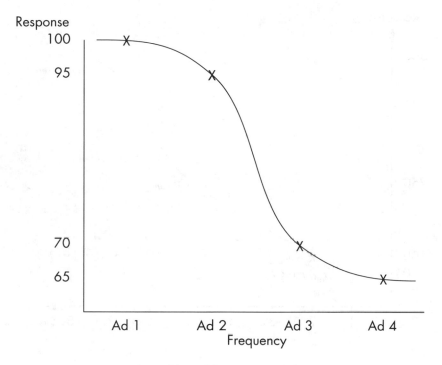

Figure 17.3 The problem of frequency and diminishing returns

volumes of response from the same media without the cost-per-response penalty incurred by continually increasing the size of space (see Figure 17.4).

The snag is that, because they pull large response volumes, they must be used at very low frequency. Furthermore, because they also tend to pull more impulse response, the average quality of response may be lower than for a conventional space advertisement.

Duplicated coverage is a real problem because inserts, being high response vehicles, suffer from its effects more quickly than space ads. One solution is to distribute the leaflets door to door instead of inserting them in newspapers or magazines. This may or may not prove more cost-effective depending on the relevance of the targeting opportunities in the product's target market. It may, for example, be easier to characterise the prospective customer as a reader of *The Sunday Times Magazine* than as the occupant of a detached house in a leafy suburb in Surrey. If so, then dropping inserts in *The Sunday Times* is likely to work better than dropping them in letterboxes. Direct response enables us to test to find out rather than waste hours in learned discussion. The testing process produces the right answer, too.

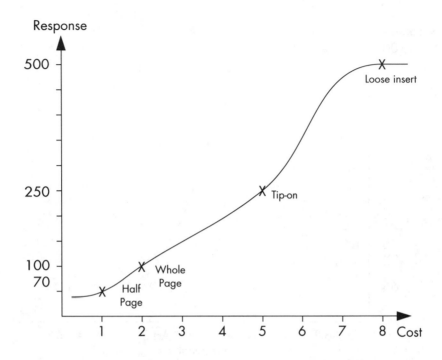

Figure 17.4 Using inserts to overcome diminishing returns

Although there can never be a foolproof way of avoiding diminishing returns, the canny direct marketer finds ways of offsetting them by using a combination of media groupings, formats and, of course, incentives to respond or buy. By doing these things we can acquire more new business before exceeding the marginally acceptable cost per new customer.

Non-standard media

Being primarily concerned with response, the direct marketer does not eschew oddball or unglamorous media opportunities that are overlooked by media research. What the direct marketer wants, above all, is a good deal. Thus inserts may appear in statement mailings, water company bills and mail order despatches. Direct response advertisers may use affinity magazines (read by customers of another company), professional journals for consumer advertising and many other media the classically trained media planner will ignore.

Each advertisement or insert in a new medium is regarded as a test. If it fails, the new medium will be discarded after one insertion or renegotiated at an acceptable rate. The approach is more pragmatic than scientific – a poorly targeted advertisement may show an acceptable return if it is bought cheaply enough. Media that conventionally trained planners ignore are likely to offer a good deal because they find it difficult to sell space.

Addressable media

The role of direct mail and telemarketing for customer acquisition is most frequently as the fulfilment media – the vehicles for offering further information once other media have generated the enquiry. However, direct mail in particular may play a significant role as a new business generator, either by stimulating enquiries or, very often, by attracting orders, applications or free trial requests.

At, say, 50 pence per recipient, direct mail may cost 40 times as much per primary 'reader' as a colour page advertisement. However, almost every recipient may read some or all of the message and many will spend minutes studying it, shuffling the pieces and becoming sufficiently involved with it to remember the contents fairly clearly in a month's time. More importantly to the direct marketer, the recipient is many times more likely to respond to it. Furthermore, the mailing package can contain far more information in words, pictures, sounds or samples.

Whether these advantages are sufficient to justify the high unit cost may depend on the relevance of the message to the recipient. This in turn will depend on whether the methods used to target direct mail are appropriate to the case. Can the prospect be characterised by previous purchasing behaviour, by lifestyle group, by membership of an affinity group, by job title, by size of employer's company or by residence within a store's catchment area? These are some of the material questions. Direct mail targeting that is informed by some aspect of the recipient's previous purchase behaviour is especially powerful.

The telephone is an even more powerful medium and its intrusiveness demands that its use, particularly for customer acquisition, needs to be tempered with discretion. A particular value of the medium is that it offers two-way communication. This suggests three applications:

1) discovering and correcting business decision-maker details prior to mailing;

2) making pre-announced follow-up calls to mailings;

3) qualifying enquirers for sales visits and making appointments.

WHEELING AND DEALING

There is considerable scope for securing discounts against advertising rates in non-addressable media. As a rule of thumb this scope is highest when the charge is only loosely related to the cost, as in press space advertising, and lowest when the cost of providing the service pretty directly determines the price charged, as in door-to-door distribution.

The direct response advertiser estimates the value of each opportunity to advertise and deals accordingly. Providing that the same medium has been used previously, its estimated value will usually be accurate. The best results typically come from using a media independent, that is a specialist media buying organisation with extensive direct response planning and buying experience, and empowering this organisation to contract for enough advertising to bring in the required volume of response within pre-agreed cost-per-response parameters. This is done by agreeing response forecasts in advance of negotiations with the media.

Much direct response advertising is negotiated almost literally at the last minute but some may need to be reserved well in advance (because of potential availability problems) and may be subject to volume discounts.

Direct mail offers little scope for dealing. Advertisers may do *net names* deals with list owners from whom they rent mailing lists, paying only for the names they actually use from a gross quantity ordered. The opportunity for this arises because lists are deduplicated against one another so that no one gets mailed twice. However, the cost of a list is only, say, 20 per cent of the total cost of a mailing. Cost control is therefore exercised by ensuring that mail is posted at the lowest available rate (for pre-sorted mail) and that print costs are competitive. Mailing lists are also available via intermediaries capable of providing a planning and buying service. These are list brokers.

RESULTS ANALYSIS

This is the key to successful planning and buying. It may be carried out in-house or it may be done by the media independent. Both organisations will be the source of some of the data that will be recorded. The information will be accumulated over time and provide the back data on which future planning decisions can be based. It will help answer questions such as:

- Which of our advertisements work best in which newspapers?

- What are the trends in response – by medium, media group, period, size, copy, offer?

- Which days of the week are best for daily newspaper advertisements?

- How much extra is it worth paying for guaranteed front- or back-page positions?

- How do competitive ads affect our results?

- What is the most efficient newspaper space size or TV spot length?

- Is it more efficient to use colour pages or loose inserts?

- What effect does Freepost or an 0800 number have on response and conversion rates?

Because, as we remarked earlier, each single advertisement is an event in its own right producing evidence of its relative effect, we can collect a large body of information quite quickly. This depends on the meticulous recording of information, both the results achieved and the circumstances leading to those results. Table 17.2 is typical of good practice.

Table 17.2 Recording of results

• Product	• Offer	• Copy/creative treatment
• Medium/station	• Date	• Circulation/audience rating
• Size/length	• Position/time	• Ratecard cost
• Cost paid	• Production cost	• Total cost
• Identifying code	• Response total	• Response by phone
• Response by fax	• Response by post	• Cost per response
• Conversions (total)	• Conversion %	• Conversions (by response type)
• Forecast response	• Forecast conversions	• Forecast conversion %
• Sales value	• Ad:Sales cost ratio	• Variance vs forecast %
• Competitors (number)	• Competitors (who)	• Weather

There may be variations to these items depending on the circumstances of the advertiser and the media used. For example, some telephone responses to broadcast media can be lost because blips cause the call volume to exceed the call centre's handling capacity. If the number of lost calls is not recorded, management may base future decisions on specious information, being unaware of the true problem.

Results analysis may use classification data to help identify patterns and to make results easier to understand. For example, press media will usually be classified by type, such as daily newspapers, women's weeklies and so on. Broadcast media analysis will use day part and door-to-door distribution analysis will use postal regions or postcode sectors. Classifications of this sort may reveal patterns that would otherwise be obscured by detail.

Results analysis and league tables

Figure 17.5 shows a fragment of a results analysis report. We can see that this is a ranking report in which the advertisements have been removed from the date order in which they would have originally been shown and reassembled in order of their efficiency, measured by advertising cost per £100 sales. This is, of course, only one measure of efficiency. Another would be cost per new customer and this might take precedence if we were more concerned with ongoing business than immediate return on advertising investment.

Publication	Size	Cost (£)	Sales (£)	Cost per £100 sales (£)
The Star	10 x 2	2195	14,000	15.65
The Times	10 x 2	863	4875	17.70
Independent	10 x 2	1306	4485	29.11
Daily Mail	10 x 2	7186	23,560	30.50
The Sun	10 x 2	10,749	34,800	30.89
Daily Express				

Figure 17.5 Response analysis – press: October 1996

The example shown is fairly simple. We could elect to have more headers across the top of the chart to add other pieces of information such as average sales value or sales per thousand circulation. If the cost of handling responses were significant, we would need to add this to the cost of each advertisement to produce a total customer acquisition cost. Even given the limited number of headers we have chosen, it is possible to gain a great deal of useful information from the analysis, serving it up in a wide variety of forms.

Analysis of addressable media adds a further dimension. As we saw in Chapter 5, the selection of a mailing list may be only one of several selection criteria for addressable media targeting. Thus results analysis will, ideally at least, compare responders with the mailing base, using such factors as job title, company suffix (Plc, Ltd, Partners, etc), postal area and so on. Or, for consumer lists, factors such as gender, title and address type could provide good information. Careful analysis will permit accurate selection *within* lists for future campaigns, not simply selection *of* lists.

Our analysis will give a good general impression of what is working most efficiently. However, it is unlikely that it contains no biases. For example, *The Daily Globe* may appear to be the best medium simply because we placed our most effective ad in the *Globe* more often than we did in the *Comet*. Perhaps the *Globe* ads appeared on Mondays and Tuesdays (our most responsive days) more often than the *Comet* ads. To be absolutely sure we know what is working best, we must either weight the results to remove such biases or, better still, test each critical variable independently. In the next chapter we consider testing.

TO SUM UP

Although the wheeling and dealing is generally best left to those who specialise in it, the process of direct response planning is inextricably linked to marketing. It is about acquiring customers and selling products.

There are three ways in which direct response planning differs fundamentally from conventional advertising media planning:

1) It includes results forecasts that are based on extrapolations from past results.

2) It prioritises actions by projected return on investment.

3) It treats each advertisement in each medium as a separate event that must be justified by its individual contribution.

The business of planning and buying is essentially pragmatic. Value for money is what counts. The direct response media buyer will cheerfully buy space in the 'wrong' newspaper if the discount is big enough.

Most customer acquisition campaigns have an optimum level. This is set by the optimum format, the optimum frequency and the number of media that can be relied upon to produce good results. Beyond this optimum level results begin to suffer. Ideas for new offers, media, formats and creative treatments are tested in an effort to counteract diminishing returns.

The planner will use any medium that seems appropriate. Planners like to avoid having too many eggs in one basket as media and formats grow tired easily. Media that carry ephemeral messages, such as TV, radio and posters, are at a disadvantage compared with media that stay around the home or office. However, this will not prevent their use providing they offer value for money.

In this chapter I have deliberately avoided any reference to secondary advertising objectives, such as establishing awareness of the product. It is impossible to meet two objectives without compromise. That is why integrated marketing communications plans allocate roles to specific activities.

18

CONTINUOUS LIVE TESTING

IN THIS CHAPTER

Except in the most fraught of circumstances, perhaps when your future is riding on the result, testing is the most fun you can have in direct marketing. For every occasion when you can say, 'I knew that would happen,' there is at least one other when you have to admit that the result is a complete surprise. Fortunately, human response is not easily predictable.

This chapter follows on from the last because we are still concerned with recording and analysing results. It also follows on from Chapter 7 because it was in that chapter that the idea of split-run testing and the formulae for establishing confidence intervals were introduced.

In this chapter we take a practical look at testing. What should we test? What are Terry Forshaw's seven benefits of testing? How should we test? Should we adapt the formula for multi-way splits? How should we assess test results from low response media? All will be revealed as you read on...

A direct marketing campaign has been described as a series of events, each with its own outcome. Let's say the event is a 15 centimetre double column (15 dc) advertisement in a daily newspaper. What will be the immediate outcome? Naturally, we expect it will be a number of responses. We expect, too, that the eventual outcome will be a smaller number of customer relationships, each with its own value. These outcomes will be affected by the newspaper selected, the product/package featured, the promotional offer, the size of space, the page and position, the week of the year, the day of the week, the advertisement copy and design and, possibly, other factors outside the advertiser's control, such as competitive ads, the weather and so on.

Recalling Chapter 7, you can think of the outcome as the dependent variable. It depends on at least ten contributing factors, or independent variables, in the case of our 15 dc ad. Thus the mere fact of knowing the outcome does not make it easy to guess the outcome of the next event. Because most of the independent variables recur in many separate events, the response analysis we referred to in Chapter 17 can help to unscramble the effect of each one. This will usually be obvious from looking at a table. However, if it is not, we can use a modelling technique of the type featured in Chapter 7.

Our response analysis is limited to examining the variables we have introduced.

Each introduction represents a risk. We don't want to keep repeating this risk just to collect enough evidence, so we need a purer form of testing to give us a quick result cheaply.

The purpose of testing is therefore to find ways of improving the outcome while minimising the cost of making mistakes. To conduct a test, we select one variable at a time, choosing one that we believe plays a significant part in determining the result. Against this variable we test an alternative possibility that we believe might produce a better result. The isolated variable is called the control and the alternative is called the test. The testing process being continuous, the control is usually the winner of the last test.

WHAT TO TEST?

Except at test market stage, it will be necessary to keep test expenditure to a minority of all marketing communications expenditure, leaving the outcome of the majority of expenditure as predictable as possible. Usually, testing occupies between 10 and 20 per cent of the total and, therefore, priorities for testing must be established.

There are two bases for doing this. The first is to select the most significant variables more often than the least significant. Some may not warrant testing at all. The most significant variables are more likely to be near the top of this list:

- *product/package* – the combined product, specification and price offer;

- *targeting* – the media or database selection;

- *offer* – the promotional offer, for example free brochure, video or sample;

- *format, size or length* – type of mailing pack, space size, spot length, etc;

- *creative treatment* – for example headline, illustrations;

- *timing* – week of year, day of week, time of day, etc.

Selecting alternatives for testing from near the top of the list ensures that the chances of making changes that have a real impact are increased. Furthermore, the tests are more likely to produce results that are statistically acceptable as the differences between test and control are likely to be maximised.

The second basis for awarding test priority is the presumed strength of the alternative to be tested. High priority might be awarded to an alternative that has been suggested by marketing research or by continued and, therefore, presumed successful competitive usage. On the other hand, an apparently original idea might be selected purely because it seems peculiarly apposite. There is nothing wrong with intuition when there is also some logical reason why the idea should work.

THE LOGIC OF TESTING

In *The Practitioner's Guide to Direct Marketing* (1992), Terry Forshaw lists seven benefits of testing as follows:

1) Minimises financial risk – by restricting outlay and coverage.

2) Protects your greatest asset, customers – by restricting exposure.

3) Helps to maximise response – by replacing weakness with strength.

4) Helps to trim costs – by helping to find cheaper solutions.

5) Validates research – quantifies qualitative research findings.

6) Predicts the future – assists accurate forecasting.

7) Stimulates creativity – provides a spur to development.

Possibly the most important benefit of all is the last one. Direct marketers get to use ideas that would have been ruled out if it were impossible to test them cheaply. Testing paves the way to continuous improvement. The odds favour it. If four ideas are tested and only one succeeds, the gains made from the one success will usually recover the whole of the loss made on the three failures.

TYPES OF TEST

There are two types of test: those that are based on perfect random samples and those that are not. The former are called split-run tests or *n*th name tests. Printing two alternative advertisements for the same product in alternate copies of the same newspaper is an example of a split-run test. Because only two alternatives can be tested, it is called an A/B split-run. Testing a new mailing package by sending it to every tenth name selected from a mailing database (sending the control to the other nine names) is an example of *n*th name testing.

A/B split-run tests can be run in most national newspapers and some magazines. Because these publications are printed two-up, that is simultaneously on two machines, it is possible to print two different advertisements for the same product in alternate copies of the same newspaper. Clearly, the same applies to loose inserts, providing that they are supplied by the printer in A/B sequence. When it is not possible to secure an A/B split-run, an advertiser may place ad A in the northern edition of a newspaper and ad B in the southern edition in week number one. In week number two, ad B runs in the northern edition and ad A in the southern edition. The percentage of the total response attributable to each ad is then used to decide the winner.

The telephone response problem

As more direct response is received by telephone and less by mail than was once the case, the correct attribution of response is becoming more difficult to achieve. Telephone response ads usually carry a response code or key number and the responder is asked to quote this. Unfortunately, the responder may not have the ad handy. It is easier to test different media than different ads in the same medium because the operator can ask where the ad was seen. It is easier to test split-run ads that make different offers than split-run ads where the only change is to the headline. That is because the operator can ask which offer the respondent is requesting. On the whole it is a good idea to repeat a test at least once, particularly when a fair proportion of the response is received by telephone.

When to use random sample tests

Random sample testing can be used for testing items 1, 3 and 5 on our list of six variables: (1) product/package, (2) targeting, (3) offer, (4) format, (5) creative treatment and (6) timing. It can also be used for testing item 2, as long as we are testing an addressable medium. That is to say, we can test a mailing list or a tele-marketing list by contacting every *n*th name on the list. But we cannot limit an ad in the *Daily Mirror* to every *n*th copy. To test the *Daily Mirror*, we must take a national or regional edition space.

In direct mail we can also test item 4 on a random sample basis. But we can't test different sizes of advertisement in alternate copies of the same newspaper. We can't random sample test alternative sizes of loose insert either, because they cannot be interleaved in A, B order as they leave the printers. In broadcast media we can't random sample test anything.

When random samples can't be used

No other form of testing is as accurate as random sample testing. However, media tests and format tests are sufficiently important for direct marketers to put up with the inadequacies of alternative testing procedures.

A medium such as a newspaper or a radio station has to be tested as an entity. However, the advertiser who uses loose inserts can contract for a test run in news-papers and magazines. This test run must be in consecutive issues, so it does not provide a random sample. The sample is likely to be regional, perhaps being con-fined to one or two wholesale distribution areas, so is likely to be biased. Further-more, because magazines and newspapers are distributed on a sale-or-return basis, there is a danger that some of the test inserts may be in unsold copies. Whenever random sampling is not a possibility it is advisable to run the test more than once before committing to a roll-out.

The user of door-to-door leaflets may specify a series of postcode sectors in different regions to add stability to a test and will probably specify types of area, using geodemographic profiling or other information. Although the sampling technique is not random, it is akin to quota sampling commonly used in market research and is fairly reliable.

Users of loose inserts, direct mail and door-to-door distribution are not confined to A/B split-run tests when it comes to testing the offer or the creative treatment. They can run A–H tests if they want, providing the sample sizes are sufficient. Most leaflets will be printed, say, 8-up (eight to a sheet) and there is no reason why all eight images need be the same. This facility is extremely useful when there are many feasible alternatives to test and it is used occasionally for testing advertisement headlines. Although the headline may be destined for use in a space advertisement, seven alternatives can still be tested against the control headline by printing each on an insert, split-run on an A–H basis.

Multi-way test procedures

In Chapter 7 reference was made to the sample size formula for ensuring that results are acceptable to a given confidence level. The magic numbers used (1.645 for 90 per cent and 1.960 for 95 per cent confidence) hold good for two-way tests but not for the increased risk of rejecting losers wrongly in multi-way tests. The following adjustment is recommended:

n-way tests when n =	Confidence level	
	90%	95%
2	1.645	1.96
3	1.92	2.21
4	2.06	2.37
5	2.16	2.47
6	2.23	2.55
7	2.28	2.59
8	2.31	2.62

As well as testing a number of alternatives at the same time, we can also simultaneously test different elements. For example, we might want to test two new mailing package variants against the control pack while also testing a low- and a high-value incentive to respond, both being A/B/C tests.

Mailing pack:	No gift	Low-value gift	High-value gift	Total quantity
Control:	5000	5000	5000	15,000
Test A:	5000	5000	5000	15,000
Test B:	5000	5000	5000	15,000
Total:	15,000	15,000	15,000	45,000

By testing two elements, the mailing package and the offer, simultaneously we can cut the total test quantity. Had we run the tests separately, needing 15,000 samples, we would have tested 15,000 of pack A and 15,000 of pack B against 15,000 of the control mailing – that is 45,000, all with no offer. Using the same 15,000 control mailings we would then have tested an additional 15,000 with a low-value incentive and another 15,000 with a high-value incentive, adding a further 30,000 to our mailing quantity.

By combining the tests of the two elements, we can cut the mailing quantity from 75,000 to 45,000 without reducing the sample sizes. Furthermore, we have built in a check against the possibility that there may be interactions between the offer and the creative elements. This is not very likely, but would certainly be a possibility if the two tested elements were price and targeting.

TESTING WHEN RESPONSE RATES ARE LOW

Earlier, in Chapter 7, we warned that the confidence level test of sample size does not work when response rates are very low (below 0.1%). This applies in the case of almost all space advertising and all other advertising in which either the response rates are low or testing must be regional. Broadcast advertising qualifies on both counts: response is low and we must test in two regions or on two non-terrestrial channels. The statistical tool used in this situation is one already mentioned when discussing tree-segmentation in Chapter 7. This is the chi-squared test. To apply this test we must first add up the response to both A and B halves of the split-run. Then we calculate how many per cent either A or B (whichever is the larger) is of the total. Finally, we need to decide if we want to work to 90 per cent confidence or 95 per cent.

	Significant % share for confidence level of:	
Total response	90%	95%
100	60	61
150	58	59
200	57	58
250	56	57
400	55	$55\frac{1}{2}$
600	54	$54\frac{1}{2}$
1000	53	$53\frac{1}{2}$

The figures in the two right-hand columns indicate the percentage of the total response that the more successful half of the split-run has to reach before we can be confident the same ad would win either nine times out of ten (a 90 per cent probability) or 19 times out of 20 (95 per cent). The figures in the left-hand column show the level of total response to which these percentages apply. Thus, if total response is 200, we need the winning half of the split-run to achieve 114 replies to give us 90 per cent confidence it would win again. For 95 per cent confidence, it would have to reach 116 replies.

It seems only fair to add that few practising direct marketers of any experience actually believe tables like the one above. Most prefer to try tests two or three times if possible. The statistics may not lie, but funny things happen in the printing and distribution of newspapers, leaflets and magazines.

One direct marketing agency noticed that York kept recurring as the least successful area for direct mail in almost all of its clients' results. With clients in many different businesses, they naturally realised the odds were heavily against this and were able to work out the real reason. It was that direct mail packs are assembled in postal sort order to qualify for pre-sorted mail discounts. If there is a shortfall of, say, brochures, the packs at the end of the run will either go out incomplete or be rejected. Since York begins with Y and no postal region begins with Z, York got short shrift. The solution was to prioritise this under-mailed region and, presumably, give the over-mailed Aberdonians a break. Of course, these things should not happen but it is a condition of printing contracts that the supplier may over- or under-supply by a small percentage margin.

THE VALUE OF A COMMITMENT TO TESTING

Enthusiasm for testing has apparently diminished in recent years. There are several reasons for this. Firstly, testing focuses on immediate response and this may not be the sole, or main, purpose of a marketing communication. Secondly, the increased percentage of telephone response may make test results more dubious and certainly makes tests harder to organise, because call centre staff training is involved. Thirdly, curious or inconsistent results are sometimes obtained for reasons we have already considered, such as returned copies and printing errors.

These are, of course, all excuses. None of them are valid reasons. If we believed in their validity we might as well stop counting our response, our new customer acquisitions, our sales and our profit. First, let us deal with the excuse that testing focuses purely on immediate response. The fact is that testing accelerates our learning rate. It is inconceivable, if headline A pulls twice as many replies as headline B, that it is not also the basis of a superior advertisement in other respects. It either grabs more people's attention, or it encourages more people to read the copy, or it is more persuasive. Probably all three.

Now let us knock aside the second excuse, the telephone. Some of the most committed users of testing are the more scientific of the direct insurers. These direct marketers are only interested in telephone response. Their ads, whether on TV, radio, in newspapers or on door-to-door leaflets, do not carry postal addresses. The only way to respond is by telephone. Yet they can, and do, use split-run and other testing techniques to deliver continuous improvements to efficiency. This requires dedicated training, briefing and control of call handling. It is difficult but worthwhile.

The third excuse is inconsistent or odd results. Experience shows that A/B splits when the value of A is more than twice the value of B (or the other way round) are by no means rare. Differences of 50 per cent or more are commonplace. When differences of such value can occur, it makes no sense to deny oneself the opportunity to increase the return on marketing investment so easily. Besides, tests can be repeated or extended if their validity is in doubt.

One suspects there may be a hidden agenda tucked away somewhere and the real reason for the marked absence of testing from many campaigns may be a fear of being proved wrong. If so, it is a pity because tests can add interest, knowledge and excitement. Only one new idea in three or four needs to be a winner for the test programme to show a handsome profit. Meanwhile the losers provide learning experiences.

TO SUM UP

Testing is used in direct marketing because we accept that a campaign is the aggregate of a series of events, each with its own outcome. These outcomes are affected by a number of variables. By eliminating the interference of all except one of these variables, we can measure the effect of each variable in turn. Our preferred method is to use random sample testing. When we can't do this, we will test as best we can, but we will still test.

Our testing is similar to clinical trial procedure. It provides a superior basis for estimating future results than does marketing research or econometric modelling, although it will not, of course, measure side-effects of direct response activity, such as its influence on non-responders.

19

KEEPING CUSTOMERS

IN THIS CHAPTER

In an ideal world we would keep all our customers for ever by satisfying their every whim completely. We do not live in an ideal world and, wearing our marketing communications hats, we are obliged to keep customers for longer than we strictly deserve, extracting as much business as possible from them before they defect to a competitor.

While admitting that share of customer and customer lifetime value objectives depend on a commitment to giving value, we must also seek marginal gains by outsmarting the competition. In this chapter we will see how a series of principles, ploys and practices can help the marketer to capture an unfair share of the customer's wallet.

The words *'customer lifetime value'* somehow suggest that customer relationships are loyal and prolonged. In a few markets this may still be true, but not in most. The shopper for women's clothing will, on average, give less than one-third of her business to any one retailer over any six-month period. Doubtless, she does not see herself as being disloyal. She might describe herself as a loyal Marks & Spencer customer because she has shopped there regularly for years. But this does not oblige her to buy everything she needs from one retailer. Why should it?

On the other hand, unless she can afford to keep two or three cars in her garage, she will stick to one make at a time, her loyalty being tested only when the time comes to trade in the old model. If she is a resident of the United States, there is a near 90 per cent probability that she will have pronounced herself satisfied with their last purchase, yet a 70 per cent probability that she will defect to another maker's car next time.

The notion of customer loyalty is important to marketing people but not, on the whole, important to customers. They don't think in these terms. They don't actively seek relationships with suppliers. They don't see why they shouldn't accept a good offer from a new supplier just because they are satisfied with their present one. Such an attitude is typical of consumers and not uncommon among business buyers.

PRINCIPLES OF RETENTION AND DEVELOPMENT

Many companies like to think they manage customer relationships. Some even charge executives with this task, awarding each with a suitable job title such as *'Customer Relationship Manager'*. Of course, the awarding of such a title may simply confirm the employer's predilection for hierarchies, the customer relationship manager appearing halfway up the organisation chart and the customer at the bottom. The idea that the customer not only pays for the organisation but also manages the business relationship has little appeal to those whose keys open the door of the executive washroom.

An increasing number of companies, one example being the American-owned credit card provider, MBNA, require senior executives to spend time listening in on customer telephone calls on a regular basis. The calls may be concerned with queries, complaints or sales. Whatever the purpose, listening in reminds managers what customers are like and what it is like to be a customer. In fact, MBNA have signs up in their offices saying: *'Think of yourself as a customer.'*

Research-based customer satisfaction scores are not predictive of loyal behaviour. Although part of the problem may be imperfect research methodology, the major part of the problem is that mere satisfaction is not enough in either of two situations that are certain to arise sooner or later. The first of these two situations is a *crisis*. A crisis can occur when a complaint is unresolved, a delivery is delayed or a member of staff fails to keep a promise. It can also occur, through no fault of the supplier, when the customer moves or changes jobs.

The second situation that will certainly occur, sooner or later, may also disrupt a satisfied-customer relationship. It is a *competitive offer*. This may not be directly competitive; it may just be any alternative way to spend the time or the money. But usually it will occur when a competitor offers a new, more exciting or cheaper alternative. To resist such disturbances, something more than mere satisfaction is required.

Customer commitment and customer dependency

This may be either increased *customer commitment* or increased *customer dependency*. Increased customer commitment is produced when customer expectations are raised and delivery matches or exceeds the new, heightened expectations. Customer commitment is thus the product of high expectations plus high satisfaction. High satisfaction is not enough if our expectations are low. An unreliable courier service will lose the business. But a reliable courier service may also lose the business unless it finds ways to keep adding value to its basic service.

Customer expectations may be raised as a result of product innovations, superior terms or service improvements. To work, these improvements must be communicated to customers. They may, of course, not be offered to all customers. They may only be offered to customers whose forecast profitability merits special terms or service. Marketing communications to keep customers informed and raise expectations will generally be grouped together as *customer care* communications.

Alternatively, increasing *customer dependency* also makes the severance of the relationship less likely. This is usually achieved by cross-selling; that is, getting the customer to buy a second product line. Again, there is a role for marketing communications, but this time they will be *sales promotion* communications, expected to pay off on the basis of the direct sales value produced – almost certainly without reference to enhanced customer life expectations (see Figure 19.1).

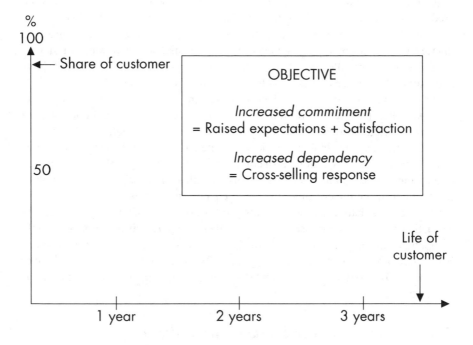

Figure 19.1 Customer retention and development

Increasing commitment and dependency are not simply ways of increasing the longevity of customer relationships. They are also ways of increasing current customer values or share of customer. The greater the share of customer, the longer the business relationship is likely to last – because it is more important to the customer and, in all probability, more inconvenient to sever. In fact, a reduction in a customer's spending is a good indicator of potential defection. Frederick F. Reichheld, head of the loyalty practice at Bain & Company, refers to such reductions as *partial defections*. To take an obvious example, a car purchaser who no longer used the appointed dealer to service his car would be more likely to change makes than one who stayed with the dealer. However, any reduction in purchase frequency, number of items purchased or value is a warning signal.

Data derived from a transactional database gives the marketer an enormous advantage in being able to identify behaviour patterns that signal increasingly loyal or disloyal behaviour. Furthermore, the data enables the marketer to target the company's best efforts towards those customers whose custom is potentially profitable. What the data cannot do is substitute for any lack of understanding of what it is like to be a customer.

PLOYS AND DEVICES

Every direct marketer knows that inertia is the enemy of response. But the customer's inertia can be turned to advantage when it comes to maintaining relationships. Staying loyal can be presented as the easy option. Direct marketers have been the pioneers of a variety of artifices designed to prolong customer relationships. Home shopping pioneered credit accounts, still the most effective way of increasing customer continuity, now also used by multiple retailers such as Marks & Spencer, House of Fraser and the Sears Group. Direct marketers pioneered continuity series publishing, now mainly used to sell collectables, and the negative option book club, also now in the guise of the negative option music club, video club and so on. Direct marketers adopted such devices as the TC (till cancelled) order and the VADD (variable direct debit) to avoid the discontinuity of asking subscribers to renew their magazine subscriptions.

All of the devices mentioned so far are features of the terms of business applied by the supplier. It is to conventional retailing that we must look for loyalty ploys unconnected with terms, invoicing or payment method. Pioneers included Co-Op dividends (issued as stamps), the dividend representing the customer's profit share. The stamp mechanism was copied by stamp trading companies (the most successful being Green Shield), whose stamps could be collected from a number of retailers. Petrol retailers, in particular, favoured collect promotions, in which customers received coupons to be saved until there were enough to redeem against a gift.

Such devices and ploys have proved insufficiently robust to hold back the tide of customer disloyalty. As choice proliferates, loyalty declines. Only a high degree of customer commitment or dependency can withstand the pressure. This does not render artificial loyalty devices useless. It merely limits their utility. This will be increased when they offer the marketer information about customers that would otherwise be hard to capture. The applications and mechanics of each device are described briefly below and a list of devices appears in Table 19.1.

Table 19.1 Retention devices

Device	Types	Used by
Credit	Store cards, credit accounts	Retailers, mail order catalogues
Negative option	Series and club agreements	Book and music clubs, collectables
Automatic payment	Direct debit, continuous authority and standing order	Clubs, charities, publishers
Lease/rental	Long-term leases, open-ended rental agreements	TV and appliance rental, motor and office equipment
Loyalty programme	Single company and cooperative	Travel and retail

Credit accounts

In business marketing, a credit account is the usual expectation of the customer. In a business context, a credit account obliges the buyer to pay in full within a stated period. In consumer marketing language, that is a charge account. More commonly the consumer will be offered an option account, offering the choice of paying in full or paying a minimum of 5 per cent of the outstanding balance each month. The shop or the home shopping company will usually accept a proprietary credit card, a Visa or Mastercard, but would much rather the shopper applied for the store's own card or used home shopping credit. The main reason for this preference is that the credit customer spends more and is more likely to remain active as a customer for longer. Credit increases both share of customer and longevity of custom.

Credit is much less effective at achieving these results than it once was. This is because the choice of credit accounts, like the choice of most other items, has proliferated. It is not difficult to clear the outstanding balance on any one account when it is only one of a number. Indeed, the majority of option account holders pay off the balance in full each month. When the balance is cleared, an account can readily be opened elsewhere.

A weakness of the credit account offer is that it cannot be unconditional. Some credit applications will represent too great a bad debt risk to accept. A number of these may be from customers who would have continued to shop had they never been offered the opportunity to apply for a store card. Once rejected, they are unlikely to shop again.

Despite this weakness, the benefits outweigh any disadvantages. Credit customers not only spend more and carry on doing so for longer, but their account provides a complete record of their transactions. Breaks in the continuity of their custom can be detected and acted upon. Their account provides a record of their purchase preferences.

The retailer has the option of providing credit from its own cash resources or contracting administration out to a bank. Providing credit involves funding application processing, credit bureau charges, collections, bad debt write-offs and cash flow deficit out of any interest charges received. Home shopping credit is often free for periods below nine months.

The value of credit as a marketing device extends beyond conventional shopping and applies to annually renewable products such as motor and household insurance, where the customer defection rate would be higher among cash customers than credit customers. Credit customers are a desirable asset and stores will offer discounts on purchases already decided upon to persuade customers to open an account.

Free approval, clubs and continuity

The device of free approval permits *negative option* marketing. Negative option marketing involves persuading the customer to accept a continued supply of items at pre-agreed intervals on free approval. Each despatch, whether it is a book or piece of china, is accompanied by an invoice. The customer is then obliged to pay the invoice or return the goods.

Although often used by publishers and collectables producers, this type of agreement lends itself to the provision of a regular delivery service of heavy or bulky commodities, particularly goods that can be ordered without comparison shopping, for example disposable nappies (diapers), cans of petfood or, perhaps, office supplies. The customer will usually have the right to cancel at any time although there may be a minimum purchase requirement as in the case of most book clubs. Clubs announce their recommended selections in advance and members have the right to choose an alternative or skip a month. The greater the customer's commitment, the more powerful must be the front-end (customer acquisition) offer.

A variation on this theme is the TC (till cancelled) agreement in which the customer pays in advance for supplies over a specified period but, instead of receiving a renewal notice, has agreed to be invoiced again once the subscription payment has expired. This type of agreement is not common in the UK because variable direct debits offer a more effective alternative.

Direct debits and continuous authority

Variable direct debit mandates and continuous authority credit card payments are ideal for subscription payments or other regular bills, whether these are payable monthly, annually or some period in between. They offer convenience to the customer, who does not need to remember to make regular payments, and improve both the cash flow and the income of the supplier. Bank standing order payments have the same effect but the payment amount cannot be varied. The direct debit and continuous authority vehicles permit the supplier to make price changes provided the customer is informed sufficiently far in advance to cancel before the next payment falls due. These vehicles can be used in business as well as consumer marketing, but many businesses will not sign mandates or are very reluctant to do so.

Consumers, too, are reluctant to enter agreements they must take positive action to cancel. The marketing cost of acquiring a direct debit customer is higher than the cost of acquiring a cash customer. But the direct debit customer is worth a lot more. When the motoring associations were experiencing an average renewal rate of about 65 per cent from cash customers, the renewal rate from VADD and continuous authority customers was about 90 per cent.

Figure 19.2 shows the effect of VADD or continuous authority payments on customer retention. In this example, the first year cash customers renew at the rate of 55 per cent, increasing to 65 per cent at the end of the second year and 70 per cent at the end of the third year. Of 100 cash customers recruited, only 25 remain by year 4. Direct debit payers do not renew as a positive action. They either cancel or do nothing. In the example, 15 per cent cancel after one year, 10 per cent after two years and 7.5 per cent after three years, leaving 70 of the 100 customers originally recruited still on board in year 4.

	Cash payer	Direct debit
Year 1	100	100
Year 2	55 (-45%)	85 (-15%)
Year 3	36 (-35%)	77 (-10%)
Year 4	25 (-30%)	70 (-7.5%)

Figure 19.2 Cash payment vs direct debit – typical four-year result

	Cash payer	**Direct debit**
Year 1	100 x 60 **£6000**	100 x 55* **£5500**
Year 2	55 x 60 **£3300**	85 x 60 **£5100**
Year 3	36 x 60 **£2160**	77 x 60 **£4620**
Year 4	25 x 60 **£1500**	70 x 60 **£4200**
	£12,960	**£19,420**

* £60 less £5 for gift

Figure 19.3 The effect of direct debits on revenue

Figure 19.3 takes the same example but expresses it in financial terms. Here, we assume customers are paying an annual fee of £60 and that cash customers also pay a £5 joining fee, waived for those agreeing to pay by direct debit. However, we can see it would be worth paying a great deal more than an extra £5 in concessions or other marketing expenses to increase the population of VADD customers and reduce the cash-paying population.

Direct debit and credit card continuous authority payments, although devised largely with utility bill payments in mind, are used as a marketing device by membership organisations, by charities and by magazine publishers with considerable success. Nevertheless, customers are becoming less reluctant to cancel than once they were.

Lease and rental agreements

Although customer loyalty was not the primary reason for the introduction of rental and lease agreements, they can have this effect. This type of agreement is most appealing when the item represents what would otherwise be a major purchase, perhaps depreciating severely in value. This would apply particularly to product fields in which technological development leads to rapid obsolescence. Currently, TV and video rental is a declining business, but car leasing agreements are increasing in popularity and machine rental has been extended into white goods, notably washing machines.

Loyalty programmes

Direct marketing is concerned only with schemes that capture the customer's identity, enabling some kind of one-to-one relationship to be established. Most often a plastic card will be issued to give tangible expression to the programme and to make it easy for the customer to provide an ID. The card may be a simple magnetic stripe card, permitting limited information, such as the ID and membership status, to be read at a terminal. More ambitiously, it may be a smart card containing a lot more information. The latter might be appropriate if the scheme had to permit instant, automated reaction to changes of customer circumstances or target instant offers to specific customer segments.

Although retail and packaged goods loyalty programmes are steeped in history, the modern version – permitting customer segmentation or even one-to-one treatment – originates from travel and credit card incentive programmes, of which American Airlines' *AAdvantage* scheme was by far the most influential.

There is clearly a limit to the number of such schemes the customer will take the trouble to join. The greater the proliferation of loyalty schemes, the less they act like loyalty schemes, appealing more to the minority of customers who are especially susceptible to promotions. In this context the truly successful scheme requires a number of key ingredients:

1) *Enrol a critical mass of committed customers.* Enabling recruitment offers to be targeted to non-customers.

2) *Pay back on increasing share of customer.* Do not depend on extending customer lifecycle.

3) *Offer opportunity to improve customer service.* Do not depend solely on rewards of a monetary value but use data collected to bring customer benefits of special relevance.

4) *Recognise individuality of customer.* Include rewards, benefits and courtesies that recognise the customer as a person.

5) *Provide absolute continuity.* A scheme that forces customers to start from scratch again each year or after each redemption is sowing the seeds of its own extinction.

6) *Offer added value benefits.* For example, a scheme operated by several non-competing retailers collectively permits faster qualification for rewards. A scheme that offers new types of reward provides fresh stimulation. A scheme that allows the utility of the membership card to be increased (eg to draw cash) is more valued.

7) *Use data collected for intelligent marketing.* Schemes can be used to provide data that drive communications recognising customer shopping patterns, preferences, breaks in continuity and so on. They can also provide useful area

data to retailers, improving catchment area definition and permitting accurate targeting of competitive customers.

The more common membership programmes of the type used by retailers and credit card providers are inappropriate to many other situations. A good loyalty programme is one that is skilfully designed to meet a specific objective. The great direct marketing pioneer Lester Wunderman provided the Ford Motor Company with a truly original idea. Knowing Ford were concerned that company executives, now able to exercise their own choice of company car within a given budget, were free to migrate from Ford to other makes, Wunderman proposed a loyalty scheme. He pointed out that, on retirement, the executive would not only lose a minimum one-third salary but also the use of a company car. Why not, he proposed, offer the retiring executive who had specified, say, ten company-purchased Fords a free one as a retirement present? What Wunderman knew, of course, was that many potential migrants would specify at least one extra Ford but few would qualify for their free retirement gift. Doubtless most accountants would have recoiled at the notion of exposing Ford to a long-term liability of uncertain magnitude and Wunderman's idea was never taken up.

OUTBOUND CUSTOMER COMMUNICATIONS

Customer retention and development marketing programmes are hard to measure. To be sure of their effect we must maintain a control group of customers who are excluded from the programme. This is not always practicable. For example, Tesco could not deny customers their Clubcard. They could compare the behaviour of cardholders with non-cardholders but, since having a card is an option available to all customers, these are self-selecting groups, not matched samples. Their behaviour cannot fairly be compared. On the other hand, Tesco can test offers or new benefits in communications to selected groups of customers within the Clubcard base. That is because a matched control group of excluded customers can be maintained. The precise effect of the tested initiative can then be gauged by comparing the behaviour of the two sets of customers. This comparison can be continued long after the end of the specific promotion.

Companies are frequently accused of spending too much on customer acquisition and not enough on keeping and developing established customers. It is difficult to be certain that such criticism is deserved in any individual case, partly because of the measurement difficulties we have touched on, but partly also because spending money, for example, to prevent defections inevitably means wasting some of it on customers who would have stayed anyway. Paradoxically, it is always harder to justify expenditure on loyal customers. The lower the loss rate, the harder it is to make loyalty marketing expenditures pay back. If we can keep a customer at a cost of £10, that is not the true cost. The £10 will also be accepted by customers who would not have defected even without the offer. If there are five such customers, the cost is £60 but, if there are ten loyal customers, the cost will be increased to £110.

It is for just this reason that the quantity of customer data and the quality of modelling are so important. The more precisely a model can predict behaviour, the more efficient will be the deployment of marketing expenditure. If our model improves our ability to recognise loyal customers, then we can reduce the true cost of preventing defections closer to the £10. A by-product may be that loyal customers will be neglected and that disloyal customers will receive favourable treatment.

While this may seem unfair, we can more easily justify expenditure to induce changes of behaviour than mere continuance of behaviour. Therefore, we need to be creative in seeking ways that loyal customers can be rewarded. One way is to reward uptrading, use of additional lines and so on. Uptrading and cross-selling are ways of changing customer behaviour, of course, and the payback is relatively easy to measure. Another way loyal customers may be rewarded is by providing service benefits, information and recognition at little or no extra cost to the company.

Broad categories of outbound communications

The two main divisions are between *seasonal* and *series* communications. The difference can be likened to the difference between sending Christmas cards and birthday cards. You will send out your Christmas cards in bulk to reach all of your friends and relatives at the right time. But to send each of them a birthday card at the right time, you must post your cards singly. The timing in the case of birthday cards is determined by the birth date of each individual on your list. As you would expect, a Christmas card is a *seasonal* communication. Less obviously, a birthday card is a *series* communication because your birthday cards have to be sent out, one after another, on predetermined dates. Series communications are also known as *event-driven* communications.

Keeping the greetings card analogy in mind, you will see that series (or event-driven) communications require more knowledge of the recipient and a good memory or diary system and make greater demands on accurate record-keeping. That is one reason why you may send out far fewer birthday cards than Christmas cards. But, for someone really close to you, just sending a Christmas card would not be enough.

The marketing communications equivalent of a Christmas card might be the announcement of a January sale. Here the timing is driven by the retailer or by demand from customers in general, rather than any one customer in particular. All the customers will be informed of the sale at the same time. It is a seasonal communication. The equivalent of the birthday card might also be an anniversary, such as the end of the second year since you took delivery of your car. Perhaps the dealer will use the opportunity to offer a test drive for a replacement or to sell an extended warranty. Alternatively, the timing might be driven by the interval since your last purchase from a shop or catalogue. Statistical analysis might show that your supplier is now at risk of losing your custom. This will have triggered the communication.

Thus a series or event-driven communication may be driven by a specific event or a specific interval after an event, but it may also be driven by a statistical process. The marketer may, for example, be using regression analysis to drive a *dynamic scorecard* that predicts the relative value of sending a specific message today to alternative customers. The purpose of the message may be to reduce the risk of customer defection, to cross-sell or to award a loyalty bonus. Whatever its purpose, the decision to send or not send the message will be automated and the automated decision system will have to be designed to act with common sense. Without common sense, the system will keep on selecting much the same group of customers every day because they will consistently produce the highest scores. Common sense is supplied by combining score-based selection with rule-based selection. Rule-based selection contains '*unless*' instructions. These instructions prevent the same customers being selected over and over again.

In 1996, Peter Simpson, Commercial Director of First Direct, was quoted in the magazine *Precision Marketing* as saying:

> Relationship marketing will become one-to-one marketing in which, rather than choosing a product which needs promoting and identifying customers to target it to, it will become a matter of identifying which customer is ready to be marketed to and then choosing a product which will fulfil his or her needs.

This ideal requires series or event-driven communications. The idea is that targeting cannot be perfected unless messages arrive at the right time.

Advantages and disadvantages of series communications

Unlike the birthday card, not all series communications will be delivered at the right time because deciding on the right time usually depends on a calculation of odds or a best guess at what will be appropriate. Paradoxically, some seasonal communications will be at exactly the right time because they fit into a framework of habits that have become established, the January sale being a perfect example.

The three main advantages of series communications are:

- They (mainly) target the right people at the right time.

- Their relevance conveys recognition of the individual customer.

- They lend themselves to telemarketing.

Readers will appreciate that series communications lend themselves to telemarketing because delivering them is a continuous activity. While it is possible to mail 5 million seasonal messages the same day, it is not possible to telephone so many people all at one time. Less obviously, the power of series communications also suits telemarketing. Telemarketing is expensive and is best used for highly targeted dialogue. A point to note, however, is that series communications can be delivered within inbound calls, too. A scorecard or event can trigger a prompt for call centre operators. The most immediate version of this is a detail within a customer's order. In one test carried out by a mail order company, customers' orders of Manchester United regalia or related merchandise triggered the offer of a book about Ryan Giggs, a United player. Every customer receiving this offer agreed to order the book. One advantage of such immediate reaction to an event is that the system may demand nothing of the customer database because it can operate without reference to historical customer data. All that is required to make it work is software that will react instantly to the trigger.

Series communications also have their disadvantages:

- They require more historical data.

- They are more expensive.

- They raise the penalty for getting it wrong.

- They can clash with seasonal communications.

- They may not meet company objectives.

Series communications require more customer data and may demand the use of statistical modelling. Outgoing messages, if delivered by mail, will usually be more expensive per unit than seasonal mailing output because volumes will be lower, affecting printing and postage costs. Any errors will prove more irritating because series mailings assume knowledge of the individual customer and mistakes convey the opposite. Another problem is that series mailings can clash with seasonal mailings and a complex set of rules may need to be written to prevent the same customer receiving different messages on the same day. Finally, series communications are not the ideal vehicle for dealing with such expediencies as offloading a quantity of redundant stock or countering some competitive initiative.

Assigning roles to customer communications

Customer communications may be needed to drive sales and also to maintain good relations. In a business marketing context the target groups for these two communications tasks may be different. For example, senior managers of a client company might receive occasional seasonal mailings to keep them informed of new product developments, whereas executives dealing directly with the supplier company might (also or instead) receive series mailings and telephone calls triggered by orders, cancellations and enquiries. Seasonal mailings might be in the form of customer magazines or newsletters. On the other hand they might include invitations to seminars, technical briefings or events of a more social nature.

The choice of seasonal and series communications will depend on their appropriateness to the task in hand and the supply of information needed to drive them. There may also be an opportunistic consideration to apply. For example, statements, bills and other correspondence may provide free rides to marketing communications. These will generally be seasonal and not highly targeted but it is not uncommon for a tailored message to be driven by details contained on an invoice or statement.

OUTBOUND COMMUNICATIONS IN ACTION – AN EXAMPLE

We can now apply some of this theory about outbound communications to a practical marketing problem. For this purpose we will adopt the identity of a bank and take on the persona of a manager charged with the task of building up a portfolio of personal loan customers from within the current (cheque) account base. This will require us to recruit reliable customers who have not borrowed in this way from us before, to retain those customers already borrowing from us and to recapture customers who used to borrow from us but no longer do so.

Where should we begin? With customer acquisition or customer retention? You know the answer, of course. We should begin with the cheapest way to add to the value of our customer base and work outwards from there. To do this we need to refer back to past experience or make some assumptions. Let's consider the opportunities.

1. Current customers
Looking first only at those whose loan agreements are not nearing the end of their life, what are the opportunities to improve business? We must begin by excluding the small minority of customers who are not paying to terms and concentrate on the good payers. Naturally, our predecessor in this job was sensible enough to build up goodwill by writing to thank each customer for their business and by offering them a hotline contact number they could ring with any query or if experiencing any difficulty in meeting scheduled repayments.

Because we can access current bank account data, we can divide our customers into those who can afford their monthly repayments with something to spare and those who are very fully committed. The danger with the former is that they will not allow their loan agreement to run to the full term (average two-and-a-half years) but pay off the outstanding balance early and without warning. By the time we know it will be too late to save the agreement. By analysing previous customer loss data, we can predict the odds of losing any customer early. All we need to do is to profile early paid-ups against full-term borrowers, using loan, bank account, credit score and application data. The results will allow us to sharpen up our targeting and our timing. So what should we do? Clearly, the potential early paid-up borrower is a good risk for a larger loan. Furthermore, a borrower is a borrower. Someone who already borrows from us is more likely to borrow again than someone who usually saves up for what they want. By offering the customer another loan we give ourselves the chance of increasing the customer's value and reduce the chance of losing the loan agreement early.

Now what about the customers who are repaying their loan to terms but are struggling to do so? Since they are reliable payers the risk of extending the period of their loan would be small. This would have the effect of reducing their monthly repayments but also have the effect of increasing our total interest earnings from the customer. Credit technicalities being what they are, no doubt a new agreement would be required and the customer's outstanding balance would be transferred to a new loan account.

In these two ways we will increase the value of the loan customer asset without adding a single new customer or recovering a single lost customer. We might also try to get our happy customers to recommend friends. This would be a standard direct marketing ploy but one we may wish to be cautious about adopting in this case. Personal loans are a confidential matter and, of course, there is a real risk that a recommended friend might not meet our acceptance criteria. We would be wise to undertake small-scale customer research before even testing a referral (member-get-member) scheme.

Our established customer programmes will consist entirely of series communications, each customer being contacted at what we have established as being the best times from back data and from current live testing. Doubtless we will test both the telephone and direct mail in various combinations.

2. Customers approaching end of term

We need a programme beginning, say, three months before the agreement runs its course. We are about to lose our favourite customers, bona fide borrowers who have been repaying to terms for over two years.

Beginning by looking at the results of our predecessor's efforts to defer customer dormancy, we will plan to do better. We can be almost sure that the previous effort was feeble as most managers are not logical but are ruled by precedent. As you now already know, unless the cost of retaining an extra customer had risen close to the cost of getting a new one, insufficient retention effort had been made. There is just one proviso: the effort must not be so intensive as to damage customer relations.

Looking at the back data, the difficulty we might expect to encounter would be in measuring the true marginal cost:benefit of the retention effort unless our predecessor had maintained a control group of non-promoted customers. However, in this case, a customer must make a positive effort to reapply and we can be reasonably confident that the net gain is therefore very close to the gross gain. In other words, without the offer, few customers would have reapplied on their own initiative.

Once again all our communications will be on a series basis and once again we will use the telephone as well as direct mail, the latter possibly, but not necessarily, in the form of statement mailings. Our approach will not appear pushy. Our customer may feel pleased to have repaid the loan and may be in no mood to borrow again for a while.

3. Lapsed customers

We are only concerned with the good payers, of course, and although, in general, previous borrowers will make better prospects than other bank customers, Pareto's principle is sure to apply to our previous borrower file. Some customers will have reached a life stage when they will expect to pay as they go for everything except their house or a home extension. They will remain in the mortgage (or secured loan) market but will have dropped out of the unsecured loan market. Let's consider some ways in which our previous borrower base might be segmented:

- number of previous agreements;
- recency of last agreement;
- recency of final payment;
- early paid-up/loan ran to full period;
- value of last loan;
- previous contact history;
- previous response history;
- remains/not remains as bank customer;
- credit score;
- current account status;
- turnover band on current account.

Naturally, if our customer also used one of our credit cards we would have a lot more useful information. The most valuable marketing information we will have is back data referring to previous success in recovering lapsed borrowers. We are not dependent on previous resolicitation efforts being directed to segmented target groups, each carrying a response code. Providing always that all the data about who was contacted and who responded is still held, we can undertake some data mining and analysis to make sense of it all. We do not even mind how customers responded. They might have agreed on the phone, replied to a mailing or visited a branch. Although this is of interest in determining their contact preferences, it need not disturb our analysis. All we need do is compare responders with non-responders and see how they differ.

We can be sure there will be differences in potential between different groups of lapsed customers. For example, we may have enough information about some customers to make them a guaranteed loan offer. In other cases our information may not be sufficient (or sufficiently up to date) for us to guarantee to lend whatever sum is requested. Naturally, customers are more likely to accept a guaranteed loan offer than a mere invitation to apply.

Then again, the longer a customer has managed without a loan from us and the more previous invitations which have been refused, the more likely it is that the customer will continue to manage without our help. The customer whose account tips into the red at some point each month is probably more likely to borrow than the one who is always in credit. However, we don't need to make assumptions. All we need do is analyse the data.

Having analysed the data, we could use it to plan a recovery campaign consisting of bulk seasonal mailings. On the other hand our analysis may tell us that there are critical times when we should contact customers. Naturally, we will have sent a thank you letter as soon as the previous loan had been paid up. This would naturally have offered a new agreement even though the customer had resisted previous efforts to retain his or her loan business. Some customers would have responded to this. We might find that customers were disproportionately inclined to borrow again on or about the same time of year as they did before, or within six months of paying off their last loan. All this information can be used to generate series mailings or, perhaps, telephone calls. We might also be able to justify bulk seasonal mailings to deliver the business volumes we can create on a profitable basis. Considerations here are the prevailing retail climate (are customers in a spending mood?) and the relative cheapness of achieving high volumes from lapsed loan customers compared with new customers.

4. Other customer segments

Still in no hurry to chase after customers we know less about, can we think of any other groups of customers who are disproportionately likely to be potential borrowers? We may have kept a record of customers who enquired about a loan but refused our offer. We will also have a file of customers whose loan applications were declined. Some of these people could now be rescored and possibly offered a guaranteed loan.

5. Cross-selling

Finally, we must turn our attention to new-to-loan customers and, here again, the data derived from their current account dealings and our analysis of previous response will help enormously to get the targeting right. Our ideal new loan prospect could be someone whose credit score enables us to guarantee a loan yet whose overdraft indicates hunger for credit. No doubt we will have to settle for less obvious opportunities and, once more, we are likely to find a need for both seasonal and series communications. For example, a change of address could signal the need for funds. This one piece of information could drive a series contact programme and it might override other segmentation, such as previous loan usage. Other series communications could be driven by dynamic scoring systems running off data extracted from current account transactions. A dynamic score could be altered by a sudden change in the turnover or debit balance of the customer's current account.

Contact management

The practical example of personal loan marketing could easily raise complex issues of multi-channel contact management. You will recognise the scope for error arising out of the use of series and seasonal communications in combination. In this case the objective of each type of communication is the same and so a clash would be embarrassing, particularly if the two communications vehicles were the same (eg direct mail). Such clashes are quite difficult to avoid as seasonal mailing files are selected some time in advance of a bulk mailing because the production lead time is seldom less than weeks.

One solution to the problem is to place all series contacts in the hands of an outbound telemarketing unit, reserving direct mail for seasonal communications. Another approach is to respect the customer's previous choice of sales channel and permit series contact only through this one channel.

However, increasingly, we can expect to see all direct approaches with an immediate sales objective to be delivered on a series basis. As the richness of data increases and our ability to analyse and use it advances, the need for seasonal promotion should diminish. Seasonal communications would then be confined to obviously seasonal topics or more generalised customer information.

TO SUM UP

In this chapter it is suggested that customer loyalty depends not on mere satisfaction but on either commitment, dependency or both. Commitment is increased by raising customers' expectations and ensuring their raised expectations are satisfied. Dependency can be increased by the use of devices that make doing business with us easier, more convenient or more rewarding. Rewards can be given by loyalty promotions. These will work better if they make intelligent use of the customer information they produce to award service benefits, not simply bribes.

The roles of two types of outbound customer communications – seasonal and series communications – were considered and I advanced the notion that the future lies with the latter, time sensitive communications.

THE HENLEY COLLEGE LIBRARY

20

INTERACTING WITH CUSTOMERS

IN THIS CHAPTER

If today's hi-tech aids permit large companies to match the corner store's service standards, they don't make it obligatory. Every so often, a trade magazine or a direct marketing agency will 'road test' enquiry or order fulfilment, putting famous-name companies' service standards on trial. Invariably the results show wide discrepancies, the worst examples never being less than disgraceful. Managers who guard brand images with almost fanatical zeal somehow lose interest at the point when the customer puts their standards to the test.

In this chapter we will consider the ever-growing choice of ways in which a customer can communicate with a supplier. Yet the most important message of the chapter has nothing to do with Interactive Voice Response, the Internet or any of the other methods by which a customer may make his or her wishes known. It is to monitor service standards continuously, rewarding good performance and stamping out bad performance.

Any company that does not monitor service performance continuously will come out nearer the bottom than the top the next time a trade magazine publishes the results of a service standards test. A potential customer's first and, very possibly, only experience of dealing with the company will create a more abiding impression than any amount of advertising. The impression is likely to be conditioned by three aspects of handling:

1) *Efficiency:* Was the enquirer satisfied within a reasonable/unexpectedly short time? Was the phone answered reasonably quickly?

2) *Accuracy:* Was the nature of the enquiry correctly identified and the right information supplied?

3) *Quality:* Was the enquiry experience pleasant and businesslike, making it easy for the enquirer to become a customer?

These simple aspects of service are easy to monitor and outweigh any competitive advantage that can be gained from high technology. However, in a competitive marketplace, it is necessary to keep pace technologically as well. The ability to call up data such as customer records, stock information and service engineer schedules on screen has made the telephone the preferred way of dealing with many companies. The technology is essential to empower a call centre to provide good service but it need not, as far as the customer is concerned, be intrusive.

INITIATING DIALOGUE

In Chapter 1 we declared that direct marketing was built round interaction with customers. Direct marketing, even within an integrated or multi-sales channel environment, implies response to messages and reaction to responses. A dialogue of some sort, however rudimentary, is provoked.

Initially, the first objective of the dialogue is to establish a fit between what the potential customer wants and what the supplier is able and willing to provide. The second objective is to acquire information that can be used to foster the development of a mutually satisfactory business relationship. Even when the supplier has a dealer or branch network, the potential customer will often prefer to deal remotely with a central source of information or service, particularly when he or she is in fact-gathering mode rather than purchase mode. This will apply in both business-to-business marketing and consumer marketing.

Reasons for preferring information centres include:

- the belief that centrally sourced information is authoritative;

- the ability to keep potential suppliers at arm's length;

- the confidentiality/privacy: eg loan or health enquiries.

The supplier, too, has a vested interest in providing help from the centre. Doing so increases the company's availability to customers and makes it less likely that potential customers will leak out of the bucket. The information centre may also be able to book appointments for sales visits, thus maximising the effective use of field sales time. Less obviously, except to us, the information centre does not just dispense information to customers, it gathers information about customers. It reports on the effectiveness of marketing communications because it collects response data and generates conversion data. It enables marketers to stay in control of their investments and helps them to find out what the customer is most likely to want next. In his book *Telemarketing in Action* (1995), Michael Stevens lists ten telephone service delivery points and eight opportunities to enhance the service image through the use of the telephone. His lists appear in Table 20.1.

Items of marketing information that can be collected from call centres are so important that companies need to find ways of collecting them when customers bypass central information or sales centres and deal with branches, dealerships or field sales personnel. Providing always that the contact details of every customer are captured, however that customer receives service, an outbound courtesy call can be made to establish contact, discover any outstanding problems and provide a helpline contact. Unobtrusively, technology has helped by providing methods of exchanging data between remote sites, with or without cable linkage. Thus the individual salesperson can access technical data from a product database and enter customer and order data using cellular data transmission or e-mail.

Table 20.1 Opportunities for service delivery by telephone

Service delivery points
Providing product/service information (eg product specifications, pricing, stock availability, outlets, booking information)
Appointment making/arranging demonstrations
Sales/sales promotion
Credit approvals/cash collection
Order hotlines
Customer account servicing
Transaction queries, eg delivery, invoice
Complaint handling
Helplines and service requests
Crisis management

Impacting on service image
Carelines
Welcome calls and courtesy calls
Ancillary information services
Post-crisis comfort calls
Invitations to events
Customer satisfaction surveys
Product/service improvement surveys
New product/service testing

FULFILMENT MEDIA

The process of satisfying enquiries or direct orders is called fulfilment. In days gone by there were few ways of doing this from a remote location. By far the commonest was the use of the postal service and this remains crucially important, for example to despatch brochures, even when the request has arrived by telephone, fax or some other means. As it is, many enquirers use the post when they wish to keep a distance between themselves and a potential supplier. The supplier not respecting this wish may exclude some longer-range enquiries. This is most likely to occur when the purchase is planned and rehearsed for some time ahead of the event. On the whole it is better to include a coupon or other postal response device unless the post cannot offer a satisfactory way of handling the enquiry.

The major fulfilment media may be summarised as:

- postal service/facsimile/couriers;

- telephone/IVR;

- e-mail/Internet

The postal service is a two-way distribution channel permitting the receipt of information requests or orders and the despatch of information or goods. Alternatively, urgent requests may be received by fax and urgent despatches made by courier. The Post Office offers postage-paid (Freepost) reply services to encourage enquiries. The advertiser applies for a licence, pre-pays for an estimated number of enquiries and is charged for any balance of enquiries received.

The post offers a cheap and practicable method of communicating simple information requests and responding to them. It is an invaluable way of encouraging accurately stated orders because a printed advertisement or mailing pack can contain an order form that obliges the customer to complete the essential details. It permits companies to send official orders requesting supplies in hard copy. It enables companies to request customers or enquirers to complete questionnaires or application forms. It can be used effectively for prize draws or other contests. It can be used for promotional offers such as mail-in premiums or cash-back discounts. Furthermore, it enables customers to stay at arm's length if they wish. There is nothing intrinsically pushy about the medium although it can be used in a fairly aggressive way.

The telephone has long since overtaken the postal service as the favoured enquiry and order channel in the home shopping business, for leisure travel and for many other direct response advertising orders and enquiries. We have become less used to writing and more demanding of instant service. We are now confident to shop around for motor and home insurance, for cheap flights, for second-hand cars and even for mortgages or personal loans by telephone.

The telephone allows home shopping companies and banks to give better service. The home shopping company can tell the customer if the goods are temporarily out of stock, say what the expected delay will be and offer an immediately available alternative. The bank can call up any data about the customer's account or accounts on screen, discuss the best course of action and follow the customer's instructions within a few minutes' private conversation – at two in the morning, if that is what the customer wants. In either case, and in many others, the customer is empowered to make rational decisions because information held on one or more databases can be put at the customer's disposal. Transactions of this sort value a customer's time. Any method of delivery that requires the customer to come to where the information is held or the goods are stocked does not value the customer's time. Similarly, the customer's time is not valued if out-of-stock notifications are sent by post in response to handwritten and posted orders.

The telephone is also preferred by many people. It provides person-to-person contact, even though the dialogue is not face to face. Dialogue facilitates rapid transactions, mutual understanding being achieved quickly through questions and their answers. A well-equipped call centre with well trained and motivated staff will usually outperform most retail branch operations in terms of service quality and customer satisfaction. For one thing, having all the sales staff under one roof and on tape enables superior coaching. For another, call centre staff can call up the information they need to deal with queries and can be enabled to compensate the customer for minor service lapses. Unfortunately not all call centres operate to such high standards.

Call centres, even with the best technology, are labour-intensive operations and are not cheap, whether maintained internally or outsourced. An alternative to human operators is *IVR* – Interactive Voice Response. An IVR system can be used for accepting simple messages, for example a request for call from a live operator when the call centre is less busy, to quite complex enquiries. Some bank customers use an IVR system to make enquiries about their account and leave simple instructions. The customer can communicate with such a system using speech or a DTMF (dual tone multi-frequency) telephone. Either way is no substitute for human contact to many of us.

The telephone cannot (yet) show us things and *e-mail, Internet* and *Intranet* communications may lend themselves to dialogue when the answer to the enquirer's question could be a diagram or a picture, or could be sufficiently long and complex to be studied on-screen or as a printout for some time. There is a potentially very wide range of business applications (for example, scientific papers are now published electronically) and consumer applications will become more popular with the increased use of modems. As has been asserted often before, the Internet is intermediate technology and it is the PC/TV (or whatever it will be called) that will take over downline information delivery and dialogue in consumer markets, assuming demand is sufficient. Meanwhile, electronic publishing is well suited to urgently (or internationally) required complex information delivery, especially when it permits an enquirer to select from a menu rather than wade through unwanted information. Obviously, its application is limited to markets with Internet (or CD-ROM) access.

Whatever the future holds, there is no doubt that demand for person to person contact, both on the telephone and face to face, will continue indefinitely. Technology does not alter human psychology, but it will be necessary to continue making shopping more entertaining and teleshopping more rewarding as the alternatives increase in number and attraction.

CUSTOMER POWER

The general direction in which fulfilment is heading is towards enabling the customer to make better informed purchase decisions with less effort and closer to the desired time of delivery. Some improvements are made as an act of faith, there being no sure way of researching the demand, 24-hour banking being an example.

If we are to harness our ability to tailor almost any engineered product, many other manufactured products and nearly every service product, we must find better ways of allowing customers to exercise their preferences. What appears to work best is some kind of simplified dialogue in which the consumer keeps on selecting from a menu until the precise configuration he or she wants is produced. This is potentially a very fast way to choose between tens of thousands of alternatives. For example, if you chose one item from a menu of six and repeated such a choice six more times, your final selection would have been from 279,936 alternatives although you would only have seen 42 of them. The dialogue can be conducted on a keyboard, with a mouse, by touching a screen or with a DTMF telephone from home or the office. Alternatively, the dialogue might take place, using similar technology, at a car showroom.

Similar dialogues can be conducted to make other kinds of purchase decision. For example, the shopper might want to begin by choosing a menu from alternative recipes. Then, for the chosen recipe, the ingredients can be listed, located and priced. The shopping list could be printed out or the shopper could merely signify acceptance by touching a screen. The transaction could take place at a kiosk in-store or it could take place at the shopper's home. Preparation of the meal could be demonstrated down the telephone line.

We can see that, just as technology can help the marketer to generate relevant messages at the right time, ultimately its greatest effect may be to empower the customer to select from increasing numbers of alternatives with greater confidence and, equally importantly, with less time spent on research or travel. The major issue is one of public demand. Even small businesses are already conducting electronic dialogues because doing so makes sense.

The completely satisfied customer

The difference between customer satisfaction and customer commitment is something we have already discussed. You will recall that the satisfied customer will defect if given an acceptable offer by a competitor. The committed customer is less likely to defect. Commitment is the product of delivering to enhanced customer expectations.

In the November–December 1995 issue of the *Harvard Business Review*, readers were startled by a paper that expressed this notion in rather different terms. The paper was intriguingly entitled 'Why Satisfied Customers Defect'. Its authors, Thomas O. Jones and Earl W. Sasser Jr, introduced a new category of satisfied customer, the completely satisfied customer.

Jones and Sasser became aware of the importance of this category through a discovery made by the Xerox Corporation. Xerox found that its completely satisfied customers were six times as likely to repurchase Xerox products over the next 18 months as its satisfied customers. Using a five-point scale, satisfaction surveys usually describe as satisfied those respondents whose satisfaction scores are between four and five. But Xerox found a huge difference in the behaviour of those who hit the top score and those who were within a few per cent of it. Was this a peculiarity of the office equipment market or could this be true of other markets, too? Jones and Sasser were determined to find out. They examined data from 30 companies in five markets. The five markets were cars, hospitals, personal computers for business, airlines and local telephone services. The satisfaction data for cars, PCs and airlines came from J.D. Power and Associates. In the UK, Toyota regularly score top in J.D. Power's annual satisfaction surveys of car owners.

What Jones and Sasser found was that the difference in behaviour between satisfied and completely satisfied customers was extreme in the car market and very marked in the PC market. In both these markets, the buying intentions of satisfied customers exhibited far lower degrees of loyalty. A market in which competition did not work, local telephone services, showed no correlation between satisfaction and loyalty. Airlines and hospitals lay in between these extremes. The case of airlines is interesting. Customers who were not completely satisfied would switch without hesitation when they had a genuinely free choice; that is, there was an alternative at a convenient time. Furthermore, they would also switch after reaching a specific frequent-flyer reward qualification. Thus the loyalty scheme would work up to a point – that is, only to defer the inevitable defection.

The pattern in the car market is, they believe, caused by increasing commoditisation. Today's technological masterpieces are all reliable, all perform well, are all free from corrosion and are all but indistinguishable. In this market and, say Jones and Sasser, most others, service is everything. Service is the discriminator, the most common point of difference between one brand and another.

So what are the key elements in providing complete satisfaction? There are four:

1) The product or service must offer the basic elements customers expect from all competitors in the marketplace.

2) There must be basic support services such as customer assistance and order tracking that make the product more useful or easier to use.

3) A recovery process must be provided for countering bad experiences.

4) Extraordinary services must be offered that so excel in meeting customers' expectations that they make the product or service appear to be tailor-made.

All four of these ingredients are required to create complete satisfaction although there would be little point in worrying about the fourth one if the process fell down earlier on. To find out, formal satisfaction research is necessary.

The fourth element links closely with direct marketing. Here we can see that Jones and Sasser have introduced the idea of the tailor-made. That is because it is impossible to deliver complete satisfaction if we don't know precisely what each individual customer wants most. Furthermore, Jones and Sasser see no reason why a company should not differentiate between its profitable customers and those who are not. Indeed, bringing in the wrong customers, customers it could not satisfy, is, they say, a prime cause of low satisfaction performance and the waste of resources that goes with it.

> Although it is important... to understand the satisfaction and loyalty of customers as a group, it is equally critical to understand the attitudes and behaviour of individual customers...
>
> ... customers behave in one of four basic ways: as loyalists, as defectors, as mercenaries or as hostages.

We are familiar with loyalists and defectors as categories. Mercenaries are customers a company is better off without. Their business can always be bought by a competitor. Hostages are customers who are stuck, by absence of competition, by a credit agreement or some other binding condition. They may show their resentment by making time-wasting or frivolous complaints.

AND THE WINNERS WILL BE ...?

At the beginning of the first chapter, we posed the question: 'Who will win the battle of the giants – the global brand proprietors, who were so dominant in the mass marketing era, or the retailing technocrats who know every detail of their customers' preferences?' No doubt both sides would say they are in partnership, that there is no conflict. If so, it's been an uneasy partnership. Firstly, packaged goods were advertised to the retailer's customers to enforce stocking; then the retailer created me-too own-label brands. The truth is that each side will always try to exercise dominance and dictate terms.

Manufacturers or distributors who do not sell directly to end users are, in reality, business-to-business marketers. However influential their brands may be in creating consumer franchises, their customers are really the retail and wholesale trade. They lack the transactional data that describes how their end-users are behaving because, except when they are running a promotion, the transactions are carried out on their behalf by others. The people with the transactional data will always be at an advantage. Data can be turned into customer knowledge and with knowledge comes power.

This does not mean that global brands are on the way out or that direct mail will supplant television or billboards as the best means of advertising soft drinks. It does suggest that the global brands proprietor should consider establishing a corporate brand in new markets, particularly markets in which the company can deal direct. A brand can signify a lifestyle; it does not have to signify one specific product.

A company that deals directly with its end-users represents, all other things being equal, a more attractive investment than one that does not. Only such a company can manage the whole process of raising end-user expectations, satisfying those raised expectations and securing end-user commitment. The company that deals through multiple retailers can lose a million end-user customers at once. However, having the end-users on the database will make that less likely.

In certain markets, including the automotive market, the need for dealers or retailers is being called into question. When the customer can choose between a million alternatives, the retail service of carrying stock becomes irrelevant. All that is needed is somewhere on the ground or, maybe, in cyberspace where the customer can exercise choice.

The marketer who controls or, rather, influences the whole process stands the best chance of survival and prosperity. Direct marketing is about influencing the whole process. It is the ultimate in integrated marketing.

POSTSCRIPT

In the late 1980s I was running a direct marketing agency which I had started with two partners back in 1976. I did a rough count of the total response in enquiries and orders we had helped our 28 clients to generate over a full year. It came to 5 million, more or less one for every eight adults in the UK. I thought this was pretty astonishing then and it was possibly a record for any UK agency at the time.

As I was writing this chapter I received news of how many people had responded to one British Telecom campaign. This had taken the form of a personalised mailing to 13 million customers. The mailing package reviewed each customer's individual savings opportunities, quoting how much the customer had spent on calling the household's five most used telephone numbers. The mailing showed the reader which these telephone numbers were. The customer was invited to sign up for BT's Friends & Family scheme, offering a 10 per cent discount on calls to these numbers. It was supported by a TV campaign that achieved 90 per cent coverage of the adult population.

In the first three months, the campaign achieved a 26 per cent response rate and a total of 6 million orders were received. BT's telemarketing and customer service centres handled 4.5 million calls from customers. By the end of the campaign BT had over 7 million BT Chargecards in circulation.

Most of BT's residential customers have never seen anyone from the company except a service engineer. That is the power of a customer marketing database.

21

DIRECT MARKETING IN ACTION II

CASE STUDY 1

SEAGRAM UK: LIST-BUILDING FOR MARTELL COGNAC

Background

Increasing advertising costs and the possibility of restrictions gave impetus to consumer name-gathering activity within the market. In October 1993, Seagram UK launched a direct marketing campaign for Martell Cognac to determine how many qualified consumer names could be collected at a given cost. Packaged consumable goods manufacturers and distributors are not preoccupied with collecting names of regular buyers of their own brand. The names are just as likely to be used for an aggressive campaign designed to win over competitive brand users as they are to be used for a defensive campaign designed to reinforce brand loyalty. Apart from the cost of data collection, the critical factor is the accuracy of the data. Is the contact data accurate and are the names genuine users of the product category? The answers to these questions will determine the value of the names and, hence, the payback on data collection.

Objectives

1) To build a database of loyal and competitive cognac drinkers.

2) To convert as many competitive drinkers as possible into Martell Cognac trialists.

A budget was allocated to make it possible to mail 120,000 people with a high-quality pack, to run once-only ads in quality and mid-market weekend supplements and to fund the offer. The budget also allowed for a follow-up programme targeted to respondents only.

Payback

The price that can be paid for a cognac drinker's contact information depends on the required payback period for the investment and the estimated success of a programme to stimulate demand. Demand may be stimulated by increasing consumption of cognac in opposition to other alcoholic beverages or it may be stimulated by increasing consumption of the brand at the expense of directly competitive brands. The most rapid payback is likely to be achieved from regular cognac consumers who use directly competitive brands. Thus, success is likely to depend on correctly identifying these consumers so that the relationship-building effort is accurately targeted.

It may be more cost-effective to discard some of the names collected than to mail them. The British Market Research Bureau's annual TGI survey results indicate why:

- 10 per cent of cognac drinkers account for 50 per cent of consumption;

- 39 per cent of cognac drinkers account for 44 per cent of consumption;

- the remaining 51 per cent account for only 6 per cent of consumption.

These figures cover consumption of monitored brands only and include bar sales.

Nevertheless they illustrate the futility of attempting to build a one-to-one relationship with customers who may buy a half bottle every Christmas to serve to the guests and improve the flavour of the pudding. Consumers in the top decile (10 per cent) are on average worth 42 times as much (in volume of consumption) as those in the bottom half of the market.

In this case, the targeted payback period was three years.

Positioning

Martell – a legend since 1715.

Attributes include its high quality, its approachability and its long history. Although the product is distributed all over the world by Seagram, there is in France a Martell family who remain actively associated with its production.

> Positioning is what someone is really buying when they buy your product or service, and conveying those impressions and motivations to the buyer.
> Mark McCormack, *What They Don't Teach You at Harvard Business School*

Targeting

It was decided to test media advertising in weekend colour supplements. This would provide a yardstick of comparison with direct mail. However, response data from each individual publication would also provide a measure of its effectiveness in producing qualified respondents.

Direct mail used outside (cold) lists and names collected from previous Martell promotions. The 90,000 cold list names were primarily from the NDL database of respondents to questionnaires inserted mainly in product packs. The questionnaires are the lengthy 'lifefstyle' type the reader will have seen inserted in prod-

THE HENLEY COLLEGE LIBRARY

uct packs, magazines or mailings, or else delivered door-to-door. The huge size of the response base (which would have been well over 3 million at the time) permits quite large segments to be extracted even with refined selection. In this case the selected names were almost all brandy or liqueur drinkers aged 35–55 or people within the same age band who were interested in wine. NDL names are qualified to the extent that they are representative of the minority of recipients who responded to the questionnaire – and of the majority of those respondents who were willing to receive commercial offers in the post.

The 30,000 Martell promotional names had in the main responded to one major on-pack promotion. This promotion offered two Air France tickets for the price of one in exchange for proof-of-purchase of one 70 cl bottle of Martell Cognac at Christmas time. Thus respondents to this promotion were at least trialists of Martell Cognac but they were not necessarily regular buyers. Many people who do not buy spirits at most other times of the year do so at Christmas. On the other hand the law of probabilities dicates that any sampling of buyers is likely to over-represent higher frequency users.

The offer

The creative style adopted for both press and mail was the same. Respondents to the space advertisements and the mailings were made the same offer. This was a free copy of *The Art of Entertaining*, a specially commissioned illustrated booklet written by Miles Kington, resident humourist with *The Independent*. To qualify, respondents had to complete a short drinks purchasing questionnaire that included brands purchased and purchase frequency data. Thus Seagram would be able to gauge the relative value of the names gathered and make appropriate offers reflecting this value. As confirmation of the genuineness of the response, Seagram also requested the neck foil from a bottle of the respondent's favoured tipple. Finally, direct mail respondents were also asked to give the names and addresses of any friends who they believed would be interested in receiving similar offers (see Figure 21.1).

The response

The percentage requesting the book from each source was:

	Target	Actual
Press advertising	0.15%	0.07%
Cold list mailing	12%	14%
House list mailing	16%	23%

Although some people tried to claim the book without volunteering any information at all, the overall response was ahead of target. Respondents were asked to

Figure 21.1 Elements of mailing package

contribute friends' names at each stage and the eventual total of friends' names represented an increment of 77 per cent to the response. Even allowing for the great difference in the unit cost of direct mail compared with space advertising, the direct mail was relatively much more successful.

Fulfilment of offer

With their free book, respondents received two further attractive offers. A self-liquidating offer of six Martell tulip glasses at the special low price of £10.95 was offered in exchange for proof-of-purchase of one 70 cl bottle of Martell Cognac. A 50 per cent sample of respondents received a £2 voucher valid against the purchase of a bottle. The opportunity was also taken to request friends' names once more.

The self-liquidating offer attracted an average response of 3.2 per cent.

Follow-up

Using the questionnaire response primarily from the cold mailing, it was possible to identify 9000 high-value competitive brand purchasers. A competition was devised and the 'hot list' of 9000 was mailed with an invitation to enter. Respondents were asked to devise two lists of their ideal dinner party companions. One list was to include the names of five famous people and the other list was to be of five friends. Naturally, full address data for the friends was requested. Entrants had to send in proof-of-purchase of one bottle of Martell Cognac. The prize was also appropriate. It was a weekend in the Château de Chanteloup, the private residence of the Martell family. Altogether 206 people entered, providing a total of about 1000 names.

Gains

Returning to the NDL source of the data for the cold direct mailing, it was possible to maintain an unmailed control group as a matched sample to the mailed group. In this way, the effect of the mailing on all the recipients (not just those who responded) could be measured through research.

The main results are shown below in gains chart form. This means that the percentages following the plus signs are the gains when the mailed population's brand awareness, purchase behaviour or preferences are compared to those of the unmailed control population.

Usually buy Martell	+27%
Bought Martell last time	+13%
Will buy Martell in future (responders only)	+24%

Will buy Martell in future (non-responders only)	+23%
Unaided recall of brand name	+21%
Unaided recall of advertising	+27%

Of those who received the mailing 72 per cent could recall it at an interval of one month, when the research was conducted. This compared favourably with the best ever result of 46 per cent achieved by House of Seagram in the United States. Among recipients, the mailing moved Martell up their league table of premium brands – altogether a very gratifying result for Seagram UK and its agency, Ogilvy & Mather Direct.

Sequel

Encouraged by the high rate of response to the 1993 activity, Seagram continued to collect names in 1994, now using a larger mailing quantity of 225,000. This has led to the construction of a fairly substantial database of own and competitive brand users, permitting 1995 activity to concentrate on development of business from the names already gathered.

Naturally, since there is no transactional data other than promotional response, it is important to maintain contact with the more valuable names to help defer address decay, as well as of course to maintain a productive dialogue with customers and prospects. If customers move every five years, a one-year-old list that has not been mailed is already 20 per cent out of date.

It is fairly common practice to clean a file of this sort by overlaying it on an edition of the Electoral Register maintained by a computer bureau. Older names that no longer match Electoral Register names and addresses are then deleted. Unfortunately it is impossible to achieve a 100 per cent match rate and this process inevitably leads to the wastage of some valid names and addresses. The cleanest lists are those that are mailed frequently, partly through undelivered mailings being returned and, generally a rarer event, when forwarded mailings provoke a response. At least one packaged goods manufacturer discards non-responding names after four years but names can be written off after whatever period (or number of mailings) experience suggests is the end of their effective life. In 'pure' direct marketing operations such as mail order or magazine subscription sales, a name will be written off when it is no more likely to respond than a new name.

The discipline of working out the effective average life of a name and the owner's potential lifetime value as a customer is crucial to making solid name-gathering investment decisions. In the early days, companies such as House of Seagram had to embark on these ventures as an act of faith in the validity of their preliminary calculations. This process is made more difficult because heavy users of a product are more valuable than light users and competitive users have a different value to own-brand users. For some years, House of Seagram has been a committed direct marketer in markets scattered around the world and has a large reservoir of direct marketing knowledge as well as many thousands of valuable customer and prospect names.

This case illustrates that direct marketing communications can have a strong advertising effect even when the task involves making promotional offers. The fact is that there is a concealed payback to direct marketing communications that are supportive of the product's positioning within the marketplace. It requires research to reveal this bonus. A non-response does not necessarily signify a wasted contact and the mere fact that direct mail is nearly always used as a direct response medium does not signify it has no advertising value.

The advertising value of direct mail has traditionally been obscured by its high delivery cost. Concern with this cost probably has its roots in the traditional 'drip, drip' theory of how advertising messages are absorbed. Chapter 15 includes a brief discussion of this.

CASE STUDY 2

AUDI: THE UK LAUNCH OF THE A4

Background

In 1995 the successful Audi 80, Audi's entry model in the upper medium sector of the car market, was due for replacement. It was Audi's volume model, accounting for about 70 per cent of Audi's 1.3 per cent volume market share. The launch of the new A4 would therefore be the marque's most important launch since the 80 itself.

Because of the peculiarity of the UK car registration system, August is the key month, accounting for about 25 per cent of annual new car sales. This is the ideal time to launch a new model.

The product

The Audi A4 is designed to give the impression that the car is raring to go even when it is stationary. This dynamic look reflects real and purposeful technical innovation. The A4 is powered by the first mass-produced four-cylinder engine with five valves per cylinder. This gives higher power output without any fuel consumption penalty.

It is claimed that the redesigned front suspension offers the driver the control and precise steering of front-wheel drive without sacrificing the sheer driving pleasure previously associated only with rear-wheel drive. The A4 also benefits from an ABS braking system adapted from the bigger and more expensive Audi A8.

The target market

Less showy than its main German rivals in the upper medium sector, the Audi has always appealed to drivers who appreciate a degree of understatement. However, the ageing 80 was now a little too sensible to be attractive and might even be seen as rather dowdy. The A4 was obviously an Audi and would appeal to the faithful, but it also had a chance of appealing to drivers who might have considered Audi before but had eliminated it in favour of a sexier model.

The target market was described as follows:

Unpretentious, mature, discriminating and confident, they see themselves as 'free-thinkers' and admire the slightly maverick and alternative. They get great pleasure from owning 'thought-through', well designed things. They like the idea of form following function. They aim to project a 'sorted' attitude to life – that is, they feel they are beyond the desperate need to prove they are achievers. This results in a more sophisticated attitude to 'prestige' cars – they want to drive a car that says they are different, but in a way that's understood by the people around them.

They think of Audi as well-made German quality cars but might reject the marque because of the reservations we noted above.

Launch campaign objectives

- To generate awareness of the new Audi A4.

- To broaden and reinvigorate the appeal of the marque.

- To generate enough test drives during 1995 for the sales targets to be met.

To meet these objectives an integrated marketing communications strategy was adopted. This would allow potential customers to develop a relationship at their own pace. The strategy spelled out how each medium might best be used in the context of all communications. It also described how Audi should behave at each stage of the proceedings in order to develop the relationship while still allowing the customer a respectful distance.

Creative execution

Nearly all marketing communications featured the unique advantages of five valve per cylinder engine technology and the four-link front suspension system. Rather than descend into technicalities, these were associated strongly with Audi's heritage of racing technology and of innovation: '*Vorsprung durch Technik*'.

Black and white photography was used throughout, as it had been in Audi advertising for some two years previously. This helped the advertising to stand out and was empathetic with Audi's understated positioning. It also helped give a distinctive family look to the many different elements, ranging from a $7\frac{1}{2}$ minute demonstration video to space ads the size of a postcard. The result was a very cohesive campaign, with each element reminiscent of another, even though freedom was allowed to adapt the precise message to suit each particular medium and situation.

Media roles

- *Television (60 per cent of budget):* To build awareness of the car, permitting Audi to reach a wider target market. Exploiting the dynamic nature of TV, to add depth and understanding of the car, to showcase its sporty look. To accept response from those wanting more information now (through an 0800 telephone response option). Although all enquirers would be offered a brochure or video, the leads would be qualified, only the serious enquirers being referred to dealerships. For the campaign 60-, 40- and 10-second spots were used.

It comes in several versions, including feature length.

If you'd like the film of the new Audi A4, call 0800 998877.

Figure 21.2 One of the direct response press ads

The new Audi A4 is on its way from Germany.

Figure 21.3 Swing ticket hung in Audi 80s awaiting collection from service

- *Press (25 per cent of budget):* To substantiate the campaign theme by dramatising the benefits of specific innovative features, using double-page spreads. To accept response from those wanting more information now, again using an 0800 number. All enquirers to this advertising were offered a brochure or a video.

- *Direct response press (7 per cent of budget):* To encourage prospects to make the first move and extend the life of the launch campaign. In this instance 10 cms x 4 column direct response ads were used to attract response for the 7½ minute video and subsequent conversion to test drive. The response mechanism was an 0800 number. These leads were issued to dealers. An example ad is shown in Figure 21.2.

- *Direct mail – pre-sell (3 per cent of budget):* To provide dealerships' customers and prospects with advance information and the chance to be first to test drive the new A4. This mailing was centrally prepared and assembled but was addressed from the dealer, not from Audi. In all, dealers mailed 80,000 customers and prospects, an average of 500 per dealer. Customers could respond by pre-registering for a test drive before the new model came in.

Naturally, customers visiting dealerships for routine service work were prime prospects and on-site materials included a novel device, like an overgrown swing-ticket, that could be hung inside Audi 80s before they were collected by their owners. This showed the A4 and invited the customer to be one of the first to test-drive the new car (see Figure 21.3).

- *Direct mail – national (1 per cent of budget):* To secure enquiries from buyers and enquirers for the Audi 80, the car the A4 replaced. Readers were invited to phone for the video and the contact details of their nearest Audi dealer. The mailing included a wallet with pull-out mini-brochure and letter (see Figure 21.4).

Be honest. Can you see yourself in a car with unique five-valve per cylinder engine technology and innovative four-link front suspension?

Figure 21.4 Past enquirers received a walleted mini-brochure and letter

- *Fulfilment material, including video (3 per cent of budget):* To move enquirers responding to the advertising on to the next stage towards purchase. There was sufficient information to excite (for example, the video) and inform. The recipient was encouraged to go to the next stage and take a test drive but the approach was soft – courtship, not hard sell. The video juxtaposed action sequences of the A4 with old footage of the Audi Quattro World Championship winning rally car and prewar racing cars, heavily exploiting Audi's credentials as an innovative car maker.

Results

The A4 launch was the most successful in the marque's UK history. The August sales target was 3800 units but this was passed with 800 units to spare. Audi market share for the month climbed from the usual 1.3 per cent to a record 1.9 per cent.

The 12,000 or so direct responders to national advertising and direct mail were asked to leave certain details, including their telephone number. They were then phoned (by a telemarketing agency) to establish the extent of their interest, only high quality leads being passed on to dealerships. Of the responses received from national advertising and direct mail, about 1500 were judged to be immediate prospects and a further 4500 or so were judged to be genuine prospects also, but not immediately likely to buy.

Those failing to meet the qualifying criteria were mailed a complimentary copy of the Audi magazine and a questionnaire designed to establish their intentions. In this way it was possible to handle all enquiries courteously and to ensure any serious enquirers would not fall through the net. All deciding not to pursue their interest at any stage were mailed later in the year, the mailing including a copy of the Audi magazine.

Davina West, Advertising and Direct Marketing Manager of Audi, commented: 'The launch of the A4 was an extremely important event for Audi UK, not only because it was to replace our volume model but because we had a relatively new and young marketing team working together on their first major project.' This fully integrated launch campaign was the first of its kind for Audi and enough research, response and prospect tracking data was obtained to give Audi confidence in achieving even greater success from future campaigns. Work on the campaign was executed by a team drawn from Audi's advertising agency Bartle Bogle Hegarty, Limbo (BBH's direct marketing and sales promotion arm) and media planners and buyers BBJ Media Services.

Conclusion

This launch was conventional to the extent that it followed a proven formula of using relatively heavyweight media exposure to create an event, thus establishing the importance of the new car. It was unconventional to the extent that no communication left the audience without an easy way to enter a dialogue. This dialogue could then be extended or discontinued, according to the prospect's level of interest and without any pressure being applied.

Although each medium was responsible for generating enquiries, the specific role of each medium was carefully considered and described in briefing. In this example, we see a response mechanism being used as a service to the would-be enquirer. The role of TV advertising was not to generate enquiries but it offered viewers the opportunity to become enquirers if their interest was immediate.

No advertisement was diminished in effectiveness by being cluttered with devices to qualify responders. Responders could be qualified discreetly later, leaving each ad as a clear, sharp, simple piece of communication. Here we see direct response being considered as a bonus. It was known from the outset that the majority of sales would probably be made to people phoning and visiting the dealerships without any intervening head office enquiry stage. Therefore, the priority was to ensure that the campaign worked at the level of creating interest and excitement about the A4 as the next car to own. The telephone response device adds to the drama and the video offer to the excitement. They are entirely supportive of the main communication need.

CASE STUDY 3

ROYAL MAIL: SELLING DIRECT MAIL TO SMALLER ADVERTISERS

Background

By the middle of 1994, increased competition from fax, e-mail and couriers had begun to chip away at both first- and second-class postal traffic with volume losses creeping up month by month. It was decided to counter the adverse trend by attempting to accelerate the growth of direct mail volume. Although efforts to stimulate Mailsort (larger-scale bulk mailings) were continuous, the smaller direct mail user had been somewhat neglected.

Mailsort offers discounts against postal rates for pre-sorted mailings of 4000 items or more. However, the Direct Marketing Association advises that pre-sorting is not worthwhile on volumes below 15,000 and, in practice, almost all mailers who use quantities of 10,000 or less post at the ordinary second-class rate. These users (or potential users) represented an under-exploited opportunity for Royal Mail.

Objectives

The immediate objective was to grow the number of companies using low-volume direct mail, specifically by increasing direct mail's share of current advertising spend. The traffic loss was sufficiently serious for Royal Mail to truncate a process that would normally have included careful testing of targeting, offers and communications channels. Nevertheless, careful monitoring and simultaneous testing of alternatives would enable lessons to be learned and applied in later campaigns.

Therefore, secondary objectives included:

● demonstration of payback on investment overall;

● measurement of contribution from each component of the campaign.

Achievement of these objectives would establish a basis for extension of the plan using similar or modified campaigns depending on the outcome of the various tests.

Approach

The campaign would reach users, trialists/considerers and non-users. The job was to keep users, convert trialists and find interested non-users.

The role of the campaign for each group was therefore distinct:

● **Users:**

  – promote increased usage;

  – promote more effective usage.

● **Trialists/considerers:**

  – heighten awareness and interest;

  – establish recognition and relevance;

  – promote benefits and establish positioning;

  – convert: prompt usage and trial.

● **Non-users:**

  – create awareness/plant seeds;

  – educate;

  – arouse needs;

  – encourage trial.

Although the bulk of small users would employ between ten and 20 people, a small direct mail user could easily be a moderately substantial company and the cut-off for targeting purposes was 200 employees, larger companies being excluded. Companies already on the Royal Mail direct mail user/prospect database were also excluded. These would receive regular mailings and occasional salesforce contacts. Positive selection was of companies that would be actively advertising to attract business. Thus advertisers in Yellow Pages and Thomson Directories, users of local press advertising and door-to-door leaflet users would be prime targets. The actual selection process was based on SIC (Standard

Industrial Classification) codes. (An explanation of how Standard Industrial Classifications work can be found in Chapter 8.)

The individuals to be addressed within each company were managing directors of companies with 100 employees or less and marketing directors of companies with 101–200 employees.

The offer

A close-dated trial offer was needed. Firstly, it would increase immediate usage of direct mail among considerers. Secondly, redemption of the offer would aid measurement of the campaign's immediate effect on volume. Because of the difficulty in discounting metered postage or stamps it was decided to give away 100 stamped envelopes for a mininum qualifying order of 500 stamped envelopes, up to 800 free for the maximum qualifying order of 4000. Users could also ask Royal Mail to collect the filled envelopes for postage.

The offer included free advice on direct mail through Royal Mail Business Centres and Go Direct, a Royal Mail advisory service dedicated to direct mail.

Media

The campaign was coordinated. The leads were issued to the outbound telemarketing team members and the offer was available to all qualifying customers, whether responding directly to the campaign or not. An important target for the campaign was therefore Royal Mail's own sales staff, posters and other materials being used to establish awareness of the offer and enthusiasm for the campaign. Clearly, the campaign would reach many people who would be contacted by (or already be in contact with) sales staff and it was essential to deliver the same message and offer through all channels.

The main enquiry generation medium would be direct mail, about 500,000 mailings being directed to the targeted small business users and potential users. A test of loose inserts and product cards (postcards in card decks mailed out to businesses) was included and, more unusually, an extensive PR campaign exploited the pioneering offer. This included press releases and recordings (featuring direct mail experts in conversation about direct mail and the offer) syndicated to local radio stations.

Communications plan

A multi-stage communications programme was planned. The mailing (or insert) would invite enquiries by post or telephone. The offer of up to 20 per cent extra stamps was to be featured and the free collection closing date was set as 31 March 1995, the mailings being staggered over ten days (to facilitate good lead management and timely follow-up) early in January. Respondents were to be asked to give a few basic details to confirm the size of their business, to give their telephone number and to volunteer information about their advertising spend and any previous use of direct mail. Those not interested in taking advantage of the immediate offer but nevertheless interested in staying on the mailing list were to be given this option.

It was planned to post a fulfilment pack to enquirers, giving all the necessary details on the offer and some basic hints on using direct mail. Those not taking immediate advantage of the offer were to be telephoned. Prospects not successfully contacted by phone, or not responding as a result of the call, were to be sent a follow-up mailing on 6 March with a 'just in case you lost yours' message. Finally, a reminder postcard was to be sent to residual non-responders on 20 March to remind them of the closing date. The plan is displayed graphically in Figure 21.5.

Contact Strategy

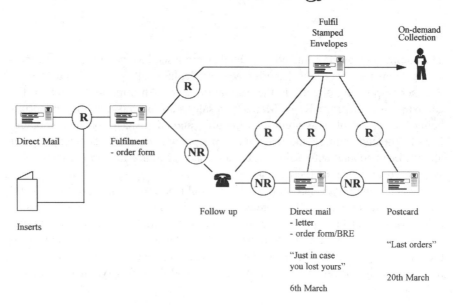

Figure 21.5 Contact strategy

Creative strategy

The proposition was: 'Royal Mail gives you a simple way to do more business.'
The communication objectives were:

● To create awareness and interest.

- To establish recognition and relevance.

- To prompt trial and usage.

- To promote the benefits of direct mail.

The tone of voice was straightforward, non-technical and inspiring.

The enquiry-generating mailing pack was enclosed in a C5 window envelope. On the reverse of the window, a black and white photograph of a sandwich-board man stood out starkly from a solid red background. The sandwich-board carried the message: '*THERE HAS TO BE AN EASIER WAY TO ADVERTISE*' (see Figure 21.6). Inside a half-page enquiry form was attached to a personalised letter. The letter was on a conventional A4 sheet and carried over to the reverse. Another enclosure was a six-page leaflet featuring a brief 'sell' for direct mail and a description of the offer. The final enclosure was a Freepost reply envelope.

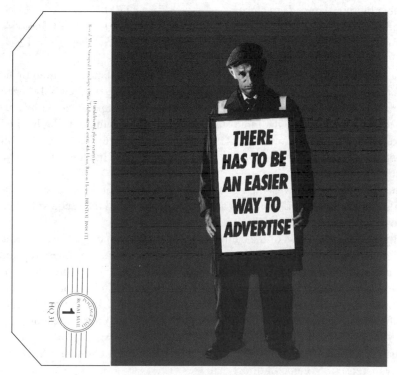

Figure 21.6 The reverse of the mailing envelope

The letter began:

I'm delighted you have picked up this envelope and are now reading this letter. You see, you have proved how effective direct mail can be.

Even if you don't take up the intriguing offer I am about to make you, at least this pack has proved one thing: it grabbed your attention.

The results

Although no pre-testing had been possible, it was necessary to forecast take-up of the offer so that a cost estimate could be made and a cost justification proposal prepared. The forecast included number of firms enquiring, number accepting the offer (conversion), immediately attributable revenue and average revenue per customer. These forecasts became the targets with which the actual results were compared:

	Target	Actual
Number of businesses enquiring	19,165	20,157
Number buying stamped envelopes	2700	4369
Revenue generated directly from offer	£769,500	£1,364,664
Average order value	£285	£308

These results include enquiries from all sources and acceptances secured by field sales personnel. In fact, the insert test proved to be unsuccessful, possibly because the mailing touched down first, and the success of the campaign could be attributed to direct mail and to the three-stage follow-up programme, using both telemarketing and reminder mailings. The telephone follow-up increased the offer acceptance ratio from approximately 9 per cent to approximately 11 per cent, a worthwhile increase.

The PR coverage represented about 4 million opportunities to see or hear details of the campaign. If bought as advertising at rate card rates, equivalent coverage would have cost £61,657.

Ultimately, the success of the campaign cannot be evaluated correctly without taking into account the eventual genuinely new to direct mail business resulting. This can only be measured over a considerable timespan. Therefore, in order to arrive at some estimation of the longer-term effects, buying intentions research was used among those accepting the offer and those enquiring but not accepting the offer. Both groups were compared with a control group of non-responders:

Measure	Responders	Control	Variance
Likely increase in volume of direct mail – deferrers	52%	33%	+19%
Likely increase in volume of direct mail – purchasers	45%	33%	+12%

Deferrers are those who enquired but did not go on to accept the immediate offer of stamped envelopes. The apparent anomaly between this group being more positively influenced than the purchasers is explained by the fact that, naturally, purchasers included more companies that had already used direct mail. Overall, 70 per cent of enquirers had never used direct mail before, while 60 per cent spent between £500 and £3000 a year on advertising.

Analysis of the results showed that 70 per cent of enquirers had ten employees or less and about 80 per cent were engaged in service industries.

Conclusion

The campaign produced sufficient evidence to demonstrate that it could be cost-effective to continue to develop direct mail business in a similar way. Specifically, it was concluded that:

● direct mail targeting could be refined and direct response press advertising used in support;

● the product offer should be widened to include pre-paid postage;

● methods of helping deferrers to become users should be explored.

The campaign was voted best Integrated Campaign in the Business Direct Marketing category of the Direct Marketing Association Awards for 1995. The direct marketing agency responsible for the campaign was Ogilvy & Mather Direct.

This case illustrates the importance of evaluating the whole effect of a campaign, not simply counting promotional redemptions. If we assume that one half of the users ran mailings they would not otherwise have run, then the immediate payback is just under £700,000 in new gross revenue. However, if – as the buying intentions research indicates – enquirers would spend about 50 per cent more on direct mail as a result of the campaign, then a payback of £3 million additional revenue in the first year alone would be a reasonable expectation.

CASE STUDY 4

ROYAL MAIL: EDIpost LAUNCH

Background

EDI (Electronic Data Interchange) is a system for transmitting data over the telephone. It is used to send information such as price lists from one site to another, for example from head office to branches or from a company to its distributors. Royal Mail identified a potential need by companies to send data to some sites without EDI reception. The idea of EDIpost was for Royal Mail to receive the data for these sites and deliver it. Royal Mail took a stand at the EDI '92 exhibition and wanted to invite EDI users to one of two seminars that were to be held during the exhibition. The snag was that they didn't have an invitation list.

Ogilvy & Mather Teleservices, a division of O&M Direct, planned the campaign described below and supplied all the information contained in the figures. The case was first described in Stevens (1995), a source containing many instructive telemarketing cases.

List research and qualification

The exhibition was to be held in the first week of October 1992 and no time was to be lost when work began in August. Two lists of EDI users were available offering a gross quantity of 4170 names, although market research indicated that there were probably only about 1000 companies originating EDI data. The first step was to verify the address/contact data and deduplicate the two lists so that no name appeared twice on the final edited list. The quality of one of the lists was poor and only 2106 company names were left on the contactable file. Contact was made with 1842 of the 2106 (about 87 per cent). This is a good rate by teleresearch standards – even cleaned-up lists are not 100 per cent contactable.

The research brief was firstly to verify the contact's personal details – name, job title and contact data – and to establish if the contact was the EDI decision-maker. If not, the contact was to be asked for the decision-maker's details. The second part of the brief was to establish the potential value of the prospect company as a Royal Mail EDIpost customer. This was done by asking if EDI had already been implemented and if so, when, how many messages had been sent and received, to and from how many sites, per cent of sites with EDI, volumes of EDI/non-EDI documents despatched, how non-EDI documents were sent and how many were sent overseas. Respondents were asked to place number answers in bands, not to give open-ended answers. Table 21.1 shows a summary of the results. Altogether, it was decided there were 1120 individuals worthy of receiving an invitation mailing.

The invitation

Figure 21.7 shows the contact sequence. Twenty-one days prior, the invitation mailings were sent. The 321 selected non-responders were telephoned one week later. The original invitation produced 38 acceptances and the follow-up telephoning produced a further 54, that is 82 companies. From the figure we can see that by no means all the refusals were wasted contacts, four producing sales appointments and 156 literature requests. Three days before the seminars, each acceptance was telephoned about catering arrangements and this produced an estimated number of individuals attending. This number differs from the number of companies accepting the invitation because more than one person from some of the companies wished to attend and some other companies (eight) dropped out. Actually, as we can see, this attendance estimate was only one out, 98 of the 99 promises being kept. This is quite remarkable for a free seminar and reflects the high degree of qualification at each stage in the process.

Table 21.1 Summary of qualification data gathered for the launch of Royal Mail's EDIpost service

	Number of contacts	% of effective calls
Effective calls (named contact spoken to):	1842	100%
EDI implemented for 12 months +	132	7.2
EDI implemented for less than 12 months	21	1.1
High potential (250,000 + documents per year)	153	8.3%
EDI implemented for 12 months +	302	16.4
EDI implemented for less than 12 months	71	3.9
Medium potential (25,000–250,000 documents per year)	373	20.3%
Low potential (<25,000 documents per year)	299	16.2%
Total companies with potential for EDIpost	**825**	**44.8%**
EDI not implemented, planned 6 months plus (potential undefined)	249	13.5
Do not use, no plans to implement EDI	175	9.5
Use EDI but all transactions via EDI	24	1.3
Use EDI but only to receive	434	23.6
Individual queries for Royal Mail action	17	0.9
Incomplete call/partial information	118	6.4
Total others	**1017**	**55.2%**
Total non-effective calls	**264**	
Total contacts attempted	**2106**	

Source: Stevens (1995), Table 8.2 (reproduced courtesy of Ogilvy & Mather Teleservices).

Follow-up

Table 21.2 displays the contact strategy immediately following the seminar attendances. The contact records would now be held on a sales lead management system of the type described in Part Two of this book.

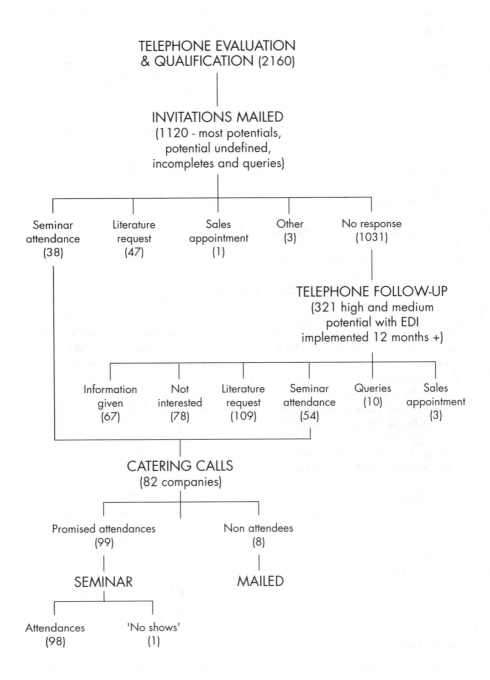

Figure 21.7 First-stage contact strategy for the launch of Royal Mail's EDIpost service (Reproduced courtesy of Ogilvy & Mather Teleservices. *Source*: Stevens, 1995, Figure 8.1.)

Table 21.2 Initial follow-up contact strategy after the launch of Royal Mail's EDIpost service

Segmentation criteria	Potential	Follow-up action*
1. Requested appointment	(High)	Salesforce direct contact
2. Attended seminar	High, medium, low	Thank you letter/brochure with telephone follow-up
	Misc. 'don't know'	Thank you letter/brochure with telephone follow-up to qualify potential
Planned to attend	High, medium, low	Thank you letter/brochure with telephone follow-up
3. Requested information	High	Telephone to follow-up information
	Medium	Call when possible
	Low	No immediate follow-up
4. Non-responders to mailing	High, medium	Thank you letter/brochure with telephone follow-up
	Low	No contact at present
	Future	Keep in touch programme
5. Queries	(Unknown)	Contact to establish if query can be answered
Stand attendees		
– requested appointment	(High)	Salesforce direct contact
– other	(Unknown)	Letter with telephone follow-up

* Groups 2 to 5 screened for appointment request prior to action.
Source: Stevens (1995), Table 8.3 (reproduced courtesy of Ogilvy & Mather Teleservices).

Apart from the attendances, the final total of useful contacts made included four sales appointments and 15 specific queries. It had provided additional product information to 224 prospects.

The case demonstrates the usefulness of the telephone in market evaluation, contact list building and securing a commitment from prospects. It would have been impossible to provide detailed information about EDIpost to 30 per cent or more of the target market any other way. Each step in the O&M Teleservices plan was essential, yet the entire exercise from plan to seminars took only two months, illustrating another benefit of telemarketing. Telemarketing campaign lead times are short and the response is immediate.

CASE STUDY 5

THE LAUNCH OF THE NEW RANGE ROVER

Background

The Range Rover had been on the market for 25 years. Naturally, it had undergone many refinements and updates. But basically it was still the same car, which was the way many of its customers wanted it to remain – utterly distinctive, aloof from the fads and fashions to which lesser vehicles conformed.

To replace the Range Rover would be a delicate matter. Yet it could not be postponed for many more years. The technology on which the original design had depended had been largely superseded, making real updating impossible. The Land Rover company held many of the clinics that are much used in the automotive industry to gauge preferences, tastes and reactions to ideas. Those invited to the clinics included Range Rover owners, the people on whose loyalty the Range Rover depended and the people whose judgement would decide the fate of its successor.

According to Jon Voelkel, Planning Director of Craik Jones Watson Mitchell Voelkel, Land Rover's direct marketing agency: 'There is huge customer loyalty to Range Rover, and people keep buying their vehicles over and over again. In launching the new model, it was essential that owners accepted it as the natural evolution of the Range Rover.'

The new car was developed in complete secrecy. It was to be launched simultaneously around the world, using interactive satellite TV as a worldwide link, part of an event involving dealers, Land Rover staff, key influencers and, of course, customers. The launch was to take place in September 1994.

The agency brief

It was decided to return the extraordinary loyalty of owners by launching the new model to them on a personal basis.

The UK direct marketing agency, Craik Jones, was briefed to devise a pre-launch campaign targeted to 12,000 people only: owners of Range Rovers, former owners of Range Rovers and a few owners of competitive luxury cars. These 12,000 people were to be invited to the launch event, held simultaneously at 125 dealerships.

To launch a new model with no conventional media advertising was as inventive as the car itself. But the originality of the brief did not end there. The car could not be shown, or even mentioned, in the pre-launch invitation material. The embargo was to remain in place until the launch day. The last twist in the tail was that Craik Jones were asked to produce something 'that's never been done before.'

The solution

It had been decided to demonstrate the capabilities of the new Range Rover in spectacular style by sending it, in the care of driver teams, on epic journeys around the world. As this was a media event, the teams included celebrity drivers but also environmentalists and scientists, each adventure having a serious purpose. Naturally, the journeys were covered by the embargo.

Still, here was a straw that could be grasped. The agency found out what it could about the destinations, in particular what happened in Vermont, Patagonia and Japan in September, especially anything that could symbolise the idea of change.

The plan was to use these symbols to fix the dates of the launch (there were two – 28 and 29 September) in recipients' minds. This was done by sending three-dimensional postcards, incorporating clear, plastic bubble packs, containing the symbols. Three postcards, one a week, each one appearing (from the design of the stamp) to be sent from a far-flung corner of the world (see Figure 21.8). The first was an autumn leaf, the message saying: 'As green turns to gold in the villages of new England, what was merely glorious becomes spectacular. Witness the transformation on September 28th/29th.' This was followed by a seashell from Patagonia. Then a chrysanthemum from Japan. Each of these ideas supported the theme – the season of change.

In the fourth week came the invitation pack. This echoed the postcard design but was, in fact, a window envelope containing a letter and personalised RSVP card. This was timed to arrive a month before the event and appeared to come from the dealer, not from Land Rover. Finally, a reminder was sent the day before the event. This was the launch pack. It was sent only to those who had confirmed they would attend.

At the event all became clear as live satellite broadcasts focused on the expeditions. Afterwards, guests were sent a test drive reminder and a video containing highlights of the satellite programme (see Figure 21.9).

Logistics and costs

Given the small size of the target group, the campaign was immensely complex. There were some 4000 variations of message, these variations being a multiple of dealers, days, events and status (owner, former owner, prospect). The range of variations was large, involving the use of 126 dealers' stationery. Some dealers had up to eight separate events and these events were not all held at the dealers' premises.

An even greater degree of difficulty arose from such original ideas as sending autumn leaves at the end of July. The leaves had to be petrified to prevent decomposition en route. The flowers had to be dried and only the more attractive specimens were used.

Figure 21.8
Postcard one: Vermont. The Fall
Postcard two: a shell from Patagonia
Postcard three: a chrysanthemum from Japan

Figure 21.9 The follow-up included a video

Some of the centre petals had to be plucked out so that the flowers would fit the bubble pack. Surprisingly, the shells caused the biggest problem. Some were too deeply curved and had to be rejected. Many were covered in seaweed or barnacles and smelt terrible. Each shell had to be thoroughly scrubbed before it was fit to be sent. The reason real flowers, shells and leaves had to be used was that authenticity is a Land Rover marque value.

The whole cost of the campaign (not including the launch events themselves) was £340,000. At close to £30 per recipient, this would be enough to make the more conventionally minded direct mail user reach for the smelling salts. But, of course, each new Range Rover sold represented a gross turnover of about £40,000, more than a thousand times as much as was expended on each potential buyer.

Furthermore, what of the alternatives? According to Craik Jones, a conventional multi-media car launch might cost as much as £6 million. Such a launch would not, of course, capitalise on and reward the loyalty of the Range Rover owner population nearly so well as Land Rover's inventive strategy.

The result would depend on whether the right 12,000 people had been selected and on their response to the invitation. As every direct marketer knows, what matters is not the cost per contact, it is the cost per result.

The result

Some dealerships reported 100 per cent response to the invitations. The average was 94.3 per cent. The cost per person attending, at £30, was little more than the cost per contact. Over the two days of the launch, the dealerships were packed, not with tyre-kickers, but with the right people, people who had bought Range Rover before or were owners of cars similar in value. The prospects were, of course, surrounded by advocates – people who had bought Range Rover not once before, but twice, three times or four times before.

The Coventry dealership took orders for three months' supply at the launch itself. The event was resoundingly successful in terms of immediate sales. However, people do not replace their cars to suit the convenience of the manufacturer and it was of even greater importance that the event should be memorable, and that the right memories should be taken away from it.

It was crucial that owners and prospects should see the new model as the rightful heir to the Range Rover they knew and loved. In fact, the car was larger, faster, more sophisticated and more expensive than its forebears. But it was accepted as a true Range Rover, the real thing. The fact that no clue was supplied as to its appearance or specification in advance prevented the car from being pre-judged. The launch strategy allowed judgement to be suspended until the car could be presented in the best possible light – a daring strategy, cleverly executed.

The campaign was awarded the Direct Marketing Association Gold Award in the UK and also won the US Direct Marketing Association's Golden Mailbox award. The agency, Craik Jones, has received many other awards for its work on Land Rover over the years.

Conclusion

The case provides an excellent illustration of how logic and self-confidence combine to enable people to break out of the trap of conventional thinking, the latter being, all too often, the absence of thinking.

More specifically, it illustrates the point that, if the targeting is sufficiently precise, the cost per contact of any communications strategy is barely relevant. Precise targeting means more than selecting the right people, essential though that is. It also means understanding those people sufficiently well to communicate with them in an influential way.

A final point: recipients of the message don't see, hear, touch or smell the original concept, brilliant though this may be. What they experience is the execution of the idea. Attention to detail is immensely important when the strategy depends on what a few very important people make of it all.

CASE STUDY 6

LAWLEYS BY POST: 'FIRE FROM THE SKY'

Background

Lawleys by Post is the trading arm of the Royal Doulton Group of Companies that was established in 1986 to deal directly with individual customers. The 200-year-old parent is famous all over the world as a producer of fine bone china gift and tableware. Lawleys by Post is not restricted to selling items bearing the Royal Doulton trademark. It also sells other Group brands: Royal Crown Derby, Minton and Royal Albert.

The items sold by Lawleys are collectables; that is, exclusive designs for plates, figures, vases, thimbles, character jugs, clocks, prints and miniatures. The buyers are often enthusiasts who specialise in collecting one or maybe two kinds of item. Dealing directly with Lawleys enables the collector to receive news of each new issue in good time. This may be important to the collector in the case of limited edition pieces and, of course, mailings about a new issue or catalogues featuring an entire range are interesting to collectors, adding an extra element to the pleasure of collecting.

The business

Lawleys by Post is a fairly small mail order business, with a turnover of about £5 million and some 130,000 active customers. Typically, an item or collection might cost between £80 and £120 payable over 5–10 monthly instalments. Anyone still paying would be classified as active, as would any recent buyer who had completed their payments. Bad debt is remarkably low at under 1 per cent. Customers can order by phone, post or fax and pay by cheque or card.

Customers will hear from Lawleys a variable number of times, depending on their particular collecting interest. On average a customer will receive six communications a year. Communications will include a catalogue, featuring about 30 collections and items, mailings offering issues of believed particular interest to the collector and other correspondence. Other correspondence will include information about, for example, a past issue when the value has increased. This information, apart from being gratifying to the collector, may affect the insurance valuation. (It is not the policy of the company to sell new issues as investments, only as items of intrinsic or aesthetic value. Nevertheless, some customers, mostly male customers, are interested in collectables as investments.) Lawleys like to send at least one non-selling mailing for every two mailings designed to win orders.

Postal research is used to collect information on customer satisfaction with service, information and delivery as well as on general preferences. Typically a response rate to a questionnaire mailing would be about 40 per cent. Satisfaction rates are consistently high with good/excellent ratings in the high 90s. Customer research is of limited value in planning new issues, the creative aspect of the business running on a mixture of inspiration and keeping a finger on the pulse of market trends. Trends towards and away from specific types of collectables (eg plates or prints) can be plotted and there also patterns in the popularity of subjects (eg wildlife or historical figures) but, inevitably, predicting the demand for any one item is fraught with difficulty.

For example, a successful character jug mailing might be expected to achieve a 10–12 per cent order rate from the customer base but a jug featuring the great cricket commentator, Brian Johnstone, generated an astonishing 37 per cent response.

New customer acquisition is primarily through sell-off-the-page advertising in the weekend magazines accompanying large circulation newspapers.

'Fire from the Sky'

In May 1994, a Royal Doulton limited edition plate was launched. As is standard practice in the limited editions field, an advance mailing and advertising appeared before production began.

The plate was called 'Fire from the Sky'. It was the second in a series of plates featuring aircraft, the first being launched in 1993. As the 50th anniversary of D-Day approached, it was decided the second plate would star the Lancaster bomber from the Second World War, but supporting parts would be played by five other bombers spanning the history of the RAF from 1924 until the Gulf War (see Figure 21.10).

The edition limit was 9500 numbered plates of $10\frac{1}{2}$ inches in diameter, crafted in bone china and encircled with 22 carat gold. The plates were designed by Geoff Hunt, RSMA, a well known aviation and marine painter. The illustrations of the six aircraft were held together by a dramatic sky background ranging from phosphorescent red to stratospheric blue. Each numbered plate was priced at £37.50 inclusive of post and packing. This amount could be paid in either one or two instalments.

With the anniversary of D-Day so close, heavy advance ordering was anticipated but, in fact, no less than 6000 of the 9500 edition limit was pre-sold, a quite exceptional demand.

Disaster

Although all the routine production tests had been undertaken without a hitch and the resulting samples had been approved as meeting Royal Doulton's quality standard, the main print delivery did not fire as it should have done. The quality was not acceptable and loss rates were far too high. The customers, of course, had

Figure 21.10 *Fire from the Sky* starring WWII Lancaster bomber

already paid either the full price or the first of two instalments. So what was to be done?

A letter was sent immediately to each customer. The letter explained exactly what had happened and forecast a delay of six weeks in despatching the plates.

When the plates were released, each one was accompanied by a standard customer service questionnaire which is enclosed with every Lawleys by Post product shipment. A high response is encouraged by means of a prize draw incentive. By the end of the year, the recorded level of customer satisfaction from this issue was higher than for any other plate.

Post mortem

Because the problem was disclosed to customers before any of them had had time to worry about their order or contact the company, they were reassured that their order had been safely received and they would (eventually) receive their plate. Since Lawleys had been proactive in breaking the bad news, there was no reason to suppose that the estimate of the delay was inaccurate. Finally, the reason for the delay was the best possible reason – it was to protect and guarantee the quality of the plate.

Apart from this by no means typical practice of sending non-selling news mailings to customers, Terry Selman, the Business Manager of Lawleys by Post, makes a point of ensuring that every customer letter is answered individually and intelligently, that is, not through standard-text form letters. When a customer requests a specific number on a plate or other numbered edition, the request is acknowledged and, whenever possible, granted. Michael Doulton will even sign plates on request.

Companies such as Royal Doulton are increasingly becoming part of the tourist industry and many of Lawleys' customers visit Stoke each year and see collectables being made. Lawleys by Post supports the values of Royal Doulton. It is not seen by management purely as a stand-alone brand although it more than pays its own way.

It is a peculiarity of direct marketing that customer relationships, at least in best practice cases, are often closer, being based on greater knowledge and mutual understanding than most face to face retail branch relationships. Communicating through a mixture of correspondence and the telephone enables more detailed information to be passed on by better informed people. A moment of truth is reached when something goes wrong. In this case, Lawleys by Post survived a moment of truth with strengthened customer relationships

CASE STUDY 7

THE ECONOMIST: SUBSCRIPTIONS AND THE BRAND

Background

Traditionally, UK magazines have relied on the news-stands to deliver, often literally, the vast majority of their sales. Yet American-owned magazines such as *Time*, *Newsweek* and, most notably, the *Reader's Digest*, have long shown that UK buyers are willing to subscribe direct in exchange for an attractive offer. In fact the *Digest* typically sells over 95 per cent of its circulation on subscription. By the 1980s, when many UK publishers at last woke up to the opportunity, *The Economist* was far ahead of the game and had already secured about 40 per cent of its UK circulation on subscription as well as selling overseas subscriptions on a considerable scale.

Unlike those British publishers which had wanted subscribers to pay more than casual buyers to cover their mailing costs, *The Economist* had long recognised the value of a loyal and influential readership. Success in promoting magazine subscription sales depends on overcoming inertia with a strong, usually money-saving, offer that includes a device to reduce the new subscriber's risk. Most often, this is a guarantee to refund the unexpired portion of the subscription if the new subscriber cancels early. The publisher's generosity is justified because more than half the revenue will usually be derived from selling advertising space. Advertising rates and demand for space are crucially affected by circulation strength and quality.

Of course, subscribers are most often drawn from the ranks of casual readers and so news-stand sales are not just an important source of revenue but also provide a sampling opportunity. In the late 1980s, *The Economist*'s advertising agency, Abbott Mead Vickers, had begun a campaign in support of news-stand sales that gained attention far beyond what might have been expected from a relatively small advertising appropriation. The opportunity to capitalise on this was not lost on *The Economist* or its new direct marketing agency, Evans Hunt Scott, who would be responsible for creating the UK subscription campaign.

'I never read The Economist.' (Management trainee, 42)

This advertisement by David Abbott, dating from June 1988, did more than any other to establish *The Economist*'s personality – witty, confident, confrontational, succinct. If you're one of the few who see the joke, it seemed to be saying, then you'll appreciate *The Economist*. The ad set the tone for a long running campaign that was made more distinctive by picking up *The Economist*'s masthead (house) style, using white type reversed out of a red background. In effect, *The Economist* took ownership of a colour combination, a device that assumed greater importance as outdoor advertising's share of the budget increased, posters becoming the main medium with simple copy-only advertisements by 1991. *The Economist*'s advertising spend had increased from about £300,000 in 1988 to somewhat less than £1.5 million in 1991.

According to a British Market Research Bureau (BMRB) survey, the advertising campaign scored an immediate hit with the socioeconomic group AB business audience. Unprompted awareness of the campaign within this segment was 37 per cent (compared with 23 per cent for *The Financial Times*' 'No FT, no comment' campaign) and prompted recall was 57 per cent.

Advertising strategy

The Economist is not a magazine. It is a weekly newspaper. Sparsely illustrated, it remains faithful to its original values of fearless objectivity, progressive liberalism and intellectual rigour. It covers politics, commerce, economics, finance, science, culture and sport.

With the wealth of alternative media available to the target market – including the FT, the business sections of weekend broadsheets, the financial and business journals and Radio 4 – one might have expected *The Economist* to have been squeezed out, relegated to the status of a worthy but non-essential institution. Yet it was bought and read by 20 per cent more people in 1996 than in 1988.

Research within the target market revealed a fundamental respect for *The Economist*, even among non-readers. Readers felt a sense of personal advantage, non-readers a sense of vulnerability. That is why David Abbott's advertisement struck a responsive note. The advertising was aimed at both readers and non-readers. Its aims were:

- to consolidate the current readership by confirming the wisdom of the readers' choice;

- to encourage occasional readers to make reading *The Economist* a habit so as not to let themselves down;

- to entice non-readers of the right profile by stressing their exclusion from those in the know.

Subscription generation

Subscribers are recruited from three sources: direct mail lists (usually subscribers to other publications appealing to readers of similar profile), loose inserts in upmarket publications (for example, *The Financial Times*) and inserts within *The Economist* itself.

Both loose and bound-in inserts are used to promote subscription sales within *The Economist* itself. The facility exists to confine inserts to subscriber copies and *The Economist* takes advantage of this to encourage subscribers to introduce friends or colleagues as subscribers. They are offered an incentive to do this, a device referred to in direct marketing as an MGM (member-get-member) Offer or, sometimes, as a referral offer. It is worth making this offer three times a year to current subscribers.

The offer to new subscribers depends on which subscription term they accept. It might be a 40 per cent discount for one year or a 60 per cent discount for three years. Although subscribers can cancel and claim back the unexpired portion of their subscription payment at any time, it is publishers' common experience that it is much harder to sell longer-term subscriptions and this explains the exceptionally generous discount for a three-year term.

Subscriptions are sold direct from inserts and mailings on a one-step (firm order, not just an enquiry) basis, although the subscriber may be billed later, not necessarily paying upfront.

At the time of Evans Hunt Scott's appointment, direct mail and inserts in *The Economist* were the only sources used. The most responsive lists had been overutilised and response rates were in decline.

Upgrading to subscriber status

Research shows the vast majority of new subscribers to be people who have read two or more copies of *The Economist* in the last 12 months. Therefore, inserts inviting subscriptions within *The Economist* itself are perfectly targeted. However, logic also dictates that outside mailing lists and insert media should overlap as much as possible with *The Economist* readership and that the invitational message should assume knowledge of *The Economist*.

The direct marketing task could be defined as *upgrading to subscriber status*. Subscribers would be those readers who felt confident enough in the product to go to a higher level of commitment.

In fact we might expect those most likely to subscribe to have a heightened interest in the advertising campaign which we might also expect to reinforce beliefs they held about *The Economist*. Certainly this was the view taken by the direct marketing agency as they set about capitalising on the advertising.

Their approach was to take the personality portrayed in the advertising, using the same confidence and humour, but to relate it specifically to the subscription proposition and offer. For example:

'The thinking man's bargain offer.'	'New Year's Offer List.'
'Valued Added Facts.'	'The All-Share Index.'
'Interest with savings.'	'Forward planning. Cost control.'
'Make a killing on the futures market.'	'Delivered wisdom.'

An insert in *The Financial Times* (see Figure 21.11) featured on the front the line: 'A rare piece of good news in these financial times.' Inside, we read: 'Trust *The Economist*. Cool, calm and delivered.'

Results

Figure 21.12 shows that subscription sales rose by about 50 per cent in the eight years under review. Part of this gain can be attributed to the successful brand advertising campaign, this helping to increase the base of regular and occasional news-stand buyers from whom the subscriber base is, very largely, recruited.

However, Figure 21.13 shows that the proportion of subscriber sales increased by about 20 per cent in the same period, from 42 to 53 per cent. Again, the brand advertising played a part, providing a style, a personality that would be recognised by those exposed to the direct marketing messages. This process, is two-way, of course, direct marketing communications having an influence beyond what can be measured through counting subscription sales gains.

Conclusion

The case supports the notion that a complementary strategy between brand advertising and direct marketing can work consistently well over a long period. The occasional user may need reassurance: 'Am I right to upgrade my commitment to this product?' Advertising can help to supply this reassurance. It may do this

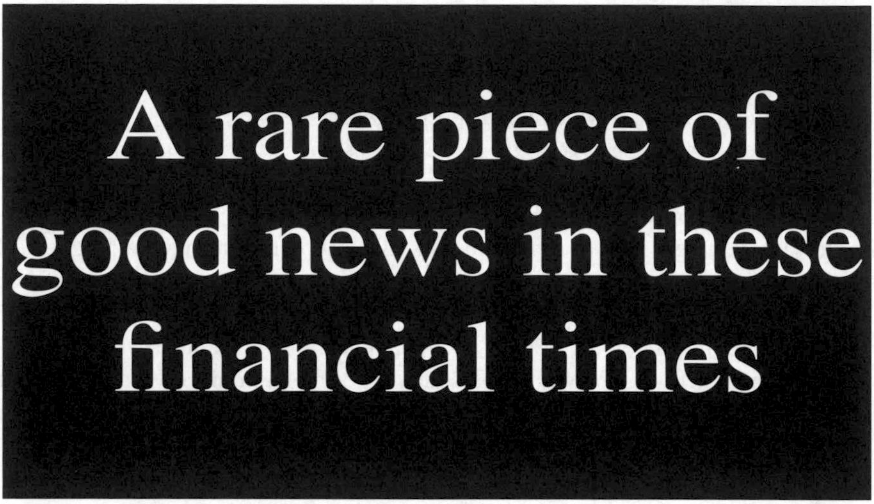

A rare piece of good news in these financial times

Figure 21.11 Insert in *The Financial Times* – A rare piece of good news in these financial times

directly through the assertions that it makes or it may do it indirectly by association, for example by associating the product with users the audience might wish to emulate. It works, generally, on an emotional level and best when it appears to confirm a notion that its audience already holds. The very public nature of advertising assists the process, implying peer group approval of the buying decision.

During the first four years of the period, *The Economist* increased its share of its sector of the media market by 27 per cent and the advertising could be said to have achieved its three aims of consolidating current readership, upgrading occasional readers to more regular readership and attracting new readers.

These aims illustrate an essential difference between most general or brand advertising and direct marketing. Because general advertising reaches regular, occasional and non-users of a product, it is often considered wasteful when the message excludes any of these groups. In sharp contrast with this, direct marketing messages are usually justified by their ability to get members of one group to migrate to another group, in this case to get occasional readers to become regular subscribers. Of course, this is also an aim of the advertising but the position is less clear-cut, firstly because the advertising has more than one aim, and secondly because the brief for advertising is less prescriptive. The relevant aim of advertising is to increase frequency of purchase. The aim here of direct marketing is to increase frequency of purchase *by selling subscriptions at an acceptable cost per subscription.*

The highly prescriptive nature of direct marketing campaign briefs affects both media planning and message content. The media carrying direct marketing messages are often more narrowly targeted than the media carrying general advertis-

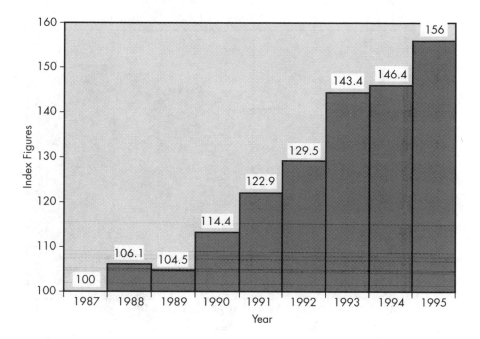

Figure 21.12 *The Economist*: subscription sales year on year (UK only)

ing messages. Even when this is not the case, the direct marketing message is addressed only to that part of the readership who may be interested in the offer that it conveys. Any beneficial side-effect of the direct marketing message will be considered as a bonus, if it is measured at all. The direct marketer must remain single-minded in the pursuit of the objective, so that a clear recommendation on how to respond is implanted in the mind of the reader.

In this case, Evans Hunt Scott delivered single-minded communications that nevertheless referred to AMV's advertising campaign, exploiting it to great effect. The example shows that integrated marketing communications do not require direct message transfer from one part of the campaign to another. If the idea or theme behind the message is clear and strong, this theme will still be recognised even when it is communicated in different words or pictures that are appropriate to the situation.

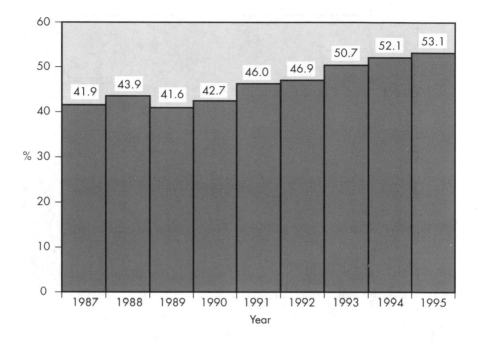

Figure 21.13 *The Economist:* subscriptions as percentage of overall sales (UK only)

CASE STUDY 8

CAMPHILL VILLAGE TRUST: BOTTON VILLAGE

Background

In the early 1950s a group of parents and friends of mentally handicapped young-sters at Camphill schools were determined to give the children a better future. They pooled their resources, bought an estate on the North Yorkshire Moors and, in 1955, Botton Village was founded. Today, Botton Village has 326 inhabitants and is the largest of 71 Camphill Communities worldwide where handicapped people live and work together, each person benefiting the community in a way best suited to their own ability.

Almost miraculously, it seemed, the funds to build and sustain Botton Village as a functioning village kept arriving at the eleventh hour. The village has its own church, a theatre, a small cafe, a bakery, a creamery, a food centre, a weavery and it has candle, doll and wood workshops. By 1983, without capital or any reserves and with serious and deteriorating infrastructural problems, it was clear to Lawrence Stroud that something had to be done. Arriving to help as a co-worker in the village ten years before, at the age of 23 after working in the computer industry, he stayed and eventually became a house-parent and village mainte-nance man. Clearing out a desk, he came across an old file of grant-making trusts. He decided to write to them, give them some news and ask them how they were. By return of post, he received £10,000 in donations. It was nowhere near enough but it was an encouraging start. Lawrence Stroud had become a fundraiser.

Early fundraising

Today, with the help of specialist fundraising agency Burnett Associates, Botton Village raises about £1.9 million a year, clear of expenses, from an active sup-porter base of some 55,000 people. The objective of the initial fundraising work was less ambitious, being to generate a supporter base of about 7500 people. However, from the start, Lawrence Stroud and Botton Village broke with con-vention. To the horror of some of his colleagues who feared a tourist invasion, he invited supporters to come and see life in the village for themselves. The invita-tion is extended to this day and research among supporters shows that the gesture is appreciated even by those who will never take advantage of it. Another feature of fundraising mailings from the earliest days is *Botton Village Life*, an illustrated, friendly and happy newsletter reporting events and bringing the village to life. The front page always features what has been achieved as a result of response to the last appeal and the next appeal is always trailed somewhere on the back page (see Figure 21.14).

Initially, everything was done by hand in the village, from sealing the envelopes to accounting for the money that came back. One day, however, a gen-erous computer manufacturer donated a system to maintain the supporter records. Unfortunately, there were no instructions and very little support. Lawrence Stroud taught himself how to install the system, even adapting the software to suit his requirements.

The database and segmentation

The first segmented mailing went out in April 1992, most of the 12 segments being very obvious divisions such as companies, trusts, groups, large covenan-tors, multiple donors, overseas donors and so on. Responses and donation values varied considerably. For example, 27.7 per cent of large donors responded, send-ing an average of £119 each, 45.1 per cent of multiple donors responded, each sending an average of £17.08 and 10.7 per cent of 'normal' donors sent an aver-age of £31.49.

Segmentation was first used creatively for the crucial appeal before Christmas the same year. By now 19 segments were being used and, instead of minor letter text variations, each segment received the most appropriate letter that could be

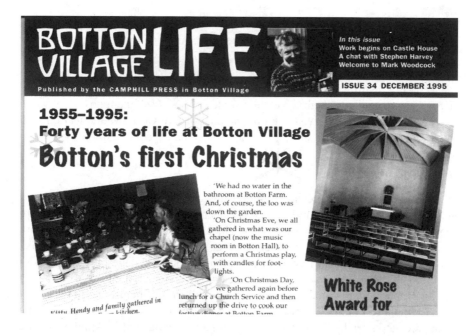

BOTTON VILLAGE LIFE

Published by the CAMPHILL PRESS in Botton Village

In this issue
Work begins on Castle House
A chat with Stephen Harvey
Welcome to Mark Woodcock

ISSUE 34 DECEMBER 1995

1955–1995:
Forty years of life at Botton Village

Botton's first Christmas

'We had no water in the bathroom at Botton Farm. And, of course, the loo was down the garden.
'On Christmas Eve, we all gathered in what was our chapel (now the music room in Botton Hall), to perform a Christmas play, with candles for footlights.
'On Christmas Day, we gathered again before lunch for a Church Service and then returned up the drive to cook our festive dinner at Botton Farm.

Kitty Hendy and family gathered in ... kitchen.

White Rose Award for

Figure 21.14 Newsletter features how the last appeal's donations have helped

written, depending on status or expressed interest. Bar coding was introduced. The appeal raised £580,000, an increase of 46 per cent on the same appeal in 1991. A segment of donors who had requested to be mailed only at Christmas produced an astonishing 55 per cent response. Another segment had requested that they be sent only information, that is unaccompanied by a request for money. Although this segment received only *Botton Village Life* and a newsy letter (no donation form or envelope, nor any request for funds) 12.5 per cent responded, enclosing a higher than average donation. Since that time, the 2000 or so 'information-only' names have been sent a covenant form on a once-only basis in case they wished to covenant money over four years, a tax-efficient way to give. This mailing produced a net £38,000.

Lapsed donors are held as a separate file segment although attempts are made to reactivate them. The ambition is to move further away from segmenting by 'performance', that is the number, recency, value and type of previous donations, and towards segmenting by expressed interest or preference. This enables mailings to be timely and relevant, respecting the supporters' wishes and increasing the bonding between Botton Village and its supporters.

This raises two points of particular interest. Most charities maintain performance-related segmentation because mailing frequency to any one segment is driven by economics. Segments that will 'stand' eight or ten mailings a year will receive this number on the basis that they are already bombarded by competing charities' appeals. The ethos of Botton Village mailings is such that very high frequency would be intolerable and every segment of the supporter base produces a surplus from each mailing, so there is no need to edit out segments unless they wish to be excluded.

The second point of interest is that the required direction of Botton Village segmentation involves asking the supporters more questions about their interests and preferences and finding more ways in which their involvement can be increased, if they wish this. Supporters can visit Botton Village, send for a video of village life, covenant their donations, introduce friends, help at events, undertake campaigning, participate in research and remember Botton Village in their wills. The corollary is that if they wish to receive information only, their wish is respected. Furthermore, because of the closeness of this charitable relationship, many write personal letters and each of these letters must receive an intelligent, courteous, warm response.

Getting the relationship right

A recent appeal requests help to make Castle House in the village into a bigger and better home. The donation form avoids the charitable cliché of suggested donation amounts with supporting tick boxes. After all, shouldn't Botton know how much you like to give by now? Instead, there are examples of what good use could be made of £10, £20, £60, £150, £500 and £1000, subtly supplying the suggested amounts.

The reverse of the form is headed 'Seven ways Botton can help you'. This is the opposite of what we expect to read. Underneath there are seven numbered offers. The first is a chance to hear from Botton only at Christmas, or to receive no appeals at all, or to carry on having four mailings a year, or to have back numbers sent of *Botton Village Life*. These offers are quite daring by fundraising standards but, of course, it is not possible to respond without returning the donation form. The remaining six offers are a guide to making a will, a video on loan or to buy, an invitation to visit Botton, an offer of historical information about Botton, an offer not to disclose the recipient's name to other charities and, finally, an offer to delete the recipient's name from the mailing list.

Testing

Although there have been as many as 71 tests within an appeals mailing, the majority of testing now is of fairly significant tactical changes, not minor creative refinements, for example the use of alternative tactics to persuade covenantors to renew or to encourage one-time-only donors to send a second donation. This is because too many tests in the past either failed to produce a statistically significant result or information of lasting value. One exception was the test of a roll-fold leaflet, featuring a popular Village resident, within an appeals mailing to new donors. It produced an uplift of 20 per cent in response (see Figure 21.15).

If I didn't
live at Botton,
I wouldn't
be needed

Figure 21.15 The front page of the successful roll-fold leaflet

Interestingly, this breaks with fundraising tradition by using a series of captioned photographs to tell a story rather than the usual, lengthy narrative copy. The front of the leaflet captions resident Lizzie's smiling face: 'If I didn't live at Botton, I wouldn't be needed.' Inside, we see a series of captioned shots of Lizzie working and relaxing. On the back page, the balance between the picture and the copy changes and it reads:

> Lizzie is 43 and has lived at Botton since she was 18. She leads a happy, busy life where she enjoys helping and where she's needed. Lizzie can lead this kind of ful-filling life because our friends, through their generosity, have made it possible. Please will you give us your support so that we can protect this way of life at Botton for Lizzie and her friends?

This appears to sum up the value of Botton and an attitude to its supporters rather well.

BIBLIOGRAPHY

Baier, M. (1996) *How to Find and Cultivate Customers Through Direct Marketing*, NTC.

Bird, D. (1993) *Commonsense Direct Marketing*, 3rd edn, Kogan Page.

Birn, R., Hague, P. and Vangelder, P. (1990) *The Handbook of Market Research Techniques*, Kogan Page.

Fifield, P. (1992) *Marketing Strategy*, Butterworth-Heinemann.

Fraser-Robinson, J. (1989) *The Secrets of Effective Direct Mail*, McGraw-Hill.

Harvard Business Review, Harvard Business School.

Institute of Direct Marketing (1995) *Direct Marketing Education Programme*, IDM.

Jackson, R. and Wang, P. (1995) *Strategic Database Marketing*, NTC.

Jenkinson, A. (1995) *Valuing Your Customers*, McGraw-Hill.

Journal of Direct Marketing, John Wiley & Sons Inc.

Kotler, P. (1996) *Marketing Management: Analysis, Planning, Implementation*, 9th edn, Prentice Hall.

McCorkell, G. (1990) *Advertising That Pulls Response*, McGraw-Hill.

McKenna, R. (1991) *Relationship Marketing*, Addison-Wesley.

Naisbitt, J. (1982) *Megatrends*, MacDonald & Co.

Peppers, D. and Rogers, M. (1993) *The One-to-One Future*, Piatkus.

Porter, M. (1980) *Competitive Strategy*, Free Press.

Rapp, S. and Collins, T. (1987) *MaxiMarketing*, McGraw-Hill.

Schultz, D.E., Tannenbaum, S.I. and Lauterborn, R.F. (1993) *The New Marketing Paradigm*, NTC.

Stevens, M. (1995) *Telemarketing in Action*, McGraw-Hill, in association with The Marketing Society.

Stone, M. and Young, L. (1992) *Competitive Customer Care*, Croner.

Stone M., Davies, D. and Bond, A. (1995) *Direct Hit*, Pitman Publishing.

Stone, R. (1994) *Successful Direct Marketing Methods*, 5th edn, NTC.

Targeting, Measurement and Analysis for Marketing, Henry Stewart Publications.

The Journal of Database Marketing, Henry Stewart Publications.

(1992) *The Practitioner's Guide to Direct Marketing*, Institute of Direct Marketing (2nd edn due 1997).

INDEX

References in italic indicate figures or tables.